A Loewenthau

50¢

ROBERT BROWNING.

A BLOT IN THE 'SCUTCHEON

AND

OTHER DRAMAS.

By ROBERT BROWNING.

EDITED, WITH NOTES,

BY

WILLIAM J. ROLFE, LITT. D.,

AND

HELOISE E. HERSEY.

NEW YORK ·:· CINCINNATI ·:· CHICAGO

AMERICAN BOOK COMPANY

PREFACE.

THIS book has been prepared on the same plan as the *Select Poems of Browning*, edited by Miss Hersey and myself last summer. The introduction is, however, much longer than in that volume, and contains considerable matter the substance of which would otherwise have been given in the notes.

The grateful acknowledgments of the editors are due to Mr. Lawrence Barrett for his interesting letter on the production of *A Blot in the 'Scutcheon* under his management, and for other information on the subject which is incorporated in the notes; also to Col. T. W. Higginson for the use of his copy of *Bells and Pomegranates* in collating the texts.

W. J. R.

CAMBRIDGE, *April* 14, 1887.

CONTENTS.

INTRODUCTION.

I. BROWNING'S DRAMAS.

BROWNING'S career as a dramatist is included between the years 1837 and 1845. The eight dramas followed each other in quick succession in this order :

Strafford, 1837 ; *Pippa Passes*, 1841 ; *King Victor and King Charles*, 1842 ; *The Return of the Druses* and *A Blot in the 'Scutcheon*, 1843 ; *Columbe's Birthday*, 1844.; *Luria* and *A Soul's Tragedy*, 1845.

It will be observed that the three plays included in this volume come from the later and riper period of Browning's dramatic utterance.

Before 1837 Browning had published *Pauline* and *Paracelsus*. *Strafford*, the first drama, was written at the request of Mr. Macready, made half by accident. Mr. Gosse, in an excellent article in *The Century* for December, 1881, gives an account of the interview which resulted in the connection between the actor and the poet, and of their subsequent relations.

With whatever impulsiveness Browning began to write drama, he abandoned the form with deliberation. The dedication of *Luria* to Walter Savage Landor opens thus : " I dedicate this last attempt for the present at dramatic poetry to a great dramatic poet." It has been said that the complications incident to the stage presentation of the plays, the disagreements between author and manager, and the consequent half-success of Browning's plays, were the chief causes for his abandonment of the drama. All these may have had their share in the result ; but no one can read those plays in chronological order without feeling that there was an inward as well as an outward reason for the change. The work grows less and less dramatic, and approaches more and more the form which Browning has made so entirely his own—the dramatic monologue. In *Colombe's Birthday* and *A Soul's Tragedy* there is scarcely anything deserving the name of action. There is not even development of character brought about by the complex influences of plot and counterplot. There is, instead, a single soul put into a single, supreme situation. Upon its choice in that crisis depends all its after-history. This *motif* is familiar to all readers of Mr. Browning's later short poems. It is the favorite theme there. *The Statue and the Bust*, "*Childe Roland to the Dark Tower Came*," *The Confessional*, *Ivan Ivanovitch*, crowd instantly to the memory as random illustrations of this method of depicting life.

In the later dramas the dialogue grows more weighty. There is little of the passion that gives its tremendous force to the scene between Ottima and Sebald in *Pippa Passes*, and none of the sprightliness which makes Guendolen the life of *A Blot in the 'Scutcheon.* These are supplanted by steady poetic fervor and lofty thought.

But even the earliest of these dramas—*Strafford* and *Pippa Passes*, for example—have a quality which, for want of a better name, we must call *remoteness.* As compared with the men and women of Shakespeare, these are removed from us by a perceptible distance. A marked difference is noticeable in the various plays of Shakespeare in this respect. *The Tempest* is much more remote than *The Merchant of Venice*, though both deal with situations unusual to our experience. It is easy to see that, in some plays, for a definite artistic reason, the characters act their parts as if on a deep stage at a considerable distance from the audience; while in others they crowd up to the very footlights to speak to us.

Browning is, even in his early career, more in love with this effect of remoteness than Shakespeare, and it becomes finally his most noticeable characteristic. In *A Soul's Tragedy* the characters are so real as to be almost identified with our own selves, yet we see them at a distance so great that one feels the stage to be the clouds of heaven, over which the actors walk as on a pavement.

In the Introduction to *Pippa Passes,* in the previous volume of *Selections* in this series, we called attention to Mr. Browning's indifference to the ordinary requirement that the *dramatis personæ* shall speak *in character.* He simply ignores the demand. Pippa soliloquizes like a poet at whose feet Shelley might have sat; Colombe, a mere girl, talks like the wisest of philosophers; Tresham finds time and breath for a flight of the imagination when he has the news of Mertoun's death to impart to Mildred. But all this, which could never have been done by Shakespeare, is a part of Browning's method, and must be judged as such. He does not crudely or ignorantly pursue it. He conceives the office of the poet to be the expression of the feelings, thoughts, and aspirations of dumb humanity. His analyses will not bear the glare of the footlights, but they bear the light of the soul. "Were we not dumb from our birth, we should so speak," his creations seem to say to us. We can do a poet no greater injustice than to set up a false standard by which to try him. Shakespeare suffered this posthumous martyrdom for years at the hands of the admirers of the classic school; but at last we judge him after his own deserts.

The fact that Shakespeare is the only name suggested as we try to deal with Browning's dramatic quality is itself a testimony to the grade of his work. If the first drama in this book does not convince the reader of Browning's right to be judged as seriously as Shakespeare, then we much overrate *A Blot in the 'Scutcheon.* But those of us who have learned to prize Browning may remember that his is not the first drama which has "pleased not the million," has been "caviare to the general," though "an excellent play, well digested in the scenes, set down with as much modesty as cunning."

While this volume was in preparation one of the editors begged an interview with Mr. Lawrence Barrett, for the purpose of asking him various questions about his experience in the production of *A Blot in the 'Scutcheon.* The play was originally brought out in London, under Macready's management, with Mr. Phelps in the rôle of Tresham. With this exception, Mr. Barrett has the honor of being the only actor who has tested the possibilities of the play on the stage.

He took at once the most cordial interest in the forthcoming book, and was ready to give a detailed account of the changes which had been made in the play for the stage, and of its success. He grew so eloquent while talking of Browning as a dramatist that the editor expressed regret at being unable to reproduce *verbatim* that part of the interview. On this Mr. Barrett, with characteristic enthusiasm, offered to put his views into writing for our benefit. The letter which was the result of this offer is valuable not only from being the only available testimony to the play from an experienced actor, but also as coming from a trusted friend of Mr. Browning.* It is now, with Mr. Barrett's consent, given a place here:

"I had learned to value Browning as a dramatic poet before I knew that he was not so considered by his critics. In the midst of a reading which had only professional aims in

---

* The various points in the play altered or omitted in Mr. Barrett's production, and the history of its American presentation, will be given in the Notes.

view my attention was called to this poet by one who shares his genius in a remarkable degree, not only as a dramatic poet, but as, indeed, our only *American* dramatic poet in its highest sense—George H. Boker.

"I had heard *My Last Duchess* and *In a Gondola* read most eloquently by Mr. Boker, and I then turned to the poet's works to find for myself the greatest of dramas in *A Blot in the 'Scutcheon.* While I was at once arrested by the majesty of the verse, my mind was more attracted by the dramatic quality of the story, which stamped the author at once as a master of theatric form of narration — the oldest and the greatest of all forms.

"I saw in Thorold a clear and perfectly outlined character suited to stage purposes; in Mildred and Mertoun a pair of lovers whose counterparts may be found only in the immortal lovers of Verona, Juliet and Romeo, while they are as distinctly original as those of Shakespeare; and in Guendolen a revival of Imogen herself. I saw that the play, like many plays of the earlier dramatists as well as those contemporary with this production, was written for an age when the ear of the auditor was more attentive than the eye, and when the appliances of the stage were less ample than now; and I saw that, with a treatment of the text such as all stage managers have freely given even to the plays of the greatest of all dramatists, the *Blot in the 'Scutcheon* would take a front rank as an acting play.

"With this idea I awaited my approaching visit to London, in the hope that I might meet the poet and persuade him to make certain slight alterations, or permit me to stage it in the modern way. I found him as eager for the glory of the theatre as when he produced his *Strafford*, forty years before, and while he was unable, as he said, to go over the text extensively to meet the stage requirements, he would gladly consent to its presentation with the ordinary changes which the stage manager makes in such matters.

"I had gained only a part of my purpose, but I determined to make the best of such license as he gave me ; and the result was that, with a few verbal inversions and a slight cutting of the text, the play was given in Washington before a most distinguished audience with remarkable effect, and it has since taken its place in my repertoire with the other great plays of kindred dramatists.

"The difficulties have been in finding proper persons to represent the parts. Mertoun and Mildred are especially hard to fill, but in Mr. Mosley and in Miss Allen these characters had adequate representatives, while the Guendolen of Miss Gale and the Gerald of Mr. Rogers were portraits worthy of the author.

"Looking back over the literary and biographical history of the past half-century, no event seems to have borne greater misfortune to the stage and the drama generally than the misunderstanding between Mr. Browning and Mr. Macready over the initial performance of this play. It is all the more to be regretted that it arose from no ill-intent on the part of either; but it drove from the stage a poet who only needed the experience at the manager's table which all the great dramatists have found so valuable to have given us a new gallery of stage portraits. Here was, again, a poet whose thoughts fell at once into the dramatic form, whose characters unfolded themselves by act and speech, whose treatment of subject involved a rising interest and a progressive movement, terminating in an adequate denouement, while the verse bore the impress which lives in Shakespeare and his contemporaries, and in 'Marlowe's mighty line,' an heir to the fellowship of those writers who have made the drama's history sublime and achieved the highest fame.

"A little familiarity with the mechanism of the theatre, such as Shakespeare, Alfieri, or Goldoni had, such as all the successful dramatists have had, and we should possess great plays as well as great poems from the pen of Robert

Browning. Then the grand traits of his two heroines in the dramatic poem *In a Balcony* would have shone in the theatrical frame resplendent with the Antoinette of Giacometti or the Ophelia and Portia of Shakespeare ; while the *Flight of the Duchess* and other remarkable poems would have obeyed the grand laws of the dramatic form, and gone into line with the creations of those great poets with whom only Browning may be classed— 'the immortal names that were not born to die.' LAWRENCE BARRETT."

II. CRITICAL COMMENTS ON BROWNING AS A DRAMATIST.

[From James Russell Lowell's Paper on Browning.*]

Are we to suppose that the genius for poetry is entirely exhausted? Or would it not rather be wiser to admit as a possibility that the poems we are criticising may be new and great, and to bestow on them a part at least of that study which we dare not refuse to such as have received the warrant of time? The writings of those poets who are established beyond question as great are constantly inculcating upon us lessons of humility and distrust of self. New depths and intricacies of meaning are forever unfolding themselves. We learn by degrees that we had at first comprehended, as it were, only their astral spirit. Slowly, and, as it might seem, almost reluctantly, their more ethereal and diviner soul lets itself become visible to us, consents to be our interpreter and companion. The passage which one mood of our mind found dark and shadowy, another beholds winding as between the pillars of the Beautiful Gate. We discover beauties in exact proportion as we have faith that we shall. And the old poets have this advantage, that we bring to the reading of them a religious and trustful spirit. The realm of Shake-

---

* *North American Review*, April, 1848 (vol. xlvi.). The brief passage from this paper given in our *Select Poems of Browning* (p. 19) is included in the present longer extract, from which it could not be omitted without injury to the context.

speare, peopled with royal and heroic shades, the sublime
solitudes of Milton, bid us take the shoes from off our feet.
Flippancy is abashed there, and conceit startles at the sound
of its own voice ; for the making of true poetry is almost
equally divided between the poet and the reader. To the
consideration of universally acknowledged masterpieces we
are willing to contribute our own share, and to give earnest
study and honest endeavor. Full of meaning was that ancient belief, that the spirits of wood, and water, and rock,
and mountain would grant only an enforced communion.
The compulsion they awaited was that of a pure mind and a
willing spirit.

The critic, then, should never compress the book he comments on within the impoverishing limits of a mood. He
should endeavor rather to estimate an author by what he is
than by what he is not. He should test the parts of a poem,
not by his own preconceptions, but by the motive and aim
of the whole. He should try whether, by any possibility, he
can perceive a unity in it toward which the several parts
centre. He should remember that very many excellent and
enlightened men, in other respects good citizens, have esteemed poetry to be, not only an art, but the highest of all
arts, round which the rest of what we call the fine arts re-
volve, receiving light and warmth. He should consider that
only they whose understandings are superior to and include
that of the artist can criticise his work by intuition. He should
feel that his duty is to follow his author, and not to guide
him. Above all he should consider that the effort which the
poor author has made to please the world was very likely
not intended as a personal insult to be indignantly resented,
but should make an attempt to read the book he is about to
pronounce judgment upon, and that, too, with a civil attention.

The difference between a true poet and a mere rhymer is
not one of degree, but of kind. It is as great as that be-

tween the inventor and the mechanician. The latter can make all the several parts of the machine, and adapt them to each other with a polished nicety. The idea once given, he can always reproduce the complete engine. The product of his labor is the highest finish of which brass and steel are capable, but it remains a dead body of metal still. The inventor alone can furnish those strong, weariless limbs with a soul. In his creative intellect resides the spirit of life which shall inspire this earthborn Titan, which shall set him at work in the forge and the mill, and compel him to toil side by side in friendly concert with the forces of nature. There, in the dark, patiently delves the hundred-handed Pyrophagus, and it is this primal breath of the master's spirit which forever gives motion and intelligence to that iron brain and those nerves of steel.

The first thing that we have to demand of a poet is that his verses be really alive. Life we look for first, and growth as its necessary consequence and indicator. And it must be an original, not a parasitic life—a life capable of reproduction. There will be barnacles which glue themselves fast to every intellectual movement of the world, and seem to possess in themselves that power of motion which they truly diminish in that which sustains them and bears them along. But there are also unseen winds which fill the sails, and stars by which the courses are set. The oak, which lies in the good ship's side an inert mass, still lives in the progeny of its chance-dropped acorns. The same gale which bends the creaking mast of pine sings through the tossing hair of its thousand sons in the far inland. The tree of the mechanic bears only wooden acorns.

Is Robert Browning, then, a poet? Our knowledge of him can date back seven years [from 1848], and an immortality which has withstood the manifold changes of so long a period can be, as immortalities go, no mushroom. How many wooden gods have we seen during that period transformed into chopping-blocks, or kindled into unwilling and sputtering sacrificial fires upon the altar of other deities as ligneous as themselves! We got our first knowledge of him from two verses of his which we saw quoted in a newspaper, and from that moment took him for granted as a new poet. Since then we have watched him with a constantly deepening interest. Much that seemed obscure and formless in his earlier productions has been interpreted by his later ones. Taken by itself, it might remain obscure and formless still, but it becomes clear and assumes definite shape when considered as only a part of a yet unfinished whole. We perceive running through and knitting together all his poems the homogeneous spirit, gradually becoming assured of itself, of an original mind. We know not what higher praise to bestow on him than to say that his latest poems are his best.

His earlier poems we shall rather choose to consider as parts and illustrations of his poetic life than as poems. We find here the consciousness of wings, the heaven grasped and measured by an aspiring eye, but no sustained flight as yet. These are the poet's justifications of himself to himself, while he was brooding over greater designs. . . .

Let us now turn to the *Bells and Pomegranates.* And here we are met on the very threshold by the difficulty of selection. Not only are the lyrics singularly various in tone and character, but, in the dramas, that interdependence of the parts, which is one of their most striking and singular merits, makes any passage taken by itself do great injustice to the author. These dramas are not made up of a number of beauties, distinct and isolate as pearls, threaded upon the string of the plot. Each has a permeating life and spirit of its own. When we would break off any fragment, we cannot find one which would by itself approach completeness. It is like tearing away a limb from a living body. For these are works of art in the truest sense. They are not aggregations of dissonant beauties, like some modern sculptures, against which the Apollo might bring an action of trover for an arm, and the Antinoüs for a leg, but pure statues, in which everything superfluous has been chiselled away, and whose wonderful balance might seem tameness to the ordinary observer, who demands *strain* as an evidence of strength. They are not arguments on either side of any of the great questions which divide the world. The characters in them are not bundles of different characteristics, but their gradual development runs through the whole drama and makes the life of it. We do not learn what they are by what they say of themselves, or by what is said of them, so much as by what they do or leave undone. Nor does any drama seem to be written for the display of some one character which the author has conceived and makes a favorite of. No undue emphasis is laid upon any. Each fills his part, and each, in his higher or lower grade, his greater or less prominence, is equally necessary to the rest. Above all, his personages are not mere mouthpieces for the author's idiosyncrasies. We take leave of Mr. Browning at the end of *Sordello*, and, except in some shorter lyrics, see no more of him. His men and women *are* men and women, and not Mr. Browning masquerading in different-colored dominos. We implied as much when we said that he was an artist. For the artist-period begins precisely at the point where the pleasure of expressing self ends, and the poet becomes sensible that his highest duty is to give voice to the myriad forms of nature, which, wanting him, were dumb. The term *art* includes many lower faculties of the poet ; but this appears to us its highest and most comprehensive definition. Hence Shakespeare, the truest of artists, is also nothing more than a voice. We seek in vain in his plays for any traces of his personal character or history. A man may be even a great poet without being an artist. Byron was, through all whose works we find no individual, self-subsistent characters. His heroes are always himself in so many different stage-costumes, and his *Don Juan* is his best poem, and approaches more nearly a work of art, by just so much as he has in that expressed *himself* most truly and untheatrically.

Regarding Mr. Browning's dramas in this light, and esteeming them as so excellent and peculiar, we shall not do him the injustice of picking out detached beauties, and holding them up as fair specimens of his power. He may be surpassed by one contemporary in finish, by another in melody; but we shall not try him by comparison. We are thankful to him for being what he is, for contriving to be himself and to keep so. Why, in ordinary society, is it not sometimes the solitary merit of Smith, and all that makes him endurable, that he is not exactly Brown? We are quite willing to be grateful for whatever gifts it has pleased God to bestow on any musically-endowed spirit. The scale is composed of various notes, and cannot afford to do without any of them, or to have one substituted for another.

It is not so much for his expression of isolated thoughts as for his power of thinking, that we value Browning. Most readers prefer those authors in whom they find the faculty of observation, to those in whom power of thought is predominant, for the simple reason that sensation is easier than reflection. By observation we mean that quality of mind which discriminates and sets forth particular ideas by and for themselves alone. Thought goes deeper, and employs itself in detecting and exemplifying the unity which embraces and underlies all ideas. A writer of the first class reaches the mass of readers because they can verify what he says by their own experience, and we cannot help thinking tolerably well of those who put us in mind of our own penetration. He requires them only to feel. A writer of the other kind takes the understanding, and demands in turn an exercise of thought on the part of his readers. Both of these faculties may, of course, differ in degree, may be more or less external, more or less profound, as it may happen. They co-exist in the same mind overlapping one the other by a wider or more limited extent. The predominance of the one or the other determines the tendency of the mind. There are exceptional natures in which they balance each other as in Shakespeare. We may instance Browne and Montaigne as examples in one kind, Bacon as an illustration of the other.

It is because we find in Browning eminent qualities as a dramatist, that we assign him his place as a thinker. This dramatic faculty is a far rarer one than we are apt to imagine. It does not consist in a familiarity with stage effect, in the capacity for inventing and developing a harmonious and intricate plot, nor in an appreciation of passion as it reveals itself in outward word or action. It lies not in a knowledge of character, so much as in an imaginative conception of the springs of it. Neither each of these singly, nor all of them together, without that unitary faculty which fuses the whole and subjects them all to the motion of a single will, constitute a dramatist. Among the crowd of play-writers contemporary with Shakespeare, we can find poets enough, but can we name three who were dramatists in any other than a technical sense? In endeavoring to eliminate the pure dramatic faculty, by precipitating and removing one by one the grosser materials which it holds in solution, we have left the Greek drama entirely out of the question. The *motive* of the ancient tragedy differs from that of the modern in kind. Nor do we speak of this faculty as a higher or lower one, but simply as being distinct and rare.

[*From Rev. John Weiss's Review of Browning.**]

We do not find the condensed energy and meaning of Mr. Browning an objectionable trait. Hamlet has to be studied a little, and we remember that Beethoven's symphonies do not possess us till we have heard each half a dozen times.

* *Massachusetts Quarterly Review*, June, 1850 (vol. iv.).

Mr. Browning seems to take his poems, after writing them, and crush them together at both ends, till he gets the well-knit symmetry and consistency of a Bedouin ; he succeeds in making a sort of intellectual and spiritual pemmican. Sometimes, indeed, the desire to produce something dense and nervous gets only obscurity for its result instead of an effective vivacity. When Mr. Browning began to write, we say with deference, that this was his besetting sin. . . . The fancies throng to the pen's point, throwing dashes and commas behind them, till they get out of sight of their arch instigator in the first lines. We love to linger over such passages, grudging no time, till we tie the two ends together ; then we can enjoy the picture so munificently grouped. It is no condemnation of these pages to say that few people will consent to bestow so much time and labor upon them. The lovers of a smooth poetry, which can be caught at a glance, or of an easy flow of didactic talk which does not harass the average intellect, cannot sit in judgment upon Mr. Browning's involutions and lengthy crescendoes, for they are not the persons who wait to see whether the picture, at first so confused and apparently destitute of a leading group or idea, is worth the contemplation which may finally reproduce the poet's point of view, and thus call a beautiful order out of the prodigal chaos. . . .

The fast diminishing space admonishes us that we have yet the greater part of this new archipelago to sail through, and taste the different fruits, while we have hardly indicated the beauties that remain behind. Visit the Jardin des Plantes to appreciate the hopeless bewilderment of the critic fairly turned into Mr. Browning's menagerie, aviary, flower-garden, and halls of relics, with the door slammed behind him. None of the plays have yet been noticed ; nothing said yet about the innocent Pippa, with her holiday ministry, a pure voice of nature, Heaven's opportunity to redeem many sinful hearts, and each of these hearts, too, worth our sympathy ; no love yet expressed for Guendolen, who is God's grace and woman's fidelity to the erring Mildred, and one of Mr. Browning's most natural characters, beckoned apart from the living throng of the street before she has learned the tricks of self-consciousness; no hint of the subtle developments in the *Soul's Tragedy*, with its racy prose, pitting sly papal reaction against a patriotism none of the purest; and not yet a line of Valence's integrity, enamoured of Colombe, another real woman, unspoiled by a year's splendor, resigned to the legal claimant, Valence, the true Duke's generous rival in love, but at last the husband of simple Colombe—Valence, the man, left alone with her undisturbed content when the courtiers rushed like motes to the new magnet. . . .

To our perception this play [*Luria*] is not so artless and human as the *Blot in the 'Scutcheon;* its fortunes do not touch our feelings so deeply. Guendolen and Mildred uncover the heart's well, they draw for us the pathos of home, and the same draught mingles sadness for the catastrophes of sin with gratitude for home's loyalty and mercy. Yes, we thank Guendolen with our eyes and hearts, for she succeeds in assuring us that God will yet find the sullied Mildred lovable. . . . *Luria* is a lesson; *A Blot in the 'Scutcheon* is an experience; the one is a drama; the other is a heart's or home's interior. Luria is stately and inspiring; but Mildred and Guendolen are of us—women kiss them; all sit and weep with them. . . .

Is it too much to say that, with this pen for sceptre, Mr. Browning can exact the homage of all hearts? He will permit us to apply to his conceptions of truth and beauty what he says of the chief, best way of worship:

> " Let me strive
> To find it, and, when found, contrive
> My fellows also take their share."

' We deem that he possesses all the gifts and the exuberant life needed by the great artist, and he makes us conscious of a religiousness that can command their services for the good of men. "Give the world a direction toward the good," Schiller says to the artist. "You have given it this direction, if as a teacher you elevate its thoughts to the necessary and eternal ; if, while acting or composing, you transform the necessary and eternal with an object of its impulse. Create the conquering truth in the modest stillness of your soul, array it in a form of beauty, that not only thought may pay it homage, but sense lovingly comprehend its presence."

Last words of admiration and gratitude linger on our pen. We bespeak for every future line of Mr. Browning a cordial welcome here. And it is pleasant to think that he cannot regard the warm personal friendships he has unconsciously established here with indifference. . . .

> "Contrive, contrive
> To rouse us, Waring ! Who's alive ?
> Our men scarce seem in earnest now ;
> Distinguished names !—but 'tis somehow
> As if they played at being names
> Still more distinguished, like the games
> Of children. Turn our sport to earnest."

[*From " Putnam's Magazine." *]

Robert Browning's poetry is certainly very hard reading, like Cowley's and Dr. Donne's. But the difference between him and such obscurists is, that with the earlier poets, both the style and the sentiment were equally conceits—while Browning's style is the naturally quaint form of a subtle or sinewy thought. In any general classification of English poetry, Browning must be ranked with the modern school for his profound reality and humanity and faithful reliance upon nature. In any classification of poetry in general, he is strictly a dramatist — the most purely dramatic genius in English literature since the great dramatic days.

A great deal of the difficulty in reading his poetry arises from its purely dramatic conception and form. The man

* April, 1856 (vol. vii.).

Browning is not to be found in his poems, except inferentially, like Shakespeare in his dramas. The various play of profound passion is his favorite realm. He loves the South, and Southern character, as Byron loved the East. But Byron's passion, however fiery and intense, is a passion of the senses—Browning's is the passion of the soul, including and deepening the other. In other great English poets there is more daring indecency ; but in none such startling audacity of passionate expression. It is the emotional nature of man with which he deals, and with man everywhere, and under all circumstances. Thus, while the quaint structure of his mind, and his rare and curious reading, show, for instance, his natural abstract sympathy with the fantastic horrors of the Middle Ages, springing, as they did, out of a kind of cold, religious logic ; yet he dashes in the scene with a living picturesqueness, which invests it with a lurid but appropriate splendor. . . .

The fact of occasional obscurity is not to be denied. Upon the whole, Browning's poetry is harder to follow than that of any other great English poet. But the chief reason is, that he boldly aims to express what is, in its nature, so evanescent and shadowy—to put into words processes of thought and feeling, so delicately inwrought and fluctuating that only sharp self-observers and students of human character can pursue them. For instance, *Luria* and *A Soul's Tragedy* are like transverse sections of human life and human souls. As in the wax physiological models every exquisite detail is preserved, so the finest fibres of feeling, so to speak—the most intricate, and, at the same time, delicate convolutions of impulse, policy, and principle—are laid open in this poetry. The poet shrinks from expressing nothing, and there is, therefore, a variety of the profoundest passionate experience in Browning's poetry, not to be surpassed out of Shakespeare.

Critics complain that they find no difficulty in understand-

ing Pope and Thomson, and Cowper and Dryden, and Goldsmith and Byron ; but the modern school, Keats, Shelley,
Coleridge, Tennyson, and Browning, they declare to be beyond them.   They find, in the modern men, a tendency to
euphemism, a dazzling range of splendid and voluptuous
words, but nothing else.   It is contended that the modern
men mistake obscurity for profundity, and a glittering epithet for a beautiful thought.   Now, that Pope and the other
poets are, in a certain sense, easier reading than the others,
is true enough.   But it is easier reading, because it is easier
thinking.   Shakespeare is no primer, nor so shallowly intelligible.   The greatest things are simplest, certainly ; but ease
is not necessarily simplicity.   Tom Moore never perplexes
us about his meaning ; but then, Tom Moore never has much
meaning.   To insist that, if a man has anything to say, he
must say it so that everybody can understand it, is merely
idle ; for only experience can understand what experience
inspires.   To complain of Browning, because he is not so
intelligible, at a glance, as Pope, is like complaining that
Plato is not so easy as Steele.   It is as impossible that
Browning should write as Pope wrote as it is that Pope
should have written like Byron.   The truth is, that no poet's
style is more profoundly individual and appropriate than
Browning's.   The very form of his expression helps us often
to the significance of the thought ; and when we bear in
mind what the character of his mental action is ; how sudden and unexpected, and vigorous, and subtle, and romantic ;
that he is peculiarly a psychologist—it may be better, instead
of calling him turgid and blind, and asking him to say what
he means, to reflect that he has as much to say as any recent
poet, and says it as perfectly, although entirely in his own
way. . . .

The power which appears in the quaint and horrible poems of our author, which is a power working to most legitimate ends—for what a prodigious moral in human history

and development is thundered from each of the poems we have quoted—is no less evident through all his dramas, dramatic lyrics, and pure love poems. Love is peculiarly his inspiration. Not the love of girls, or sick striplings, but the terrible love of great, strong, passionate natures. Of all modern poets, Browning is the most subtle analyst of the passion, and yet, singularly enough, his poetry is full of its finest fire ; for his knowledge does not come from philosophical investigation, but from the acutest perception. Akin to this is his remarkable appreciation of the passion as it appears in women. No other English poet but Shakespeare has given expression to so many and different moods of love. He is sternly true to nature and experience. The slight influences that so strongly affect deep feeling, the inconsistencies, caprices, irrationalities, and surprises of human love, are shown by the poet in their most delicate and evanescent forms and relations. . . .

Browning's dramas would amply supply material for another article. Our present object has been rather to show the general character and affluent variety of the poet's genius, and to remind the reader that, if there is much of his verse which will demand close study to understand, there is very much which is really as simple and original and beautiful as any poetry. Browning is an objective poet in an age of subjective poetry. His heart beats strongly for the noblest truths. With all his profound sympathy with the spirit of many countries and times, he is never, for a moment, recreant to the loftiest spirit of his own age and country. Yet this sympathy never appears directly ; never, by any chance, in the way of preaching. He holds the mirror to mediæval Germany, Italy, France, and England, and so firmly that the picture is perfect, and is its own criticism. He holds the mirror to his own day as truly, and the reflection is a profound commentary upon the time. . . .

A poet's poet he has been called. But if a poet's poet, then how much a poet ! We beg the reader not to judge this man unheard, nor to believe him only a phrase-monger, because some critics cannot slip along his verses as smoothly as they do upon some others. Browning is not less a poet because he is not like other good and true poets. He would be less a poet if he were more like them; for he would then be less original and individual. His individuality is not a spasmodic use of words for thoughts; but it is the exquisite perception of a strong and rich mind, using words with a delicate skill and an inward music.

[*From the " Book of the Poets," by Elizabeth Barrett Browning.**]

It is advantageous for us all, whether poets or poetasters, or talkers about either, to know what a true poet is, what his work is, and what his patience and success must be, so as to raise the popular idea of these things, and either strengthen or put down the individual aspiration. "Art," it was said long ago, "requires the whole man," and "Nobody," it was said later, "can be a poet who is anything else;" but the present idea of Art requires the segment of a man, and everybody who is anything at all is a poet in a parenthesis. And our shelves groan with little books over which their readers groan less metaphorically; there is a plague of poems in the land apart from poetry; and many poets who live and are true do not live by their truth, but hold back their full strength from Art because they do not *reverence* it fully; and all booksellers cry aloud and do not spare, that poetry will not sell; and certain critics utter melancholy frenzies, that poetry is worn out forever—as if the morning star was worn out from heaven, or " the yellow primrose " from the grass; and Mr. D ʒraeli the younger, like Bildad comfort-

* London, 1863. This extract has a unique interest as showing the poetic value which Elizabeth Barrett gave to Mr. Browning's work even before she knew him. The papers on *The English Poets* were originally printed in 1842, in the *Athenæum.* It is scarcely straining a point to suggest that Mrs. Browning's closing quotation applies as well to Browning as to Wordsworth.

ing Job, suggests that we may content ourselves for the future with a rhythmetic prose, printed like prose for decency, and supplied, for comfort, with a parish allowance of two or three rhymes to a paragraph. Should there be any whom such a "New Poor Law" would content, we are far from wishing to disturb the virtue of their serenity ; let them continue, like the hypochondriac, to be very sure that they have lost their souls, inclusive of their poetic instincts. In the meantime the hopeful and believing will hope—trust on ; and, better still, the Tennysons and the Brownings, and other high-gifted spirits, will work, wait on, until, as Mr. Horn has said :

> "Strong deeds awake,
> And, clamoring, throng the portals of the hour."

It is well for them and all to count the cost of this life of a master in poetry, and learn from it what a true poet's crown is worth ; to recall both the long life's work for its sake— the work of observation, of meditation, of reaching past models into nature, of reaching past nature unto God ; and the early life's loss for its sake—the loss of the popular cheer, of the critical assent, and of the "money in the purse." It is well and full of exultation to remember *now* what a silent, blameless, heroic life of poetic duty this man [Wordsworth] has lived ; how he never cried rudely against the world because he was excluded for a time from the parsley garlands of its popularity ; nor sinned morally because he was sinned against intellectually ; nor, being tempted and threatened by paymaster and reviewer, swerved from the righteousness and high aims of his inexorable genius. And it cannot be ill to conclude by enforcing a high example by some noble precepts which, taken from the "Musophilus" of old Danish, do contain, to our mind, the very code of chivalry for poets :

> "Be it that my unseasonable song
> Come out of time, that fault is in the time ;
> And I must not do virtue so much wrong
> As love her aught the worse for other's crime.
> *   *   *   *   *   *   *   *

And for my part, if only one allow
  The care my laboring spirits take in this,
He is to me a theatre enow,
  And his applause only sufficient is :

" All my respect is bent but to his brow ;
  That is my all, and all I am is his,
And if some worthy spirits be pleased too,
  It shall more comfort breed, but not more **will**.
BUT WHAT IF NONE ? *It cannot yet undo*
  The love I bear unto this holy skill ;
This is the thing that I was born to do,
  This is my scene, this part must I fulfil."

[*From George Barrett Smith's Paper on Browning.**]

No contemporary poet is greater than the author of *The Ring and the Book,* and yet the world has been very fickle towards him. It reads him not, save in the spasmodic and painful effort, and if his popularity be measured by that of Tennyson or Longfellow, it may be described as the climax of neglect. His genius is powerful, but irritating ; his poems are full of entangling meshes for the unwary reader ; they are a thorn in the side of this desultory generation. Men like to have the reputation of understanding him, but are unwilling to go through the necessary amount of intellectual labor for the purpose. Critics enlarge upon his perversities of thought and diction, and yet, when all has been said against him that critical ingenuity or popular feeling can suggest, it is universally admitted that this distinguished poet's works, with all their manifest defects, are charged with passages of the very loftiest order of poetry. . . . His soul has always been aflame with poetic thought ; and his ideal and goal have never consisted in mere popular applause. He has sung because he must, and given to his song that articulation of which he was capable. . . .

The life of Browning has been such as we should wish to

* *International Review*, vol. vi. p. 176 fol.

associate always with the genuine poet—quiet, retired, uneventful. Though evidently a close student of human nature, his genius has been nurtured in contemplation rather than in the midst of those morbid forms of social and mental activity which have dwarfed and paralyzed the powers of so many men of letters. Like the oak, Browning has grown to his present stature silently and by assured natural stages ; in retirement in Italy, with the solace and communion of his wife (" Shakespeare's daughter," as a brother poet called her), and since her death, for many years in England, he has been accumulating those vast stores of knowledge which find but their merest indication in his works. . . . His friends are among the most distinguished of Englishmen ; they know his powers, his gifts, and his charms in society ; for when we say that he has shunned the common forms of mental and social activity, it must not be assumed that there is no circle whatever in society which his genius has illumined. Only he is no poser in his works or his life.

*[From the " Christian Examiner." *]*

Rich as are Mr. Browning's powers of imagination and description, his chief excellence lies in his delineation of individual character ; and we know of no other living poet who so thoroughly conceives or so finely portrays the differing shades of it found in actual life. His personages have a vitality and idiosyncrasy of their own, while they are always true to nature, and never degenerate into caricatures. Take almost any one of his principal characters, and we at once perceive this excellence, although we occasionally find them dealing quite too much in metaphysical arguments and discussions about abstract ideas. But, apart from that defect, which is, to a greater or less degree, inherent in nearly all his creations, we have little to object to in his conceptions of character. Among his female characters, the preference,

* May, 1850 (vol. xlviii.).

we suppose, will be given to Pippa, who is one of the sweetest creations of modern poetry. It is impossible to resist the beautiful simplicity and purity of her character, as it is developed in the few brief glimpses which we catch of her during her single holiday. Widely different from her and from each other are the clear-headed but faithful Polyxena, the gentle Mildred, the spotless but affectionate Guendolen, the fond mother of Luigi, the tender-hearted and patriotic Colombe, the devoted Anael, the cunning Domizia, and the thoroughly wicked Ottima; yet all are admirably conceived and sharply drawn. We at once pierce to the very heart's core of each of them, and read her whole disposition at a glance. In his delineations of male character, Mr. Browning shows equal skill. Luigi, Sebald, Monsignor, King Victor, King Charles, D'Ormea, Valence, Thorold, Austin, Henry, Gerard, Luria, Puccia, Braccio, and Tiburzio, are all living realities to the mind.

Mr. Browning's mind is eminently dramatic, and all of his works have a dramatic tone. Even his lyrical and narrative poems are very properly denominated "dramatic lyrics." Most of them, however, are dramatic poems rather than dramas, and might just as well have been cast in a different form. They lack those salient points and that briskness of movement which are needful in an effective stage-play. . . .

Colombe's Birthday is a sprightly and pleasant dramatic sketch, in which the interest centres wholly in the two principal characters, and we care little for the accessories. *A Blot in the 'Scutcheon* comes next, and is undoubtedly Mr. Browning's masterpiece; but it must be read as a whole in order to be fairly appreciated, for no extracts can do justice to its great power and beauty. It possesses a simple and massive grandeur to which none of his other works can lay claim. The reader's mind is completely overwhelmed and led captive during its perusal, and he rises from it with the full conviction that no one but a poet of the highest order could thus have chained his attention. . . .

A Soul's Tragedy is properly a dramatic poem, with little incident and only a slight attempt at characterization. The second part, however, is full of quiet humor and pointed satire. Few pieces are more characteristic of Mr. Browning's mind than this second part.

[*From Richard Henry Stoddard's Paper on Browning.**]

The characteristics of Mr. Browning are so marked, that but little critical sagacity is required to detect them. Indeed, they force themselves upon his readers, who cannot escape them, except by refusing to read him. He compels attention, even when he excites dislike. The two qualities which strike me most in his poetry are: first, an intensification of the dramatic faculty; and, second, the singularity of the method by which it is evolved. Mr. Browning is the greatest dramatic poet since Shakespeare, and, like Shakespeare's, his art is unique. The art of Shakespeare, as I understand it, is large, noble, and obvious. We are never in doubt as to his intention. There are heights in him, perhaps, which few of us can hope to scale, and depths which our plummets fail to sound; but, in the main, he is equable. We can understand his characters and his situations. Hamlet is not too profound for us, in spite of the mist with which the critics have contrived to surround him; and we readily perceive the difference between the innate jealousy of Leontes and the deceived credulity of Othello. Lear, the most stupendous of mortal creations, is a man fashioned like unto ourselves. Even Ariel and Caliban are within the range of our sympathies. I do not feel this to be the case with the *dramatis personæ* of Mr. Browning. Some few of them I understand, many I do not pretend to. Even these last, however, sometimes give me an insight into the human nature

* *Appleton's Journal*, Nov. 11, 1871 (vol. vi.).

they do not embody—clews leading into dark passages and long labyrinths — the sudden opening of doors, with lightning-like glimpses of chambers beyond. In an instant the doors are shut, the clew is dropped, and I am in the dark. . . .

I have endeavored to indicate some of the characteristics of Mr. Browning, and by comparing his method with that of Shakespeare, to show his merits and his defects. The relation which he holds to the poets of his time and the place which he holds in English Literature are not so readily determined. Certain elements at work in Poetry shortly before Mr. Tennyson arose went far to make him what he is; and of these, without entering into particulars, it is sufficient to remark that they existed in Keats; as, for example, in his *Ode to a Nightingale*, which is perhaps the most poetical poem ever written. Certain other elements went to the making of Mr. Browning; but these are not so easy to detect. They existed in no author before him, but in the literary life of the time, of which they are the result; a result the most unexpected and, so far, the least rewarded.

The renaissance of English Poetry in the first years of the present century, and the forms which it chiefly assumed, are so well known that it would be a waste of words to dwell upon them, further than to say that whatever the Form, the Spirit was always that of Story, or Narrative. From the days of Chaucer, Narrative Poetry, Story Poetry, had slumbered. It was awakened by Southey, and Scott, and Byron. Dramatic Poetry slumbered also, from the days of Shakespeare and his immediate successors, and many strove to awaken it. Miss Baillie wrote plays, which dealt with single passions. Coleridge wrote a tragedy; Wordsworth wrote a tragedy; Shiel, Milman, Croly, Maturin, Byron, Miss Mitford, wrote tragedies, some of which were played with different degrees of success. There was a demand for plays then, as there is now, and for the same reason, that there were actors who wanted plays. The actors of that period were men of genius—the Kembles, Kean, and others—and what they sought was worthy of their genius; what the actors of the present period seek is worthy, I suppose, of their genius. An attempt was made to revive the Poetic Drama, and it continued down to the "little hour" of Talfourd and Knowles, when it was abandoned. Mr. Macready was the last actor of note who had faith in it. It was "faith without works."

It is instructive to read the modern Poetic Drama—to see what beauties it has—how sweet, and tender, and manly much of it is, and—how little it really accomplished.

At last there came a poet who, in all probability, knew nothing about this— certainly a poet who cared nothing for it, if he knew it; and it is to him that we must pay homage for whatever is good, great, and profound in the second period of the Poetic Drama of England. It is not what his predecessors sought to find; it is not what Shakespeare found without seeking; it is something never found, and never sought before. That so strange a flower should spring from such roots is marvellous. It is the Body blossoming into Soul.

Such I conceive is Robert Browning and his work.

[*From the "North British Review."* *]

It will be impossible for us to do any sort of justice to Mr. Browning's dramas by quotation or otherwise. Yet these alone ought to be sufficient to build up the fame of a true and great poet. *King Victor and King Charles* is a profound study of statecraft and human nature, finely intervolved and as finely evolved. *The Return of the Druses* is likewise most subtle and intense, with its perplexity of motives solved by passionate action, and the complexity of life made all clear by death. The conclusion of this tragedy is grand as a sunset. The Duchess *Colombe* is one of our especial favorites; our 'play queen' so natural and brave on her birthday. And

* May, 1861 (vol. xxxiv.).

Pippa, everybody's favorite with her one day's holiday, going about like an unwitting missionary of heaven, doing good without knowing it. . . . *A Blot in the 'Scutcheon* is full of deep, moving power. The characters are living, breathing, loving, and suffering human souls, real enough to stir the profoundest human feelings. By the nearest and dearest ties they are bound up in the dark web of a bitter fate. We see how they might be saved, but cannot save them. We behold them striving in the toils, and the great shadowing cloud overhead coming straight down, big and black to bursting. Life and death are brought to the fine turning-point of a single word, and it cannot be spoken. Thus an interest is created intensely tragic. We have before mentioned the passionate pathos of this drama. The pathos of that last parting betwixt Arthur and Guinevere in Tennyson's fourth Idyl is very noble, but this is yet more piercing.

[*From Darmesteter's " Essais de Littérature Anglaise."* *]

The obscurity of Browning does not proceed, as with Hugo and Tennyson, in their latest period, from the vague immensity of the subjects considered, from the indefiniteness of his ideas, from the predominance of metaphysical abstractions, but, on the contrary, from the very precision of the ideas and sentiments, studied in their remotest ramifications, in all their varied complications, and then presented in a mass of abstractions and metaphors, now with the infinite minuteness of scholastic argument, now with sudden leaps over abysses of deeper significance. Browning is, *par excellence*, the psychological poet. "Mine," he says—

"Mine be man's thoughts, loves, hates !"

Hence his obscurity, because he plunges to the very depths ; but hence, also, his force. No English poet since Shakespeare—say the critics, even the most severe, who have stud-

* *Essais de Littérature Anglaise*, par James Darmesteter (Paris, 1883).

ied Browning most thoroughly— has had in a higher degree
the dramatic quality, that is to say, the power of going out
of one's self, and of entering into another soul; he is the most
objective poet in an age in which each of us has only one
soul, his own, and in which all poetry is only a confession;
he is, perhaps, the only poet of our time who creates souls.

[*From Symons's " Introduction to the Study of Browning."* *]

There is another popular misconception to which also a
word in passing may as well be devoted. This is the idea
that Mr. Browning's personality is apt to get confused with
his characters', that his men and women are not separate
creations, projected from his brain into an independent existence, but mere masks or puppets through whose mouths
he speaks. This fallacy arises from the fact that not a few
of his imaginary persons express themselves in a somewhat
similar fashion; or, as people too rashly say, "talk like
Browning." The explanation of this apparent paradox, so
far as it exists, is not far to seek. All art is a compromise,
and all dramatic speech is in fact impossible. No persons
in real life would talk as Shakespeare or any other great
dramatist makes them talk. Nor do the characters of Shakespeare talk like those of any other great dramatist, except
in so far as later playwrights have consciously imitated
Shakespeare. Every dramatic writer has his own style, and

* *An Introduction to the Study of Browning,* by Arthur Symons (London, 1886), p. 18.

This book, which has appeared since our *Select Poems of Browning* was
published, should be added to the list of the "Helps to the Study of the
Poet" given in that volume (p. 13). If the works there mentioned are
valuable to the student, this is invaluable. It is compact, clear, unaffected,
exhaustive. Of course it does not aim to say all that may well be said
of Browning, but in its well-defined sphere it is complete. There is at
present so much insincere attitudinizing which passes under the name
of enthusiasm for our poet that it is a genuine relief to meet with a work
at once simple, virile, and appreciative.

in this style, subject to modification, all his characters speak. Just as a soul, born out of eternity into time, takes on itself the impress of earth and the manners of human life, so a dramatic creation, pure essence in the shaping imagination of the poet, takes on itself, in its passage into life, something of the impress of its abode. "The poet, in short, endows his creations with his own attributes; he enables them to utter their feelings as if they themselves were poets, thus giving a true voice even to that intensity of passion which in real life often hinders expression."* If this fact is recognized — that dramatic speech is not real speech, but poetical speech, and poetical speech infused with the individual style of each individual dramatist, modulated, indeed, but true to one keynote—then it must be granted that Mr. Browning has as much right to his own style as other dramatists have to theirs, and as little right as they to be accused on that account of putting his personality into his work. But as Mr. Browning's style is very pronounced and original, it is more easily recognizable than that of most dramatists—so far, no doubt, a defect †—and for this reason it has come to seem relatively more prominent than it really is. This consideration, and not any confusion of identity, is the cause of whatever similarity of speech exists between Mr. Browning and his characters, or between individual characters. The similarity is only skin-deep. Take a convenient

---

* "Realism in Dramatic Art," *New Quarterly Magazine*, Oct., 1879.

† Allowing at its highest valuation all that need be allowed on this score, we find only that Mr. Browning has the defects of his qualities; and from these who is exempted? By virtue of this style of his he has succeeded in rendering into words the very inmost thoughts and finest shades of feeling of the "men and women fashioned by his fancy," and in such a task we can pardon even a fault—for such a result we can overlook even a blemish; as Lessing, in *Laokoon*, remarking on an error in Raphael's drapery, finely says, "Who will not rather praise him for having had the wisdom and the courage to commit a slight fault, for the sake of greater fulness of expression?"

instance, *The Ring and the Book.* I have often seen it stated that the nine tellings of the story are all told in the same style, that all the speakers—Guido and Pompilia, the Pope and Tertium Quid alike—speak like Browning. I cannot see it. On the contrary, I have been astonished, in reading and rereading the poem, at the variety, the difference, the wonderful individuality in each speaker's way of telling the same story—at the profound art with which the rhythm, the metaphors, the very details of language, no less than the broad distinctions of character and the subtle indications of bias, are adapted and converted into harmony. A certain general style, a certain general manner of expression, are common to all, as is also the case in, let us say, *The Tempest.* But what distinction, what variation of tone, what delicacy and expressiveness of modulation! As a simple matter of fact, few writers have ever had a greater flexibility of style than Mr. Browning.

I am doubtful whether full justice has been done to one section of Mr. Browning's dramatic work—his portraits of women. The presence of Woman is not perhaps relatively so prominent in his work as it is in the work of some other poets; he has nothing of that exclusive preoccupation with the subject, nothing of that adoring or reviling fascination which we sometimes see; but as faithful and vital representations, I do not hesitate to put his portraits of women quite on a level with his portraits of men, and far beyond those of any other English poet of the last three centuries. In some of them, notably in Pompilia, there is a something—I can hardly describe it—which always seems to me almost incredible in a man: an instinct that one would have thought only a woman could feel or see. And his women, good or bad, are always real women, and they are represented without bias. Mr. Browning is one of the very few men—Mr. Meredith, whose women are, perhaps, the consummate flower of his work, is the only other now living in England—who can

paint women without idealization or degradation, not from
the man's side, but from their own ; as living equals, not as
goddesses or as toys.   His women live, act, and suffer—
even think ; not assertively, mannishly—for the loveliest of
them have a very delicate charm of girlishness — but with
natural volition, on equal rights with men.   Any one who
has thought at all on the matter will acknowledge that this
is the highest praise that could be given — the highest and
rarest.   Mr. Browning's women are not indeed as various as
his men ; but from Ottima to Pompilia — from the "great
white queen, magnificent in sin," to the "lily of a maiden,
white with intact leaf" — what a range and gradation of
character !   These are the two extremes ; between them, as
earth lies betwixt heaven and hell, are stationed all the others, from the faint and delicate dawn in Pauline, Michal, and
Palma, on through Pippa and Mildred and Colombe and
Constance and the Queen, to Balaustion and Elvire, Fifine
and Clara and the heroine of the *Inn Album*, and the lurid
close in Cristina.   I have named only a few, and how many
there are to name !

III. CRITICAL COMMENTS ON "A BLOT IN THE 'SCUTCHEON."
  [*From Symons's " Introduction to the Study of Browning." * *]

A Blot in the 'Scutcheon is the simplest, and perhaps the
deepest and finest of Mr. Browning's plays.   The Browning
Society's performance, and Mr. Barrett's in America, have
proved its acting capacities, its power to hold and thrill an
audience.   The language has a rich simplicity of the highest
dramatic value, quick with passion, pregnant with thought,
and masterly in imagination ; the plot and characters are
perhaps more interesting and affecting than in any other of
the plays ; while the effect of the whole is impressive from
its unity.   The scene is English ; the time somewhere in the
eighteenth century; the motive, family honor and dishon-

* Page 62 fol.

or. The story appeals to ready popular emotions, emotions which, though lying nearest the surface, are also the most deeply-rooted. The whole action is passionately pathetic, and it is infused with a twofold tragedy—the tragedy of the sin, and that of the misunderstanding—the last and final tragedy, which hangs on a word, a word spoken only when too late to save three lives. This irony of circumstance is at once the source of earth's saddest discords, and the motive of art's truest tragedies. It takes the place, in our modern world, of the ʼΑνάγκη, the irresistible Fate of the Greeks ; and is not less impressive because it arises from the impulse and unreasoning wilfulness of man rather than from the implacable insistency of God. It is with perfect justice, both moral and artistic, that the fatal crisis, though mediately the result of accident, of error, is shown to be the consequence and the punishment of wrong. A tragedy resulting from the mistakes of the wholly innocent would jar on our sense of right, and could never produce a legitimate work of art. Even Œdipus suffers, not merely because he is under the curse of a higher power, but because he is wilful, and rushes upon his own fate. Timon suffers, not because he was generous and good, but from the defects of his qualities. So, in this play, each of the characters calls down upon his own head the suffering which at first seems to be a mere caprice and confusion of chance. Mildred Tresham and Henry Mertoun, both very young, ignorant, and unguarded, have sinned. They attempt a late reparation, apparently with success, but the hasty suspicion of Lord Tresham, Mildred's brother, diverted indeed into a wrong channel, brings down on both a terrible retribution. Tresham, who shares the ruin he causes, feels, too, that his punishment is his due. He has acted without pausing to consider, and he is called on to pay the penalty of " evil wrought by want of thought."

The character of Mildred, " more sinned against than sinning," is exquisitely and most tenderly drawn.   We see her, and we see and feel—

> "the good and tender heart,
> Its girl's trust and its woman's constancy,
> How pure yet passionate, how calm yet kind,
> How grave yet joyous, how reserved yet free.
> As light where friends are "—

as her brother, in a memorable passage, describes her.   She is so thrillingly alive, so beautiful and individual, so pathetic and pitiful in her desolation.   Every word she speaks comes straight from her heart to ours.   "I know nothing that is so affecting," wrote Dickens in a letter to Forster, "nothing in any book I have ever read, as Mildred's recurrence to that 'I was so young—I had no mother.'"*   Not till Pompilia do we find so pathetic a portrait of a woman.

In Thorold, Earl Tresham, we have an admirable picture of the head of a great house, proud above all things of the honor of the family and its yet stainless 'scutcheon, and proud, with a deep brotherly tenderness, of his sister Mildred : a strong and fine nature, one whom men instinctively cite as "the perfect spirit of honor."   Mertoun, the apparent hero of the play, is a much less prominent and masterly figure than Tresham, not so much from any lack of skill in his de- lineation, as from the essential ineffectualness of his nature. Guendolen Tresham, the Beatrice of the play — her lover Austin is certainly no Benedick—is one of the most pleas- antly humorous characters in Mr. Browning's works.   Her gay, light-hearted talk brightens the sombre action like a gleam of sunlight.   And, like her prototype, she has a true woman's heart.   As Beatrice stands by the calumniated Hero, so Guendolen stands by Mildred, and by her quick woman's heart and wit, her instinct of things, sees and seizes the missing clew, though too late, as it proves, to avert the impending catastrophe.

* Forster's *Life of Dickens*, vol. ii. p. 24.

The play contains one of Mr. Browning's most delicate and musical lyrics — the serenade beginning, "There's a woman like a dew-drop." This is the first of the love-songs in long lines which Mr. Browning has so frequently written of very recent years, and so seldom before.

[*From Forster's "Life of Dickens."* *]

This was the date of Mr. Browning's tragedy of the *Blot in the 'Scutcheon,* which I took upon myself, after reading it in the manuscript, privately to impart to Dickens ; and I was not mistaken in the belief that it would profoundly touch him. "Browning's play," he wrote, "has thrown me into a perfect passion of sorrow. To say that there is anything in its subject save what is lovely, true, deeply affecting, full of the best emotion, the most earnest feeling, and the most true and tender source of interest, is to say that there is no light in the sun, and no heat in blood. It is full of *genius*, natural and great thoughts, profound and yet simple and beautiful in its vigor. I know nothing that is so affecting, nothing in any book I have ever read, as Mildred's recurrence to that ' I was so young—I had no mother.' I know no love like it, no passion like it, no moulding of a splendid thing after its conception, like it. And I swear it is a tragedy that MUST be played ; and must be played, moreover, by Macready. There are some things I would have changed if I could (they are very slight, mostly broken lines) ; and I assuredly would have the old servant *begin his tale upon the scene;* and be taken by the throat, or drawn upon, by his master, in its commencement. But the tragedy I never shall forget, or less vividly remember than I do now. And if you tell Browning that I have seen it, tell him that I believe from my soul there is no man living (and not many dead) who could produce such a work."

* Vol. ii. p. 46.

IV. CRITICAL COMMENTS ON "COLOMBE'S BIRTHDAY."

[From Symons's "Introduction to the Study of Browning."]*

Colombe's Birthday, a drama founded on an imaginary episode in the history of a German duchy of the seventeenth century, is the first play which is mainly concerned with inward rather than outward action; in which the characters themselves, what they are in their own souls, what they think of themselves, and what others think of them, constitute the chief interest, the interest of the characters as they influence one another or external events being, however intense in itself, distinctly secondary. The point on which the action turns is this. Colombe of Ravestein, Duchess of Juliers and Cleves, is surprised, on the first anniversary of her accession (the day being also her birthday), by a rival claimant to the duchy, Prince Berthold, who proves to be in fact the true heir. Berthold, instead of pressing his claim, offers to marry her. But he conceives the honor and the favor to be sufficient, and makes no pretence at offering love as well. On the other hand, Valence, a poor advocate of Cleves, who has stood by Colombe when all her other friends failed, offers her his love, a love to which she can only respond by "giving up the world"—in other words, by relinquishing her duchy, and the alliance with a Prince who is on the road to be Emperor. Now, we have nothing to do with the question of who has the right and who has the might : that matter is settled, and the succession agreed on, almost from the beginning. Nor are we made to feel that any disgrace or reputation of weakness will rest on Colombe if she gives up her place ; not even that the pang at doing so will be over-acute or entirely unrelieved. All the interest centres in the purely personal and psychological bearings of the act. It is perhaps a consequence of this that the style is somewhat differ-

* Page 65 fol.

ent from that of any previous play. Any one who notices
the stage directions will see that the persons of the drama
frequently speak "after a pause." The language which they
use is, naturally enough, more deliberate and reflective, the
lines are slower and more weighty, than would be appropriate amid the breathless action of *A Blot in the 'Scutcheon* or
The Return of the Druses. A certain fiery quality, a thrill-
ing, heart-stirred and heart-stirring tone, which we find in
these is wanting; but the calm sweep of the action carries
with it some of the finest harmonics of line and metaphor
since *Paracelsus*.

Colombe, the veritable heroine of the drama, is, if not
"the completest full-length portrait of a woman that Mr.
Browning has drawn," certainly both one of the sweetest
and one of the completest. Her character develops during
the course of the play—as she herself says,

> "This is indeed my birthday—soul and body,
> Its hours have done on me the work of years—"

and it leaves her a nobler and stronger, yet not less charming woman than it found her. Hitherto she has been a mere
"play-queen," shut in from action, shut in from facts and the
world, and required only to be gay and amused. But now,
at the first and yet final trial, she is proved and found to be
of noble metal. The gay girlishness of the young Duchess,
her joyous and generous light heart; her womanliness, her
earnestness, her clear, deep, noble nature, attract us from her
first words, and leave us, after the hour we have spent in her
presence, with the inalienable uplifting memory that we have
of some women whom we meet, for an hour or a moment, in
the world or in books.

Berthold, the weary and unsatisfied conqueror, is a singularly unconventional figure. He is a man of action, with
some of the sympathies of the scholar and the lover; reso-
lute in the attainment of ends which he sees to be, in themselves, vulgar; his ambition rather an instinct than something

to be pursued for itself, and his soul too keenly aware of the joys and interests he foregoes to be quite satisfied or content with his lot and conduct. The grave courtesy of his speech to Colombe, his somewhat condescending but not unfriendly tone with Valence, his rough home-truths with the parasitical courtiers, and his frank confidence with Melchior, are admirably discriminated. Melchior himself, little as he speaks, is a fine sketch of the contemplative, bookish man who finds no more congenial companion and study than a successful man of action. His attitude of detachment—a mere spectator in the background—is well in keeping with the calm and thoughtful character of the play. Valence, the true hero of the piece, the "pale fiery man" who can speak with so moving an eloquence, whether he is pleading the wrongs of his townsmen or of Colombe, the rights of Berthold or himself, is no less masterly a portrait than the Prince, though perhaps less wholly unconventional a character. His grave earnestness, his honor as a man and passion as a lover, move our instinctive sympathy, and he never for a moment forfeits it. Were it for nothing else, he would win our lasting remembrance from the mere fact that he is one of the speakers in that most delightful of love-duets, the incomparable scene at the close of the fourth act. " I remember well to have seen," wrote Mr. Moncure D. Conway in 1854, "a vast miscellaneous crowd in an American theatre hanging with breathless attention upon every word of this interview, down to the splendid climax when, in obedience to the Duchess's direction to Valence how he should reveal his love to the lady she so little suspects herself to be herself, he kneels —every heart evidently feeling each word as an electric touch, and all giving vent at last to their emotion in round after round of hearty applause."

All the minor characters are very good and lifelike, particularly Guibert, the shrewd, hesitating, talkative, cynical, really good-hearted old courtier, whom not even a court has

INTRODUCTION.   47

deprived of a heart, though the dangerous influence of the
conscienceless Gaucelme, his fellow, has in its time played
sad pranks with it.   He is one of the best of Mr. Browning's
minor characters.

The performance, in 1885, of *Colombe's Birthday*, under
the auspices of the Browning Society, has brought to light
unsuspected acting qualities in what is certainly not the most
"dramatic" of Mr. Browning's plays. "*Colombe's Birthday*," it was said on the occasion, "is charming on the boards,
clearer, more direct in action, more full of delicate surprises,
than one imagines it in print.   With a very little cutting it
could be made an excellent acting play." *

[From Mr. G. F. Chorley's Review of "Bells and Pomegranates." †]

It is a question whether any creation exists more chivalrous in its tone than this legend ; that is, if we somewhat
refine the epithet, and (by courtesy of poetical fiction) admit
it to include loyalty, delicacy—a recognition that there are
few who have not some touches of a higher nature than dis-
tinguishes the churl and the worshipper of Mammon. *Colombe's Birthday* is a tale of humanity and grace and poetry,
vindicating themselves in that place where, of all others, it
has been deemed the least possible to find them—a court :
of Ambition, in the moment of its triumph, compelled to confess to itself and to the world its own haggard weariness—
its inability to rest, its indifference to attempt new conquests
—written with all the noble generosity of youth, and all the
ripe experience of middle age. This and *A Blot in the
'Scutcheon* are the only two of the dramas in Mr. Browning's
Bells which could be made available on the stage—as the
stage stands. . . .

It appears from the play that, some time in the seventeenth century, the Duchy of Juliers and Cleves fell for a

* A. Mary F. Robinson, in *Boston Literary World*, December 12, 1885.
† *The People's Journal*, vol. ii. p. 38 fol.

twelvemonth under the government of a young and fair lady, supposed to be rightful heiress to a little kingdom. She had been brought up at Ravestein, an old castle down upon the Meuse; her youth, it would seem, left to its own guidance and innocence. And so she had taken state upon her lightly—had enjoyed, like an innocent girl who has seen few pageants, a gay reception which her subjects of Cleves had prepared for her—and had queened it so brightly and gently that her presence seemed to throw something of grace and humanity over the faded, formal functionaries of her little court—the Sieurs Guibert, Gaucelme, Maufroy, and Clugnet; insomuch that it was with something more than selfish anxiety for their wands and gold chains—with a touch of regret— that they received the tidings how Duchess Colombe's claims to her inheritance were disputed by a wise and powerful rival, Prince Berthold, who was on his way to Juliers to maintain his rights. Rumors of such a revolution had been for some time menacing them; but the bolt fell (so to say) in the tidings of the immediate coming of Prince Berthold, on no luckier day than the gentle Colombe's birthday. Little conscious of such instant peril, that gracious and delicate lady was preparing to hold her court, and to receive the good wishes of her subjects. The drama opens at the moment when the four courtiers were waiting in the ante-chamber, at a loss how to break the calamity to their mistress, saving themselves the while. A coarser chronicler would have forgotten their reluctance in their selfish uneasiness—have made the troop all equally mechanical. But Mr. Browning knows that there is a difference even among automatons. Sir Guibert had a touch of better nature than his fellows. Some slight intercourse with the people, it may be, had rendered him a trifle less wooden and metallic than his mates. He had had dealings in Cleves; had been beholden to one Valence, an advocate there, in winning some contest which involved his property; and was disposed to be as generous, and considerate, and pitiful—as a weak and mean man can be. At that precise moment of his perplexity, that very advocate just mentioned had come to court on the Duchess's birthday; all her old flatterers being kept away from her presence by the rumor of her tottering fortunes. And Valence even was come to sue, not to congratulate; to present a memorial on the wretchedness of Cleves, not to soothe fair Colombe with sweet wishes of many happy returns of so fair a day. Now Valence was a sour, thin man of common presence, in a thread-bare coat, and too full, it seemed, of his business to have studied the right way of presenting himself. The ushers would not let him enter the corridor, and had driven him back again and again; till, espying Sir Guibert, Valence forced his way in, and claimed the offices of the courtier whose estate he had saved to bring him to a speech with Duchess Colombe. A bright thought struck Sir Guibert, how to pay his debt of gratitude, and relieve himself of an unpleasant responsibility in one and the same moment. He undertook to present Valence, on condition that the latter would place in the Duchess's hand the memorial of Prince Berthold's claim! The anxious advocate of the people —unsuspecting, and absorbed in his own duties—fell into the trap. The doors were opened, and the four courtiers, and with them Valence, passed into the presence-chamber.

There was waiting the sweet Duchess Colombe, and with her one faithful bower-woman, Sabyne. She must have been more, or less, than woman, not to have been vexed at the thinness of the rank who came to pay court to her, as compared with the throng of the past year. Her strugglings with her misgivings—her consciousness that, once having been made a ruler, she can no more return to the pleasures of girlhood—are beautifully expressed :

> " Well sunshine's everywhere, and summer too.
> Next year 't is the old place again, perhaps—
> The water breeze again, the birds again.—
> It cannot be ! It is too late to be !"

And then the sudden heartening of herself up to believe what
she wishes, when she sees the courtiers enter :

> " (*Aside.*) The same words, the same faces, the same love !
> I have been over-fearful.   These are few—
> But these at least stand firmly—these are mine !
> As many come as may ;   and if no more,
> 'T is that these few suffice—they do suffice !
> What succor may not next year bring me !   Plainly
> I feared too soon !"

It was new for Advocate Valence to be dazzled by an apparition of such youth and graciousness !   He had much to
do, when permitted to speak, to plead the cause of the starving people of Cleves before her !   But though bewildered, he
was not silenced.   Out spake he ! told that fair and dainty
lady that the dream in which she had lived, and the pomp in
which she had moved abroad, had hidden from her the misery of her people ; prayed her to redress their wrongs ; and,
moved by his own earnestness, though still confused by so
fairy-like a presence, placed in her hand—not the petition
of the starving sufferers of Cleves—but the memorial of
Prince Berthold !   The Duchess read ; too proud to own
herself insulted, too young and delicate not to confess her
loneliness, and to ask upbraidingly why had her courtiers
brought her from Ravenstein, if their loyalty could protect
her no better than this !   She ended by taking off her coronet, and thanking God she was no longer Duchess of such a
heartless people !   At the sight of her nobility flashed out the
generous spirit of the people's advocate—more courteous in
all his uncourtliness than any of Colombe's cowardly follow-
ers.   " Sir Guibert," said he, advancing indignantly—

> " Sir Guibert ! knight they call you !—this of mine
> Is the first step I ever set at court.
> You dared make me your instrument, I find ;
> For that, so sure as you and I are men,
> We reckon to the utmost presently !
> But as you are a courtier and I none,
> Your knowledge may instruct me.   I already

> Have too far outraged, by my ignorance
> Of courtier-ways, this lady, to proceed
> A second step, and risk addressing her.
> I am degraded—you let me address !
> Out of her presence all is plain enough
> What I shall do—but in her presence, too,
> Surely there 's something proper to be done.
> (*To the others.*) You gentles, tell me if I guess aright—
> May I not strike this man to earth ?"

This burst of generous spirit stirred Sir Guibert, mean as he was, to make humble apology, on bended knee, to the lady. It did yet more—it stirred the young Duchess to feel and to know that loyalty might mean a nobler thing than observance out of book and flattery from the lips, not from the heart. She bent at once an eager and respectful ear to her new champion and counsellor—listened to his eloquent tale of the woes of Cleves ; and, absolving the cowardly, half-penitent courtiers from further suit and service, declared that, so long as such men as Valence were among her subjects, she would not yield up her Duchy till the right was tried ! and there and then invested him with all the offices her servants had laid down.

While these things were passing, Prince Berthold arrived, unguarded ;—having left his men-at-arms at Aix, and being only accompanied by Melchior, his philosopher-in-ordinary. For Prince Berthold, though an ambitious man, marking Juliers as one step to be gained towards

"Aix, Cologne, Frankfort, Milan, Rome !"

was not the common, vulgar usurper—half swordsman, half sensualist—by aid of whom, one poorer or coarser in imagination than Mr. Browning would have wrought out his contrast. He had a taste for what was refined and beautiful—when young, had wooed a rosy maiden, Priscilla, under a gray convent wall ;—and had not forgotten, even now that he was a hard, experienced statesman, how he had wooed

in vain! Further, though desirous of conquest, none was
readier than Prince Berthold to despise the courtier crew,
who, appalled by his presence, and each man anxious to
hold fast his place, welcomed him obsequiously ; and told
him with a sneer that Duchess Colombe denied his claim,
and defied himself—advised, doubtless, by "that blustering
advocate." These glimpses of a brave spirit in the lady suggested, with lightning quickness, a measure to the Prince,
who had never forgotten his love failure. Why not woo and
wed this high-hearted Colombe? — why not win the Duchy
without discrowning its gentle Duchess? The thought
pleased ; and ere it had passed, the lady had entered with
Valence at her side ;—her pride and the new interest which
the advocate's noble words had awakened making her
beauty more beautiful. But so courteous was Prince Berthold as at once to deprive her of half her indignation. Almost he seemed to apologize to her ; he, who could have
enforced—for preferring—his claim ; put aside, with disdain,
the intervention of the cast-off courtiers ; and listened with
grave deference to the strangely-won friend to whom the
Duchess referred him. Well might he listen when Valence
could speak for his lady and himself so nobly as he did
speak. I know of few things in heroic poetry finer than the
appeal :—

> "*Berthold.*   Where
> Stand those should answer ?
> *Valence* (*advancing*).   The lady is alone ?
> *Berthold*.   Alone, and thus ?   So weak and yet so bold ?
> *Valence*.   I said she was alone—
> *Berthold*.   And weak I said.
> *Valence*.   When is man strong until he feels alone ?
> It was some lonely strength at first, be sure,
> Created organs, such as those you seek,
> By which to give its varied purpose shape—
> And naming the selected ministrants,
> Took sword and shield and sceptre,—each a man !
> *That strength performed its work and passed its way.*

You see our lady : there the old shapes stand—
A Marshal, Chamberlain, and Counsellor—
' Be helped their way, into their death put life
And find advantage !'—so you counsel us !
But let strength feel alone, seek help itself,
And as the inland-hatched sea-creature hunts
The sea's breast out,—as littered mid the waves,
The desert brute makes for the desert's joy,
So, I am first her instinct fastens on,—
And prompt I say, as clear as heart can speak,
The people will not have you, nor shall have !
It is not merely I shall go bring Cleves
And fight you to the last—though that does much,
And men and children—ay, and women too,
Fighting for home, are rather to be feared
Than mercenaries fighting for their pay—
But, say you beat us, since such things have been,
And, where this Juliers laughed, you set your foot
Upon a steaming bloody plash—what then ?
Stand you the more our lord, as there you stand ?
Lord it o'er troops whose force you concentrate,
A pillared flame whereto all ardours tend—
Lord it 'mongst priests whose schemes you amplify,
A cloud of smoke, 'neath which all shadows brood,
But never, in this gentle spot of earth
Can you become our Colombe, our play-queen
Whom we, to furnish lilies for her hair
Would pour our veins out to enrich the soil !
Our conqueror ? Yes !—Our despot ? Yes !—Our Duke ?
Know yourself, know us !"

The remainder of the tale must be told more briefly, since
the characters are now set in all their many-colored hues
before the reader, and he will be able to follow out the story
without minute explanation ; or, what is better, he is by this
time eager to turn to the book and read the rest for himself.
Enough to say that Prince Berthold courteously intrusted to
Valence the examination of his claims ; and that these, alas
for Colombe, were proved to be valid. That the Prince also
confided to the advocate's skill his project for repairing the
lady's losses, by offering to her his hand and the Duchy.

But the lady meanwhile has discovered, not only that her new chamberlain was loyal to his Duchess — but that the man of the people — who could speak so gloriously, think so nobly, was devoted to the woman who could meet danger so heroically! Somewhat of the Duchess training clung to her — somewhat of the girl's wilfulness. Prince Berthold's noble offer flattered her fancy and soothed her pride, for youth is more dazzled by grandeur than age, which has learned its utter hollowness. And then, it was sweet to try how noble her pale, earnest servitor could be! What living being thus enforced would not have wavered? The victory had been nothing without the struggle. And Colombe did waver for an hour. But there was victory; and after having fathomed to its most secret depths one of the truest and noblest hearts which ever God created — finding at every touch a new and answering fountain of high thoughts and unselfish purposes up-springing in her own — Colombe, the Duchess, ended her birthday by choosing the better part — yielding up empty power, and embracing life with its duties, love with its rewards. Prince Berthold went his way, leaving a "black Barnabite" behind him as viceroy, to enforce from the courtiers the duty they were in such agony to tender — and the advocate returned to Cleves with a fond and fair lady.

The closing act of this beautiful drama, rich in the loftiest poetry, could have been dwelt and drawn upon, to the pleasure of every one; most of all my own. But enough has been said to indicate — and that is the purpose of these poor sketches. There is small hope of any one's progress in appreciating poetry, if, after having made the slight effort which Mr. Browning's style demands, he who has begun *Colombe's Birthday* can lay it down till the play be played out and the curtain has fallen. I repeat that if it be too fine for the stage, the fault is that our actors are too coarse, not that our audiences are incapable of relishing fancies so "chaste and noble!"

V. CRITICAL COMMENTS ON "A SOUL'S TRAGEDY."

[From Symons's "Introduction to the Study of Browning." *]

The development of Mr. Browning's genius, as shown in his plays, has been touched on in dealing with *Colombe's Birthday*. That play, as I intimated, shows the first token of transition from the comparatively conventional dramatic style of the early plays to the completely unconventional style of the later ones, which in turn lead almost imperceptibly to the final pausing-place of the monologue. From *A Blot in the 'Scutcheon* to *Colombe's Birthday* is a step; from *Colombe's Birthday* to *A Soul's Tragedy* and *Luria* another step; and in these last we are not more than another step from *Men and Women* and its successors. In *A Soul's Tragedy* the action is all internalized. Outward action there is, and of a sufficiently picturesque nature; but here, considerably more than even in *Colombe's Birthday*, the interest is withdrawn from the action, *as action*, and concentrated on a single character, whose "*soul's* tragedy," not his mere worldly fortunes, strange and significant as these are, we are called on to contemplate. Chiappino fills and possesses the scene. The other characters are carefully subordinated, and the impression we receive is not unlike that received from one of Mr. Browning's most vivid and complete monologues, with its carefully placed apparatus of side-lights.

The character of Chiappino is that of a Djabal degenerated; he is the second of Mr. Browning's delineations of the half-deceived and half-deceiving nature, the moral hybrid. Chiappino comes before us as a much-professing yet apparently little-performing person, moody and complaining, envious of his friend Luitolfo's better fortune, a soured man and a discontented patriot. But he is quite sure of his own complete probity. He declaims bitterly against his fellow-townsmen, his friend, and his love — all of whom, he asseverates,

* Page 79 fol.

treat him unjustly, and as he never could, by any possibility, treat them. While he is thus protesting to Eulalia, his friend's betrothed, to whom for the first time he avows his own love, a trial is at hand, and nearer than he or we expect. Luitolfo rushes in. He has gone to the Provost's palace to intercede on behalf of his banished friend, and in a moment of wrath has struck and, as he thinks, killed the Provost: the guards are after him, and he is lost. Is this the moment of test? Apparently; and apparently Chiappino proves his nobility. For, with truly heroic unselfishness, he exchanges dress with his friend, induces him, in a sort of stupefaction of terror, to escape, and remains in his place, "to die for him." But the harder test has yet to come. Instead of the Provost's guards, it is the enthusiastic populace that burst in upon him, hailing him as saviour and liberator. The people have risen in revolt, the guards have fled, and the people call on the striker of the blow to be their leader. *Chiappino says nothing.* "Chiappino?" says Eulalia, questioning him with her eyes. "Yes, I understand," he rejoins,

> "You think I should have promptlier disowned
> This deed with its strange unforeseen success,
> In favor of Luitolfo. But the peril,
> So far from ended, hardly seems begun.
> To-morrow, rather, when a calm succeeds,
> We easily shall make him full amends ;
> And meantime—if we save them as they pray,
> And justify the deed by its effects?
> > *Eulalia.* You would, for worlds, you had denied at once.
> > *Chiappino.* I know my own intention, be assured !
> All 's well. Precede us, fellow-citizens !"

Thus ends act first, "being what was called the poetry of Chiappino's life ;" and act second, "its prose," opens after a supposed interval of a month.

The second act exhibits, in very humorous prose, the gradual and inevitable deterioration which the silence and the deception have brought about. Drawn on and on, upon his own lines of thought and conduct, by Ogniben, the Pope's legate, who has come to put down the revolt by diplomatic measures, Chiappino denies his political principles—finding a democratic rule not at all so necessary when possibly the provostship may fall to himself; denies his love, for his views of love are, he finds, widened; and, finally, denies his friend, to the extent of arguing that the very blow which, as struck by Luitolfo, has been the factor of his fortune, was practically, because logically, his own. Ogniben now agrees to invest him with the Provost's office, making at the same time the stipulation that the actual assailant of the Provost shall suffer the proper penalty. Hereupon Luitolfo comes forward and avows the deed. Ogniben orders him to his house; Chiappino "goes aside for a time;" "and now," concludes the legate, addressing the people, "give thanks to God, the keys of the Provost's palace to me, and yourselves to profitable meditation at home."

Besides Chiappino, there are three other characters, who serve to set off the main figure. Eulalia is an observer, Luitolfo a foil, Ogniben a touchstone. Eulalia and Luitolfo, though sufficiently wrought out for their several purposes, are but sketches, the latter perhaps more distinctly outlined than the former, and serving admirably as a contrast to Chiappino. But Ogniben, who does so much of the talking in the second act, is a really memorable figure. His portrait is painted with more prominent effect, for his part in the play is to draw Chiappino out, and to confound him with his own weapons: "I help men," as he says, "to carry out their own principles; if they please to say two and two make five, I assent, so they will but go on and say, four and four make ten." His shrewd Socratic prose is delightfully wise and witty. This prose —the only dramatic prose written by Mr. Browning, with the exception of that in *Pippa Passes*—is, in its way, almost as good as the poetry; admirably keen, vivacious, full-thoughted, picturesque, and singularly original. For instance, Chiappino is expressing his longing for a woman who could understand, as he says, the whole of him, to whom he could reveal alike his strength and weakness.

"Ah my friend," rejoins Ogniben, "wish for nothing so foolish! Worship your love, give her the best of you to see ; be to her like the western lands (they bring us such strange news of) to the Spanish Court ; send her only your lumps of gold, fans of feathers, your spirit-like birds, and fruits and gems. So shall you, what is unseen of you, be supposed altogether a paradise by her,—as these western lands by Spain : though I warrant there is filth, red baboons, ugly reptiles and squalor enough, which they bring Spain as few samples of as possible."

There is in all this prose, lengthy as it is, the true dramatic note, a recognizable tone of talk. But *A Soul's Tragedy* is for the study, not the stage.

[*From the " Contemporary Review." * *]

Next to this [*Pippa Passes*] in clearness, with nothing but the simplest of plots, and with hardly more than two characters, one playing on and unfolding the weakness of the other, is *A Soul's Tragedy*. A mob-leader, claiming the merit of a deed of patriotic vengeance which was not his, trading on the fame of it, rising to supreme power, then losing in that falsehood all true nobleness, becoming sensual, corrupt, servile, till at last the astute Machiavellian politician who has seen " three and twenty leaders of revolts," entraps him in his own snare, puts him to shame, and registers him as the twenty-fourth ;—this moves on simply and naturally enough, and the reader is never embarrassed, as in the other plays, by vain efforts to recollect what has gone before, and connect it with what is coming next.

In one point, however, *A Soul's Tragedy* stands almost alone in its departure from the conventional type of tragedy. It has, of course, been common enough to mingle blank verse and prose in the same drama, leaving the latter to the

* Jan. 1867 (vol. iv.).

less noble, assigning the former to the more heroic characters.   Here, however, Mr. Browning wishes to symbolize the
truth that the noble aspirations of the patriot degenerate
into the ignoble baseness of the ambitious demagogue, and
he does so by making everybody discourse in verse in the
first part of the play, and, with an equal uniformity, talk
prose in the second.   As with every bold stroke of art, there
is, at first, a certain effectiveness in this, but the second and
permanent impression which it leaves is that there is something of the nature of a trick in it, true neither to the ideal
of poetry nor the reality of actual life.

A BLOT IN THE 'SCUTCHEON.

A TRAGEDY.

PERSONS.

MILDRED TRESHAM.

GUENDOLEN TRESHAM.

THOROLD, Earl Tresham.

AUSTIN TRESHAM.

HENRY, Earl Mertoun.

GERARD, and other Retainers of Lord Tresham.

TIME, 17—

A BLOT IN THE 'SCUTCHEON.

ACT I.

SCENE 1. *The interior of a lodge in Lord Tresham's park. Many* Retainers *crowded at the window, supposed to command a view of the entrance to his mansion.* GERARD, *the Warrener, his back to a table on which are flagons, etc.*

1 *Retainer.* Ay, do! push, friends, and then you 'll push
    down me!—
What for? Does any hear a runner's foot
Or a steed's trample or a coach-wheel's cry?
Is the Earl come or his least poursuivant?
But there 's no breeding in a man of you
Save Gerard yonder: here 's a half-place yet,
Old Gerard!
    Gerard.   Save your courtesies, my friend.
Here is my place.
    2 *Retainer.*   Now, Gerard, out with it!
What makes you sullen, this of all the days
I' the year? To-day that young, rich, bountiful,   ·   10
Handsome Earl Mertoun, whom alone they match
With our Lord Tresham through the country-side,
Is coming here in utmost bravery
To ask our master's sister's hand?
    Gerard.   What then?
    2 *Retainer.* What then? Why, you, she speaks to, if she
    meets
Your worship, smiles on as you hold apart

The boughs to let her through her forest walks,
You, always favorite for your no-deserts,
You 've heard these three days how Earl Mertoun sues
To lay his heart and house and broad lands too   20
At Lady Mildred's feet; and while we squeeze
Ourselves into a mousehole lest we miss
One congee of the least page in his train,
You sit o' one side—'there's the Earl,' say I—
'What then,' say you!

   3 Retainer.   I 'll wager he has let
Both swans he tamed for Lady Mildred swim
Over the falls and gain the river!

   Gerard.   Ralph,
Is not to-morrow my inspecting-day
For you and for your hawks?

   4 Retainer.   Let Gerard be!
He 's coarse-grained, like his carved black cross-bow stock,
Ha! look now, while we squabble with him, look!   31
Well done, now—is not this beginning, now,
To purpose?

   1 Retainer. Our retainers look as fine—
That 's comfort. Lord, how Richard holds himself
With his white staff! Will not a knave behind
Prick him upright?

   4 Retainer.   He 's only bowing, fool!
The Earl's man bent us lower by this much.

   1 Retainer. That 's comfort. Here 's a very cavalcade!

   3 Retainer. I don't see wherefore Richard, and his troop
Of silk and silver varlets there, should find   40
Their perfumed selves so indispensable
On high days, holidays! Would it so disgrace
Our family if I, for instance, stood—
In my right hand a cast of Swedish hawks,
A leash of greyhounds in my left?—

   Gerard.   With Hugh

The logman for supporter, in his right
The bill-hook, in his left the brushwood-shears!

   3 *Retainer*. Out on you, crab! What next, what next?
      The Earl!

   1 *Retainer*. Oh! Walter, groom, our horses, do they match
The Earl's? Alas, that first pair of the six—   50
They paw the ground—Ah, Walter! and that brute
Just on his haunches by the wheel!

   6 *Retainer*.   Ay—Ay!
You, Philip, are a special hand, I hear,
At soups and sauces: what's a horse to you?
D'ye mark that beast they've slid into the midst
So cunningly?—then, Philip, mark this further;
No leg has he to stand on!

   1 *Retainer*.   No? That's comfort.

   2 *Retainer*. Peace, Cook! The Earl descends. — Well,
      Gerard, see
The Earl at least! Come, there's a proper man,
I hope! Why, Ralph, no falcon, Pole or Swede,   60
Has got a starrier eye.

   3 *Retainer*.   His eyes are blue—
But leave my hawks alone!

   4 *Retainer*.   So young, and yet
So tall and shapely!

   5 *Retainer*.   Here's Lord Tresham's self!
There now—there's what a nobleman should be!
He's older, graver, loftier, he's more like
A House's head!

   2 *Retainer*.   But you'd not have a boy—
And what's the Earl beside?—possess too soon
That stateliness?

   1 *Retainer*.   Our master takes his hand—
Richard and his white staff are on the move—
Back fall our people—tsh!—there's Timothy   70
Sure to get tangled in his ribbon-ties—

  5

And Peter's cursed rosette 's a-coming off !—
At last I see our lord's back and his friend's—
And the whole beautiful bright company
Close round them—in they go ! [*Jumping down from the
        window-bench, and making for the table and its jugs*]
                        Good health, long life,
Great joy to our Lord Tresham and his House !
    6 *Retainer.* My father drove his father first to court,
After his marriage-day—ay, did he !
    2 *Retainer.*   God bless
Lord Tresham, Lady Mildred, and the Earl !
Here, Gerard, reach your beaker !
    Gerard.   Drink, my boys !   80
Don't mind me—all 's not right about me—drink !
    2 *Retainer* [*Aside*]. He 's vexed, now, that he let the show
        escape !
[*To Gerard*] Remember that the Earl returns this way.
    Gerard. That way?
    2 *Retainer.*   Just so.
    Gerard.   Then my way 's here.   [*Goes.*
    2 *Retainer.*   Old Gerard
Will die soon—mind, I said it !   He was used
To care about the pitifullest thing
That touched the House's honor, not an eye
But his could see wherein : and on a cause
Of scarce a quarter this importance, Gerard
Fairly had fretted flesh and bone away   90
In cares that this was right, nor that was wrong,
Such point decorous, and such square by rule—
He knew such niceties, no herald more ;
And now—you see his humor : die he will !
    2 *Retainer.* God help him ! Who 's for the great servant's-
        hall
To hear what 's going on inside ?   They 'd follow
Lord Tresham into the saloon.

3 *Retainer*.   I !—
4 *Retainer*.   I !—
Leave Frank alone for catching at the door
Some hint of how the parley goes inside !
Prosperity to the great House once more !   100
Here 's the last drop !
  1 *Retainer*.   Have at you !   Boys, hurrah !

SCENE II. *A Saloon in the Mansion.*

Enter LORD TRESHAM, LORD MERTOUN, AUSTIN, *and* GUEN-
DOLEN.

Tresham. I welcome you, Lord Mertoun, yet once more,
To this ancestral roof of mine.   Your name—
Noble among the noblest in itself,
Yet taking in your person, fame avers,
New price and lustre—as that gem you wear,
Transmitted from a hundred knightly breasts,
Fresh chased and set and fixed by its last lord,
Seems to re-kindle at the core—your name
Would win you welcome !
  Mertoun.   Thanks !
  Tresham.   But add to that,
The worthiness and grace and dignity   10
Of your proposal for uniting both
Our Houses even closer than respect
Unites them now—add these, and you must grant
One favour more, nor that the least,—to think
The welcome I should give ;—'t is given !   My lord,
My only brother, Austin—he 's the king's.
Our cousin, Lady Guendolen—betrothed
To Austin : all are yours.
  Mertoun.   I thank you—less
For the expressed commendings which your seal,
And only that, authenticates—forbids   20

My putting from me—to my heart I take
Your praise—but praise less claims my gratitude,
Than the indulgent insight it implies
Of what must needs be uppermost with one
Who comes, like me, with the bare leave to ask,
In weighed and measured unimpassioned words,
A gift, which, if as calmly 't is denied,
He must withdraw, content upon his cheek,
Despair within his soul.   That I dare ask
Firmly, near boldly, near with confidence,   30
That gift, I have to thank you.   Yes, Lord Tresham,
I love your sister—as you 'd have one love
That lady—oh! more, more I love her!   Wealth,
Rank, all the world thinks me, they 're yours, you know,
To hold or part with, at your choice—but grant
My true self, me without a rood of land,
A piece of gold, a name of yesterday,
Grant me that lady, and you—Death or life?
   Guendolen [*apart to Austin*]. Why, this is loving, Austin!
   Austin.   He 's so young!
   Guendolen. Young?   Old enough, I think, to half surmise
He never had obtained an entrance here,   41
Were all this fear and trembling needed.
   Austin.   Hush!
He reddens.
   Guendolen. Mark him, Austin; that 's true love!
Ours must begin again.
   Tresham.   We 'll sit, my lord.
Ever with best desert goes diffidence.
I may speak plainly nor be misconceived.
That I am wholly satisfied with you
On this occasion, when a falcon's eye
Were dull compared with mine to search out faults,
Is somewhat.   Mildred's hand is hers to give   50
Or to refuse.

Mertoun.   But you, you grant my suit?
I have your word if hers?
    Tresham.   My best of words
If hers encourage you.   I trust it will.
Have you seen Lady Mildred, by the way?
    Mertoun. I—I—our two demesnes, remember, touch;
I have been used to wander carelessly
After my stricken game : the heron roused
Deep in my woods, has trailed its broken wing
Thro' thicks and glades a mile in yours,—or else
Some eyass ill-reclaimed has taken flight   60
And lured me after her from tree to tree,
I marked not whither.   I have come upon
The lady's wondrous beauty unaware,
And—and then—I have seen her.
    Guendolen [*aside to Austin*].   Note that mode
Of faltering out that, when a lady passed,
He, having eyes, did see her!   You had said—
'On such a day I scanned her, head to foot;
Observed a red, where red should not have been,
Outside her elbow ; but was pleased enough
Upon the whole.'   Let such irreverent talk   70
Be lessoned for the future !
    Tresham.   What 's to say
May be said briefly.   She has never known
A mother's care ; I stand for father too.
Her beauty is not strange to you, it seems—
You cannot know the good and tender heart,
Its girl's trust and its woman's constancy,
How pure yet passionate, how calm yet kind,
How grave yet joyous, how reserved yet free
As light where friends are—how imbued with lore
The world most prizes, yet the simplest, yet   80
The—one might know I talked of Mildred—thus
We brothers talk !

Mertoun.   I thank you.
Tresham.   In a word,
Control 's not for this lady; but her wish
To please me outstrips in its subtlety
My power of being pleased : herself creates
The want she means to satisfy.   My heart
Prefers your suit to her as 't were its own.
Can I say more?
  Mertoun.   No more—thanks, thanks—no more!
  Tresham. This matter then discussed—
  Mertoun.   We 'll waste no breath
On aught less precious.   I 'm beneath the roof   90
Which holds her : while I thought of that, my speech
To you would wander—as it must not do,
Since as you favor me I stand or fall.
I pray you suffer that I take my leave!
  Tresham. With less regret 't is suffered, that again
We meet, I hope, so shortly.
  Mertoun.   We? again?—
Ah! yes, forgive me—when shall—you will crown
Your goodness by forthwith apprising me
When—if—the lady will appoint a day
For me to wait on you—and her.
  Tresham.   So soon   100
As I am made acquainted with her thoughts
On your proposal—howsoe'er they lean—
A messenger shall bring you the result.
  Mertoun. You cannot bind me more to you, my lord.
Farewell till we renew—I trust, renew
A converse ne'er to disunite again.
  Tresham. So may it prove !
  Mertoun.   You, lady, you, sir, take
My humble salutation !
  Guendolen and Austin. Thanks !
  Tresham.   Within there !

[*Servants enter.   Tresham conducts Mertoun to the door.
Meantime Austin remarks,*

                                        Well,
Here I have an advantage of the Earl,
Confess now !   I 'd not think that all was safe   110
Because my lady's brother stood my friend !
Why, he makes sure of her—'do you say, yes—
She 'll not say no,'—what comes it to beside ?
I should have prayed the brother, 'speak this speech,
For Heaven's sake urge this on her—put in this—
Forget not, as you 'd save me, t 'other thing,—
Then set down what she says, and how she looks,
And if she smiles, and '—in an under breath—
' Only let her accept me, and do you
And all the world refuse me, if you dare !'   120
       Guendolen. That way you'd take, friend Austin ?   What a
           shame
I was your cousin, tamely from the first
Your bride, and all this fervor 's run to waste !
Do you know you speak sensibly to-day ?
The Earl 's a fool.
       Austin.   Here 's Thorold.   Tell him so !
       Tresham (*returning*). Now, voices, voices !   'St ! the lady 's
           first !
How seems he ?—seems he not—come, faith give fraud
The mercy-stroke whenever they engage !
Down with fraud, up with faith !   How seems the Earl ?
A name ! a blazon ! if you knew their worth,   130
As you will never ! come—the Earl ?
       Guendolen.   He 's young.
       Tresham. What 's she ? an infant save in heart and brain.
Young !   Mildred is fourteen, remark !   And you—
Austin, how old is she ?
       Guendolen.   There 's tact for you !

I meant that being young was good excuse
If one should tax him—
 Tresham.   Well?
 Guendolen.   With lacking wit.
 Tresham. He lacked wit? Where might he lack wit, so
  please you?
 Guendolen. In standing straighter than the steward's rod
And making you the tiresomest harangue,
Instead of slipping over to my side   140
And softly whispering in my ear, 'Sweet lady,
Your cousin there will do me detriment
He little dreams of: he 's absorbed, I see,
In my old name and fame—be sure he 'll leave
My Mildred, when his best account of me
Is ended, in full confidence I wear
My grandsire's periwig down either cheek.
I 'm lost unless your gentleness vouchsafes—'
 Tresham. 'To give a best of best accounts, yourself,
Of me and my demerits.' You are right!   150
He should have said what now I say for him.
You golden creature, will you help us all?
Here 's Austin means to vouch for much, but you—
You are—what Austin only knows! Come up,
All three of us: she 's in the library
No doubt, for the day 's wearing fast. Precede!
 Guendolen. Austin, how we must—!
 Tresham.   Must what? Must speak truth,
Malignant tongue! Detect one fault in him
I challenge you!
 Guendolen. Witchcraft 's a fault in him,
For you 're bewitched.
 Tresham.   What 's urgent we obtain 160
Is, that she soon receive him—say, to-morrow—
Next day at furthest.
 Guendolen. Ne'er instruct me!

Tresham.   Come !—
He 's out of your good graces, since forsooth,
He stood not as he 'd carry us by storm
With his perfections !   You 're for the composed,
Manly, assured, becoming confidence !—
Get her to say, 'to-morrow,' and I 'll give you—
I 'll give you black Urganda, to be spoiled
With petting and snail-paces.   Will you?   Come !

SCENE III.   *Mildred's Chamber.   A painted window over-
looks the park.*   MILDRED *and* GUENDOLEN.

Guendolen. Now, Mildred, spare those pains. I have not left
Our talkers in the library, and climbed
The wearisome ascent to this your bower
In company with you,—I have not dared—
Nay, worked such prodigies as sparing you
Lord Mertoun's pedigree before the flood,
Which Thorold seemed in very act to tell—
Or bringing Austin to pluck up that most
Firm-rooted heresy—your suitor's eyes,
He would maintain, were gray instead of blue—   10
I think I brought him to contrition !—Well,
I have not done such things—all to deserve
A minute's quiet cousin's talk with you—
To be dismissed so coolly !
Mildred.   Guendolen !
What have I done? what could suggest—
Guendolen.   There, there !
Do I not comprehend you 'd be alone
To throw those testimonies in a heap,
Thorold's enlargings, Austin's brevities,
With that poor silly, heartless Guendolen's
Ill-timed, misplaced, attempted smartnesses—   20
And sift their sense out? now, I come to spare you

Nearly a whole night's labor.   Ask and have!
Demand, be answered!   Lack I ears and eyes?
Am I perplexed which side of the rock-table
The Conqueror dined on when he landed first
Lord Mertoun's ancestor was bidden take—
The bow-hand or the arrow-hand's great meed?
Mildred, the Earl has soft blue eyes!

  Mildred.   My brother—
Did he—you said that he received him well?

  Guendolen. If I said only 'well' I said not much—   30
Oh! stay—which brother?

  Mildred.   Thorold! who—who else?

  Guendolen. Thorold—a secret—is too proud by half—
Nay, hear me out—with us he 's even gentler
Than we are with our birds.   Of this great House
The least retainer that e'er caught his glance
Would die for him, real dying—no mere talk;
And in the world, the court, if men would cite
The perfect spirit of honor, Thorold's name
Rises of its clear nature to their lips.
But he should take men's homage, trust in it,   40
And care no more about what drew it down.
He has desert, and that, acknowledgment;
Is he content?

  Mildred.   You wrong him, Guendolen.

  Guendolen.   He's proud, confess; so proud with brood-
        ing o'er
The light of his interminable line,
An ancestry with men all paladins,
And women all—

  Mildred.   Dear Guendolen, 't is late!
When yonder purple pane the climbing moon
Pierces, I know 't is midnight.

  Guendolen.   Well, that Thorold
Should rise up from such musings, and receive   50

One come audaciously to graft himself
Into this peerless stock, yet find no flaw,
No slightest spot in such an one—
   Mildred.   Who finds
A spot in Mertoun?
   Guendolen.   Not your brother; therefore,
Not the whole world.
   Mildred.   I am weary, Guendolen.—
Bear with me!
   Guendolen.   I am foolish.
   Mildred.   Oh! no, kind—
But I would rest.
   Guendolen.   Good night and rest to you!
I said how gracefully his mantle lay
Beneath the rings of his light hair?
   Mildred.   Brown hair.
   Guendolen. Brown? why it *is* brown—how could you know
     that?   60
   Mildred. How? did not you—Oh! Austin 'twas, declared
His hair was light, not brown—my head!—and look,
The moonbeam purpling the dark chamber! Sweet,
Good night!
   Guendolen. Forgive me—sleep the soundlier for me!
                 [*Going, she turns suddenly.*
                         Mildred!
Perdition! all's discovered! Thorold finds—
That the Earl's greatest of all grandmothers
Was grander daughter still—to that fair dame
Whose garter slipped down at the famous dance!   [*Goes.*
   Mildred. Is she—can she be really gone at last?
My heart! I shall not reach the window. Needs   70
Must I have sinned much, so to suffer!
     [*She lifts the small lamp which is suspended before the
       Virgin's image in the window, and places it by the
       purple pane.*

There!
                  [*She returns to the seat in front.*
Mildred and Mertoun!   Mildred, with consent
Of all the world and Thorold, Mertoun's bride!
Too late!   'T is sweet to think of, sweeter still
To hope for, that this blessed end soothes up
The curse of the beginning ; but I know
It comes too late : 't will sweetest be of all
To dream my soul away and die upon.   [*A noise without.*
The voice!   Oh! why, why glided sin the snake
Into the paradise Heaven meant us both?   80
              [*The window opens softly.   A low voice sings.*

There 's a woman like a dewdrop, she 's so purer than the
           purest ;
And her noble heart 's the noblest, yes, and her sure faith 's the
           surest ;
And her eyes are dark and humid, like the depth on depth of
           lustre
Hid i' the harebell, while her tresses, sunnier than the wild-
           grape cluster,
Gush in golden-tinted plenty down her neck's rose-misted
           marble :
Then her voice's music—call it the well's bubbling, the bird's
           warble !
           [A figure wrapped in a mantle appears at the window.
And this woman says, ' My days were sunless and my nights
           were moonless,
Parched the pleasant April herbage, and the lark's heart's out-
           break tuneless,
If you loved me not !'   And I who—ah, for words of flame !—
           adore her,
Who am mad to lay my spirit prostrate palpably before her—
           [He enters, approaches the seat, and bends over her.
I may enter at her portal soon, as now her lattice takes me,   91

*And by noontide as by midnight make her mine, as hers she
     makes me!*

     [*The Earl throws off his slouched hat and long cloak.*
My very heart sings, so I sing, beloved!
     Mildred. Sit, Henry—do not take my hand!
     Mertoun.   'T is mine.
The meeting that appalled us both so much
Is ended.
     Mildred. What begins now?
     Mertoun.   Happiness
Such as the world contains not.
     Mildred.   That is it.
Our happiness would, as you say, exceed
The whole world's best of blisses: we—do we
Deserve that? Utter to your soul, what mine   100
Long since, beloved, has grown used to hear,
Like a death-knell, so much regarded once,
And so familiar now; this will not be!
     Mertoun. O Mildred, have I met your brother's face,
Compelled myself—if not to speak untruth,
Yet to disguise, to shun, to put aside
The truth, as—what had e'er prevailed on me
Save you, to venture? Have I gained at last
Your brother, the one scarer of your dreams,
And waking thoughts' sole apprehension too?   110
Does a new life, like a young sunrise, break
On the strange unrest of our night, confused
With rain and stormy flaw—and will you see
No dripping blossoms, no fire-tinted drops
On each live spray, no vapor steaming up,
And no expressless glory in the east?
When I am by you, to be ever by you,
When I have won you and may worship you,
O Mildred, can you say 'this will not be?'

Mildred. Sin has surprised us; so will punishment.   120

Mertoun. No—me alone, who sinned alone!

Mildred.   The night
You likened our past life to—was it storm
Throughout to you then, Henry?

Mertoun.   Of your life
I spoke—what am I, what my life, to waste
A thought about when you are by me?—you
It was, I said my folly called the storm
And pulled the night upon.   'T was day with me—
Perpetual dawn with me.

Mildred.   Come what, come will,
You have been happy: take my hand!

Mertoun [*after a pause*].   How good
Your brother is!   I figured him a cold—   130
Shall I say, haughty man?

Mildred.   They told me all.
I know all.

Mertoun.   It will soon be over.

Mildred.   Over?
Oh! what is over? what must I live through
And say, ''t is over?'   Is our meeting over?
Have I received in presence of them all
The partner of my guilty love—with brow
Trying to seem a maiden's brow—with lips
Which make believe that when they strive to form
Replies to you and tremble as they strive,
It is the nearest ever they approached   140
A stranger's—Henry, yours that stranger's—lip—
With cheek that looks a virgin's, and that is—
Ah! God, some prodigy of thine will stop
This planned piece of deliberate wickedness
In its birth even! some fierce leprous spot
Will mar the brow's dissimulating!   I
Shall murmur no smooth speeches got by heart,

But, frenzied, pour forth all our woeful story,
The love, the shame, and the despair—with them
Round me aghast as men round some cursed fount   150
That should spirt water, and spouts blood.   I 'll not—
Henry, you do not wish that I should draw
This vengeance down?   I 'll not affect a grace
That 's gone from me—gone once, and gone forever!

Mertoun. Mildred, my honor is your own.   I 'll share
Disgrace I cannot suffer by myself.
A word informs your brother I retract
This morning's offer; time will yet bring forth
Some better way of saving both of us.

Mildred. I 'll meet their faces, Henry!

Mertoun.   When? to-morrow!
Get done with it!

Mildred.   O Henry, not to-morrow!   161
Next day!   I never shall prepare my words
And looks and gestures sooner.—How you must
Despise me!

Mertoun.   Mildred, break it if you choose,
A heart the love of you uplifted—still
Uplifts, thro' this protracted agony,
To heaven! but Mildred, answer me,—first pace
The chamber with me—once again—now, say
Calmly the part, the—what it is of me
You see contempt—for you did say contempt—   170
Contempt for you in!   I would pluck it off
And cast it from me!—but no—no, you 'll not
Repeat that?—will you, Mildred, repeat that?

Mildred. Dear Henry!

Mertoun.   I was scarce a boy—e'en now
What am I more?   And you were infantine
When first I met you; why, your hair fell loose
On either side!   My fool's-cheek reddens now
Only in the recalling how it burned

That morn to see the shape of many a dream—
You know we boys are prodigal of charms   180
To her we dream of—I had heard of one,
Had dreamed of her, and I was close to her,
Might speak to her, might live and die her own—
Who knew?   I spoke.   O Mildred, feel you not
That now, while I remember every glance
Of yours, each word of yours, with power to test
And weigh them in the diamond scales of pride,
Resolved the treasure of a first and last
Heart's love shall have been bartered at its worth—
That now I think upon your purity   190
And utter ignorance of guilt—your own
Or other's guilt—the girlish undisguised
Delight at a strange novel prize—I talk
A silly language, but interpret, you!—
If I, with fancy at its full, and reason
Scarce in its germ, enjoined you secrecy,
If you had pity on my passion, pity
On my protested sickness of the soul
To sit beside you, hear you breathe, and watch
Your eyelids and the eyes beneath—if you   200
Accorded gifts and knew not they were gifts—
If I grew mad at last with enterprise
And must behold my beauty in her bower
Or perish—I was ignorant of even
My own desires—what then were you?—if sorrow—
Sin—if the end came—must I now renounce
My reason, blind myself to light, say truth
Is false and lie to God and my own soul?
Contempt were all of this!

    Mildred.   Do you believe—
Or, Henry, I 'll not wrong you—you believe   210
That I was ignorant.   I scarce grieve o'er
The past!   We 'll love on ; you will love me still!

Mertoun. Oh! to love less what one has injured!   Dove,
Whose pinion I have rashly hurt, my breast—
Shall my heart's warmth not nurse thee into strength?
Flower I have crushed, shall I not care for thee?
Bloom o'er my crest, my fight-mark and device!
Mildred, I love you and you love me!
Mildred.   Go!
Be that your last word.   I shall sleep to-night.
Mertoun. This is not our last meeting?
Mildred.   One night more.   220
Mertoun. And then—think, then!
Mildred.   Then, no sweet courtship days,
No dawning consciousness of love for us,
No strange and palpitating births of sense
From words and looks, no innocent fears and hopes,
Reserves and confidences: morning 's over!
Mertoun. How else should love's perfected noontide follow?
All the dawn promised shall the day perform.
Mildred. So may it be! but—
                            You are cautious, love?
Are sure that unobserved you scaled the walls?
Mertoun. Oh! trust me!   Then our final meeting 's fixed?
To-morrow night?
Mildred.   Farewell!   Stay, Henry—wherefore?   231
His foot is on the yew-tree bough; the turf
Receives him: now the moonlight as he runs
Embraces him—but he must go—is gone.
Ah! once again he turns—thanks, thanks, my love!
He 's gone.   Oh! I 'll believe him every word!
I was so young, I loved him so, I had
No mother, God forgot me, and I fell.
There may be pardon yet; all 's doubt beyond.
Surely the bitterness of death is past!   240

6

ACT II.

Scene.—*The Library.*

Enter Lord Tresham *hastily.*

This way !   In, Gerard, quick !
                    [*As Gerard enters, Tresham secures the door.*
                              Now speak ! or, wait—
I 'll bid you speak directly.   [*Seats himself.*
                    Now repeat
Firmly and circumstantially the tale
You just now told me ; it eludes me ; either
I did not listen, or the half is gone
Away from me.   How long have you lived here?
Here in my house, your father kept our woods
Before you?
    Gerard.   As his father did, my lord.
I have been eating, sixty years almost,
Your bread.
    Tresham.   Yes, yes.   You ever were of all   10
The servants in my father's house, I know,
The trusted one.   You 'll speak the truth.
    Gerard.   I 'll speak
God's truth.   Night after night—
    Tresham.   Since when?
    Gerard.   At least
A month—each midnight has some man access
To Lady Mildred's chamber.
    Tresham.   Tush, 'access'—
No wide words like 'access' to me !
    Gerard.   He runs

Along the woodside, crosses to the south,
Takes the left tree that ends the avenue—
   Tresham. The last great yew-tree?
   Gerard.   You might stand upon
The main boughs like a platform. Then he—
   Tresham.   Quick!   20
   Gerard. Climbs up, and, where they lessen at the top—
I cannot see distinctly, but he throws,
I think—for this I do not vouch—a line
That reaches to the lady's casement—
   Tresham.   Which
He enters not! Gerard, some wretched fool
Dares pry into my sister's privacy!
When such are young, it seems a precious thing
To have approached,—to merely have approached,
Got sight of, the abode of her they set
Their frantic thoughts upon! He does not enter?   30
Gerard?
   Gerard. There is a lamp that 's full i' the midst,
Under a red square in the painted glass
Of Lady Mildred's—
   Tresham.   Leave that name out! Well?
That lamp?
   Gerard.   Is moved at midnight higher up
To one pane—a small dark-blue pane; he waits
For that among the boughs: at sight of that,
I see him, plain as I see you, my lord,
Open the lady's casement, enter there—
   Tresham. And stay?
   Gerard.   An hour, two hours.
   Tresham.   And this you saw
Once?—twice?—quick!
   Gerard.   Twenty times.
   Tresham.   And what brings you
Under the yew-trees?

Gerard.   The first night I left   41
My range so far, to track the stranger stag
That broke the pale, I saw the man.
     Tresham.   Yet sent
No cross-bow shaft through the marauder?
     Gerard.   But
He came, my lord, the first time he was seen,
In a great moonlight, light as any day,
From Lady Mildred's chamber.
     Tresham [*after a pause*]. You have no cause—
Who could have cause to do my sister wrong?
     Gerard. O my lord, only once—let me this once
Speak what is on my mind!   Since first I noted   50
All this, I 've groaned as if a fiery net
Plucked me this way and that—fire, if I turned
To her, fire if I turned to you, and fire,
If down I flung myself and strove to die.
The lady could not have been seven years old
When I was trusted to conduct her safe
Through the deer-herd to stroke the snow-white fawn
I brought to eat bread from her tiny hand
Within a month.   She ever had a smile
To greet me with—she—if it could undo   60
What 's done to lop each limb from off this trunk—
All that is foolish talk, not fit for you—
I mean, I could not speak and bring her hurt
For Heaven's compelling.   But when I was fixed
To hold my peace, each morsel of your food
Eaten beneath your roof, my birthplace too,
Choked me.   I wish I had grown mad in doubts
What it behooved me do.   This morn it seemed
Either I must confess to you, or die:
Now it is done, I seem the vilest worm   70
That crawls, to have betrayed my lady!
     Tresham.   No—
No, Gerard!

Gerard.   Let me go!

Tresham.   A man, you say:
What man? Young? Not a vulgar hind? What dress?

Gerard. A slouched hat and a large dark foreign cloak
Wraps his whole form; even his face is hid;
But I should judge him young: no hind, be sure!

Tresham. Why?

Gerard.   He is ever armed: his sword projects
Beneath the cloak.

Tresham.   Gerard, —I will not say
No word, no breath of this!

Gerard.   Thanks, thanks, my lord! [*Goes.*

TRESHAM *paces the room.   After a pause,*

Oh! thought 's absurd!—as with some monstrous fact   80
Which, when ill thoughts beset us, seems to give
Merciful God that made the sun and stars,
The waters and the green delights of earth,
The lie!   I apprehend the monstrous fact—
Yet know the Maker of all worlds is good,
And yield my reason up, inadequate
To reconcile what yet I do behold—
Blasting my sense!   There 's cheerful day outside:
This is my library, and this the chair
My father used to sit in carelessly   90
After his soldier fashion, while I stood
Between his knees to question him; and here
Gerard our gray retainer—as he says,
Fed with our food, from sire to son, an age—
Has told a story—I am to believe!
That Mildred—oh, no, no! both tales are true,
Her pure cheek's story and the forester's!
Would she, or could she, err—much less, confound
All guilts of treachery, of craft, of—Heaven
Keep me within its hand!—I will sit here   100

Until thought settle and I see my course.
Avert, O God, only this woe from me!

[*As he sinks his head between his arms on the table,
Guendolen's voice is heard at the door.*

Lord Tresham! [*She knocks.*] Is Lord Tresham there?

[*Tresham, hastily turning, pulls down the first book
above his head and opens it.*

 Tresham.   Come in! [*She enters.*
Ha! Guendolen—good morning.

 Guendolen.   Nothing more?

 Tresham. What should I say more?

 Guendolen.   Pleasant question! more?
This more. Did I besiege poor Mildred's brain
Last night till close on morning with 'the Earl,'
'The Earl'—whose worth did I asseverate
Till I am very fain to hope that—Thorold,
What is all this? You are not well!

 Tresham.   Who? I? 110
You laugh at me.

 Guendolen. Has what I'm fain to hope
Arrived then? Does that huge tome show some blot
In the Earl's 'scutcheon come no longer back
Than Arthur's time?

 Tresham.   When left you Mildred's chamber?

 Guendolen. Oh! late enough, I told you! The main thing
To ask is, how I left her chamber,—sure,
Content yourself, she'll grant this paragon
Of earls no such ungracious—

 Tresham.   Send her here!

 Guendolen. Thorold?

 Tresham.   I mean—acquaint her, Guendolen,—
But mildly!

 Guendolen. Mildly?

 Tresham.   Ah! you guessed aright. 120
I am not well: there is no hiding it.

But tell her I would see her at her leisure—
That is, at once! here in the library!
The passage in that old Italian book
We hunted for so long is found, say, found—
And if I let it slip again—you see,
That she must come—and instantly!

    Guendolen.   I 'll die
Piecemeal, record that, if there have not gloomed
Some blot i' the 'scutcheon!

    Tresham.   Go! or, Guendolen,
Be you at call,—with Austin, if you choose,—   130
In the adjoining gallery! There, go!   ⌊ *Guendolen goes.*
Another lesson to me! You might bid
A child disguise his heart's sore, and conduct
Some sly investigation point by point
With a smooth brow, as well as bid me catch
The inquisitorial cleverness some praise!
If you had told me yesterday, 'There 's one
You needs must circumvent and practise with,
Entrap by policies, if you would worm
The truth out; and that one is—Mildred!' There,   140
There—reasoning is thrown away on it!
Prove she 's unchaste—why, you may after prove
That she 's a poisoner, traitress, what you will!
Where I can comprehend nought, nought 's to say.
Or do, or think? Force on me but the first
Abomination—then outpour all plagues,
And I shall ne'er make count of them!

              Enter MILDRED.

    Mildred.   What book
Is it I wanted, Thorold? Guendolen
Thought you were pale; you are not pale. That book?
That 's Latin surely.

    Tresham.   Mildred, here 's a line—   150

Don't lean on me : I 'll English it for you—
' Love conquers all things.'   What love conquers them?
What love should you esteem—best love?

    Mildred.   True love.

    Tresham. I mean, and should have said, whose love is
        best
Of all that love or that profess to love?

    Mildred. The list 's so long : there 's father's, mother's,
        husband's—

    Tresham. Mildred, I do believe a brother's love
For a sole sister must exceed them all.
For see now, only see ! there 's no alloy
Of earth that creeps into the perfect'st gold   160
Of other loves—no gratitude to claim ;
You never gave her life, not even aught
That keeps life—never tended her, instructed,
Enriched her—so your love can claim no right
O'er her save pure love's claim : that 's what I call
Freedom from earthliness.   You 'll never hope
To be such friends, for instance, she and you,
As when you hunted cowslips in the woods
Or played together in the meadow hay.
Oh ! yes—with age, respect comes, and your worth   170
Is felt, there 's growing sympathy of tastes,
There 's ripened friendship, there 's confirmed esteem :—
Much head these make against the new-comer !
The startling apparition, the strange youth—
Whom one half-hour's conversing with, or, say,
Mere gazing at, shall change—beyond all change
This Ovid ever sang about—your soul—
Her soul, that is,—the sister's soul !   With her
'T was winter yesterday ; now, all is warmth,
The green leaf 's springing and the turtle's voice,   180
' Arise and come away !'   Come whither?—far
Enough from the esteem, respect, and all

The brother's somewhat insignificant
Array of rights!   All which he knows before,
Has calculated on so long ago!
I think such love—apart from yours and mine—
Contented with its little term of life,
Intending to retire betimes, aware
How soon the background must be place for it,—
I think, am sure, a brother's love exceeds   190
All the world's love in its unworldliness.
    Mildred. What is this for?
    Tresham.   This, Mildred, is it for!
Or, no, I cannot go to it so soon!
That's one of many points my haste left out—
Each day, each hour throws forth its silk-like film
Between the being tied to you by birth,
And you, until those slender threads compose
A web that shrouds her daily life of hopes
And fears and fancies, all her life, from yours:
So close you live and yet so far apart!   200
And must I rend this web, tear up, break down
The sweet and palpitating mystery
That makes her sacred?   You, for you I mean,
Shall I speak, shall I not speak?
    Mildred.   Speak!
    Tresham.   I will.
Is there a story men could—any man
Could tell of you, you would conceal from me?
I'll never think there's falsehood on that lip.
Say 'There is no such story men could tell,'
And I'll believe you, though I disbelieve
The world—the world of better men than I,   210
And women such as I suppose you.   Speak!
[*After a pause.*] Not speak? Explain then! Clear it up
      then! Move
Some of the miserable weight away

That presses lower than the grave !   Not speak ?
Some of the dead weight, Mildred !   Ah, if I
Could bring myself to plainly make their charge
Against you !   Must I, Mildred ?   Silent still ?
[*After a pause*] Is there a gallant that has night by night
Admittance to your chamber ?
　　　　[*After a pause*]　　　　Then, his name !
Till now, I only had a thought for you :　　　　　　　220
But now,—his name !
　　Mildred.　　　　　　Thorold, do you devise
Fit expiation for my guilt, if fit
There be !   'T is nought to say that I 'll endure
And bless you,—that my spirit yearns to purge
Her stains off in the fierce renewing fire :
But do not plunge me into other guilt !
Oh, guilt enough !   I cannot tell his name.
　　Tresham. Then judge yourself !   How should I act ?   Pro-
　　　　nounce !
　　Mildred. O Thorold, you must never tempt me thus !
To die here in this chamber by that sword　　　　　230
Would seem like punishment : so should I glide,
Like an arch-cheat, into extremest bliss !
'T were easily arranged for me : but you—
What would become of you ?
　　Tresham.　　　　　And what will now
Become of me ?   I 'll hide your shame and mine
From every eye ; the dead must heave their hearts
Under the marble of our chapel-floor ;
They cannot rise and blast you.   You may wed
Your paramour above our mother's tomb ;
Our mother cannot move from 'neath your foot.　　240
We too will somehow wear this one day out :
But with to-morrow hastens here—the Earl !
The youth without suspicion that faces come
From heaven, and hearts from—whence proceed such hearts ?

I have dispatched last night at your command
A missive bidding him present himself
To-morrow—here—thus much is said ; the rest
Is understood as if 't were written down—
' His suit finds favour in your eyes :'—now dictate
This morning's letter that shall countermand   250
Last night's—do dictate that !
    Mildred.   But Thorold—if
I will receive him as I said?
    Tresham.   The Earl?
    Mildred. I will receive him.
    Tresham [*starting up*].   Ho there ! Guendolen !

          GUENDOLEN *and* AUSTIN *enter.*

And, Austin, you are welcome, too ! Look there !
The woman there !
    Austin and Guendolen. How? Mildred?
    Tresham.   Mildred once !
Now the receiver night by night, when sleep
Blesses the inmates of her father's house—
I say, the soft sly wanton that receives
Her guilt's accomplice 'neath this roof which holds
You, Guendolen, you, Austin, and has held   260
A thousand Treshams—never one like her !
No lighter of the signal-lamp her quick
Foul breath near quenches in hot eagerness
To mix with breath as foul! no loosener
O' the lattice, practised in the stealthy tread,
The low voice, and the noiseless come-and-go !
Not one composer of the bacchant's mien
Into—what you thought Mildred's, in a word !
Know her !
    Guendolen. O Mildred, look to me, at least !
Thorold—she 's dead, I 'd say, but that she stands   270
Rigid as stone and whiter !

Tresham.   You have heard—
Guendolen. Too much! You must proceed no further.
Mildred.   Yes—
Proceed! All's truth. Go from me!
      Tresham.   All is truth,
She tells you! Well, you know, or ought to know,
All this I would forgive in her. I'd con
Each precept the harsh world enjoins, I'd take
Our ancestors' stern verdicts one by one,
I'd bind myself before them to exact
The prescribed vengeance—and one word of hers,
The sight of her, the bare least memory   280
Of Mildred, my one sister, my heart's pride
Above all prides, my all in all so long,
Would scatter every trace of my resolve.
What were it silently to waste away
And see her waste away from this day forth,
Two scathed things with leisure to repent,
And grow acquainted with the grave, and die
Tired out if not at peace, and be forgotten?
It were not so impossible to bear.
But this—that, fresh from last night's pledge renewed   290
Of love with the successful gallant there,
She calmly bids me help her to entice,
Inveigle an unconscious, trusting youth
Who thinks her all that's chaste and good and pure—
Invites me to betray him—who so fit
As honor's self to cover shame's arch-deed?—
That she'll receive Lord Mertoun—her own phrase—
This, who could bear? Why, you have heard of thieves,
Stabbers, the earth's disgrace, who yet have laughed,
'Talk not to me of torture—I'll betray   300
No comrade I've pledged faith to!'—you have heard
Of wretched women—all but Mildreds—tied
By wild illicit ties to losels vile

You 'd tempt them to forsake ; and they 'll reply
' Gold, friends, repute, I left for him, I find
In him, why should I leave him then for gold,
Repute or friends ?'—and you have felt your heart
Respond to such poor outcasts of the world
As to so many friends ; bad as you please,
You 've felt they were God's men and women still,   310
So not to be disowned by you.   But she
That stands there, calmly gives her lover up
As means to wed the Earl that she may hide
Their intercourse the surelier ; and, for this,
I curse her to her face before you all.
Shame hunt her from the earth !   Then Heaven do right
To both !   It hears me now—shall judge her then !

   [*As Mildred faints and falls, Tresham rushes out.*
 Austin. Stay, Tresham, we 'll accompany you !
 Guendolen.   We ?
What, and leave Mildred ?   We ?   Why, where 's my place
But by her side, and where yours but by mine ?   320
Mildred—one word !   Only look at me, then !
 Austin.   No, Guendolen !   I echo Thorold's voice.
She is unworthy to behold—
 Guendolen.   Us two ?
If you spoke on reflection ; and if I
Approved your speech—if you—to put the thing
At lowest—you the soldier, bound to make
The king's cause yours and fight for it, and throw
Regard to others of its right or wrong—
If with a death-white woman you can help,
Let alone sister, let alone a Mildred,   330
You left her—or if I, her cousin, friend
This morning, playfellow but yesterday,
Who said, or thought at least a thousand times,
' I 'd serve you if I could,' should now face round
And say, ' Ah ! that 's to only signify

I 'd serve you while you 're fit to serve yourself—
So long as fifty eyes await the turn
Of yours to forestall its yet half-formed wish,
I 'll proffer my assistance you 'll not need—
When every tongue is praising you, I 'll join   340
The praisers' chorus—when you 're hemmed about
With lives between you and detraction—lives
To be laid down if a rude voice, rash eye,
Rough hand should violate the sacred ring
Their worship throws about you,—then indeed,
Who 'll stand up for you stout as I ?'   If so
We said, and so we did,—not Mildred there
Would be unworthy to behold us both,
But we should be unworthy, both of us,
To be beheld by—by—your meanest dog,   350
Which, if that sword were broken in your face
Before a crowd, that badge torn off your breast,
And you cast out with hooting and contempt,
Would push his way through all the hooters, gain
Your side, go off with you and all your shame
To the next ditch you choose to die in !   Austin,
Do you love me?   Here 's Austin, Mildred,—here 's
Your brother says he does not believe half—
No, nor half that—of all he heard !   He says,
Look up and take his hand !

    Austin.   Look up and take   360
My hand, dear Mildred !
    Mildred.   I—I was so young !
Beside, I loved him, Thorold—and I had
No mother ; God forgot me : so I fell.
    Guendolen.   Mildred !
    Mildred.   Require no further !   Did I dream
That I could palliate what is done ?   All 's true.
Now punish me !   A woman takes my hand ?
Let go my hand !   You do not know, I see.
I thought that Thorold told you.

Guendolen.   What is this?
Where start you to?
　Mildred.   O Austin, loosen me!
You heard the whole of it—your eyes were worse,   370
In their surprise, than Thorold's! Oh! unless
You stay to execute his sentence, loose
My hand! Has Thorold gone, and are you here?
　Guendolen. Here, Mildred, we two friends of yours will wait
Your bidding; be you silent, sleep or muse!
Only, when you shall want your bidding done,
How can we do it if we are not by?
Here's Austin waiting patiently your will.
One spirit to command, and one to love
And to believe in it and do its best,   380
Poor as that is, to help it—why, the world
Has been won many a time, its length and breadth,
By just such a beginning!
　Mildred.   I believe.
If once I threw my arms about your neck
And sunk my head upon your breast, that I
Should weep again.
　Guendolen.   Let go her hand now, Austin.
Wait for me. Pace the gallery and think
On the world's seemings and realities,
Until I call you.   [*Austin goes.*
　Mildred.   No—I cannot weep.
No more tears from this brain—no sleep—no tears!   390
O Guendolen, I love you!
　Guendolen.   Yes: and 'love'
Is a short word that says so very much!
It says that you confide in me.
　Mildred.   Confide!
　Guendolen. Your lover's name, then! I've so much to
        learn,
Ere I can work in your behalf!

Mildred.   My friend,
You know I cannot tell his name.
   Guendolen.   At least
He is your lover? and you love him too?
   Mildred. Ah! do you ask me that?—but I am fallen
So low!
   Guendolen. You love him still, then?
   Mildred.   My sole prop
Against the guilt that crushes me!   I say,   400
Each night ere I lie down, 'I was so young—
I had no mother, and I loved him so!'
And then God seems indulgent, and I dare
Trust him my soul in sleep.
   Guendolen.   How could you let us
E'en talk to you about Lord Mertoun then?
   Mildred. There is a cloud around me.
   Guendolen.   But you said
You would receive his suit in spite of this?
   Mildred. I say there is a cloud—
   Guendolen.   No cloud to me!
Lord Mertoun and your lover are the same!
   Mildred. What maddest fancy—
   Guendolen [*calling aloud*]. Austin!—spare your pains—
When I have got a truth, that truth I keep—   412
   Mildred. By all you love, sweet Guendolen, forbear!
Have I confided in you—
   Guendolen.   Just for this!
Austin!—Oh! not to guess it at the first!
But I did guess it—that is, I divined,
Felt by an instinct how it was: why else
Should I pronounce you free from all that heap
Of sins which had been irredeemable?
1 felt they were not yours—what other way
Than this, not yours?   The secret's wholly mine!   420
   Mildred. If you would see me die before his face—

Guendolen. I 'd hold my peace !   And if the Earl returns
To-night ?

Mildred. Ah ! Heaven, he 's lost !

Guendolen.   I thought so.   Austin !

[*Enter Austin.*

Oh ! where have you been hiding ?

Austin.   Thorold 's gone,
I know not how, across the meadow-land.
I watched him till I lost him in the skirts
O' the beech-wood.

Guendolen.   Gone ?   All thwarts us.

Mildred.   Thorold too ?

Guendolen. I have thought.   First lead this Mildred to
  her room.
Go on the other side ; and then we 'll seek
Your brother : and I 'll tell you, by the way,   430
The greatest comfort in the world.   You said
There was a clue to all.   Remember, sweet,
He said there was a clue !   I hold it.   Come !

ACT III.

SCENE I. *The end of the Yew-tree Avenue under Mildred's window. A light seen through a central red pane.*

Enter TRESHAM *through the trees.*

Again here!   But I cannot lose myself.
The heath—the orchard—I have traversed glades
And dells and bosky paths which used to lead
Into green wildwood depths, bewildering
My boy's adventurous step.   And now they tend
Hither or soon or late ; the blackest shade
Breaks up, the thronged trunks of the trees ope wide,
And the dim turret I have fled from fronts
Again my step ; the very river put
Its arm about me and conducted me   10
To this detested spot.   Why then, I 'll shun
Their will no longer : do your will with me !
Oh, bitter !   To have reared a towering scheme
Of happiness, and to behold it razed,
Were nothing : all men hope, and see their hopes
Frustrate, and grieve awhile, and hope anew.
But I—to hope that from a line like ours
No horrid prodigy like this would spring,
Were just as though I hoped that from these old
Confederates against the sovereign day,   20
Children of older and yet older sires,
Whose living coral berries dropped, as now
On me, on many a baron's surcoat once,
On many a beauty's wimple would proceed

No poison-tree, to thrust, from hell its root,
Hither and thither its strange snaky arms.
Why came I here?   What must I do?   [*A bell strikes.*
    A bell?
Midnight! and 't is at midnight—Ah! I catch—
Woods, river, plains, I catch your meaning now,
And I obey you!   Hist!   This tree will serve.   30
    [*He retires behind one of the trees.   After a pause, enter*
      MERTOUN *cloaked as before.*

Mertoun. Not time!   Beat out thy last voluptuous beat
Of hope and fear, my heart!   I thought the clock
I' the chapel struck as I was pushing through
The ferns.   And so I shall no more see rise
My love-star!   Oh! no matter for the past!
So much the more delicious task to watch
Mildred revive ; to pluck out, thorn by thorn,
All traces of the rough forbidden path
My rash love lured her to!   Each day must see
Some fear of hers effaced, some hope renewed ;   40
Then there will be surprises, unforeseen
Delights in store.   I 'll not regret the past.
      [*The light is placed above in the purple pane.*
And see, my signal rises, Mildred's star !
I never saw it lovelier than now
It rises for the last time.   If it sets,
'T is that the re-assuring sun may dawn.
      [*As he prepares to ascend the last tree of the avenue,*
        Tresham arrests his arm.
Unhand me—peasant, by your grasp!   Here 's gold.
'T was a mad freak of mine.   I said I 'd pluck
A branch from the white-blossomed shrub beneath
The casement there.   Take this, and hold your peace.   50
   Tresham. Into the moonlight yonder, come with me !—
Out of the shadow !
    Mertoun.   I am armed, fool !

Tresham.   Yes,
Or no? You 'll come into the light, or no?
My hand is on your throat—refuse!—
    Mertoun.   That voice
Where have I heard—no—that was mild and slow.—
I 'll come with you.   [*They advance.*
    Tresham.   You 're armed : that 's well. Declare
Your name—who are you?
    Mertoun.   Tresham?—she is lost!
    Tresham. Oh! silent?   Do you know, you bear yourself
Exactly as, in curious dreams I 've had
How felons this wild earth is full of look   60
When they 're detected, still your kind has looked!
The bravo holds an assured countenance,
The thief is voluble and plausible,
But silently the slave of lust has crouched
When I have fancied it before a man.
Your name?
    Mertoun.   I do conjure Lord Tresham—ay,
Kissing his foot, if so I might prevail—
That he for his own sake forbear to ask
My name!   As heaven 's above, his future weal
Or woe depends upon my silence!   Vain!   70
I read your white inexorable face.
Know me, Lord Tresham!   [*He throws off his disguises.*
    Tresham.   Mertoun!
        [*After a pause*]   Draw now!
    Mertoun.   Hear me
But speak first!
    Tresham.   Not one least word on your life!
Be sure that I will strangle in your throat
The least word that informs me how you live
And yet seem what you seem!   No doubt 't was you
Taught Mildred still to keep that face and sin.
We should join hands in frantic sympathy

If you once taught me the unteachable,
Explained how you can live so, and so lie.   80
With God's help I retain, despite my sense,
The old belief—a life like yours is still
Impossible.   Now draw!
 Mertoun.   Not for my sake,
Do I entreat a hearing—for your sake,
And most, for her sake!
 Tresham.   Ha ha, what should I
Know of your ways?   A miscreant like yourself,
How must one rouse his ire?   A blow?—that's pride
No doubt to him!   One spurns him, does one not?
Or sets the foot upon his mouth, or spits
Into his face!   Come!   Which, or all of these?   90
 Mertoun. 'Twixt him and me and Mildred, Heaven be
  judge!
Can I avoid this?   Have your will, my lord!
     [*He draws and, after a few passes, falls.*
 Tresham. You are not hurt?
 Mertoun.   You'll hear me now!
 Tresham.   But rise!
 Mertoun. Ah! Tresham, say I not 'you'll hear me now?'
And what procures a man the right to speak
In his defence before his fellow-man,
But—I suppose—the thought that presently
He may have leave to speak before his God
His whole defence?
 Tresham.   Not hurt?   It cannot be!
You made no effort to resist me.   Where   100
Did my sword reach you?   Why not have returned
My thrusts?   Hurt where?
 Mertoun.   My lord—
 Tresham.   How young he is!
 Mertoun. Lord Tresham, I am very young, and yet
I have entangled other lives with mine.

Do let me speak, and do believe my speech!
That when I die before you presently—
   Tresham. Can you stay here till I return with help?
   Mertoun. Oh! stay by me! When I was less than boy
I did you grievous wrong and knew it not—
Upon my honor, knew it not! Once known,   110
I could not find what seemed a better way
To right you than I took: my life—you feel
How less than nothing were the giving you
The life you 've taken! But I thought my way
The better—only for your sake and hers:
And as you have decided otherwise,
Would I had an infinity of lives
To offer you! Now say—instruct me—think
Can you from the brief minutes I have left
Eke out my reparation? Oh! think—think!   120
For I must wring a partial—dare I say,
Forgiveness from you, ere I die?
   Tresham.   I do
Forgive you.
   Mertoun.   Wait and ponder that great word!
Because, if you forgive me, I shall hope
To speak to you of—Mildred!
   Tresham.   Mertoun, haste
And anger have undone us. 'T is not you
Should tell me for a novelty you 're young,
Thoughtless, unable to recall the past.
Be but your pardon ample as my own!
   Mertoun. Ah! Tresham, that a sword-stroke and a drop 130
Of blood or two should bring all this about!
Why, 't was my very fear of you, my love
Of you—what passion like a boy's for one
Like you?—that ruined me! I dreamed of you—
You, all accomplished, courted everywhere,
The scholar and the gentleman. I burned

To knit myself to you ; but I was young,
And your surpassing reputation kept me
So far aloof !　Oh ! wherefore all that love ?
With less of love, my glorious yesterday　　　　140
Of praise and gentlest words and kindest looks
Had taken place perchance six months ago.
Even now, how happy we had been !　And yet
I know the thought of this escaped you, Tresham !
Let me look up into your face ; I feel
'T is changed above me : yet my eyes are glazed.
Where ? where ?

　　　　[As he endeavors to raise himself, his eye catches the lamp.
　　　　　　　　Ah, Mildred !　What will Mildred do ?
Tresham, her life is bound up in the life
That 's bleeding fast away !　I 'll live—must live—
There, if you 'll only turn me I shall live　　　　150
And save her !　Tresham—oh ! had you but heard !
Had you but heard !　What right was yours to set
The thoughtless foot upon her life and mine,
And then say, as we perish, ' Had I thought,
All had gone otherwise ?'　We 've sinned and die :
Never you sin, Lord Tresham ! for you 'll die,
And God will judge you.

　　Tresham.　　　　　　Yes, be satisfied !
That process is begun.

　　Mertoun.　　　　　　And she sits there
Waiting for me !　Now, say you this to her—
You, not another—say, I saw him die　　　　160
As he breathed this, ' I love her '—you don't know
What those three small words mean !　Say, loving her
Lowers me down the bloody slope to death
With memories—I speak to her, not you,
Who had no pity, will have no remorse,
Perchance intend her—Die along with me,
Dear Mildred ! 't is so easy, and you 'll 'scape

So much unkindness! Can I lie at rest,
With rude speech spoken to you, ruder deeds
Done to you?—heartless men shall have my heart,   170
And I tied down with grave-clothes and the worm,
Aware, perhaps, of every blow—O God!—
Upon those lips—yet of no power to tear
The felon stripe by stripe! Die, Mildred! Leave
Their honorable world to them! For God
We 're good enough, though the world casts us out.

           [*A whistle is heard.*

 Tresham. Ho, Gerard!

  Enter GERARD, AUSTIN, *and* GUENDOLEN *with lights.*

      No one speak! You see what 's done.
I cannot bear another voice.
 Mertoun.   There 's light—
Light all about me, and I move to it.
Tresham, did I not tell you—did you not   180
Just promise to deliver words of mine
To Mildred?
 Tresham.   I will bear those words to her.
 Mertoun. Now?
 Tresham.   Now. Lift you the body, and leave me
The head.
    [*As they have half raised Mertoun, he turns suddenly.*
 Mertoun. I knew they turned me : turn me not from her!
There! stay you! there!   [*Dies.*
 Guendolen [*after a pause*]. Austin, remain you here
With Thorold until Gerard comes with help;
Then lead him to his chamber. I must go
To Mildred.
 Tresham.   Guendolen, I hear each word
You utter. Did you hear him bid me give
His message? Did you hear my promise? I,   190
And only I, see Mildred.

Guendolen.   She will die.

Tresham. Oh! no, she will not die! I dare not hope
She 'll die. What ground have you to think she 'll die?
Why, Austin 's with you!

Austin.   Had we but arrived
Before you fought!

Tresham.   There was no fight at all.
He let me slaughter him—the boy! I 'll trust
The body there to you and Gerard—thus!
Now bear him on before me.

Austin.   Whither bear him?

Tresham. Oh! to my chamber! When we meet there next,
We shall be friends.   [*They bear out the body of Mertoun.*
                Will she die, Guendolen?   200

Guendolen. Where are you taking me?

Tresham.   He fell just here.
Now answer me. Shall you in your whole life—
You who have nought to do with Mertoun's fate,
Now you have seen his breast upon the turf,
Shall you e'er walk this way if you can help?
When you and Austin wander arm-in-arm
Through our ancestral grounds, will not a shade
Be ever on the meadow and the waste—
Another kind of shade than when the night
Shuts the woodside with all its whispers up?   210
But will you ever so forget his breast
As carelessly to cross this bloody turf
Under the black yew avenue? That 's well!
You turn your head: and I then?—

Guendolen.   What is done
Is done. My care is for the living. Thorold,
Bear up against this burden: more remains
To set the neck to!

Tresham.   Dear and ancient trees
My fathers planted, and I loved so well!

What have I done that, like some fabled crime
Of yore, lets loose a Fury leading thus   220
Her miserable dance amidst you all?
Oh! never more for me shall winds intone
With all your tops a vast antiphony,
Demanding and responding in God's praise!
Hers ye are now, not mine!   Farewell—farewell!

SCENE II.   *Mildred's Chamber.*   MILDRED *alone.*

He comes not!   I have heard of those who seemed
Resourceless in prosperity,—you thought
Sorrow might slay them when she listed; yet
Did they so gather up their diffused strength
At her first menace, that they bade her strike,
And stood and laughed her subtlest skill to scorn.
Oh! 't is not so with me!   The first woe fell,
And the rest fall upon it, not on me:
Else should I bear that Henry comes not?—fails
Just this first night out of so many nights?   10
Loving is done with.   Were he sitting now,
As so few hours since, on that seat, we 'd love
No more—contrive no thousand happy ways
To hide love from the loveless any more.
I think I might have urged some little point
In my defence to Thorold; he was breathless
For the least hint of a defence: but no,
The first shame over, all that would might fall.
No Henry!   Yet I merely sit and think
The morn's deed o'er and o'er.   I must have crept   20
Out of myself.   A Mildred that has lost
Her lover—oh! I dare not look upon
Such woe!   I crouch away from it!   'T is she,
Mildred, will break her heart, not I!   The world
Forsakes me: only Henry 's left me—left?

When I have lost him, for he does not come,
And I sit stupidly— O Heaven, break up
This worse than anguish, this mad apathy,
By any means or any messenger !
   Tresham [*without*]. Mildred !
   Mildred.   Come in !   Heaven hears me !
       [*Enter* TRESHAM.]   You ? alone ?
Oh ! no more cursing !
   Tresham.   Mildred, I must sit.   31
There—you sit !
   Mildred.   Say it, Thorold—do not look
The curse ! deliver all you come to say !
What must become of me ?   Oh ! speak that thought
Which makes your brow and cheek so pale !
   Tresham.   My thought ?
   Mildred. All of it !
   Tresham.   How we waded—years ago—
After those water lilies, till the plash,
I know not how, surprised us ; and you dared
Neither advance nor turn back : so, we stood
Laughing and crying until Gerard came—   40
Once safe upon the turf, the loudest too,
For once more reaching the relinquished prize !
How idle thoughts are, some men's, dying men's !
Mildred,—
   Mildred. You call me kindlier by my name
Than even yesterday : what is in that ?
   Tresham. It weighs so much upon my mind that I
This morning took an office not my own !
I might—of course, I must be glad or grieved,
Content or not, at every little thing
That touches you.   I may with a wrung heart   50
Even reprove you, Mildred ; I did more :
Will you forgive me ?

Mildred.   Thorold? do you mock?
Or no—and yet you bid me—say that word!
   Tresham. Forgive me, Mildred!—are you silent, sweet?
   Mildred [*starting up*].   Why does not Henry Mertoun
      come to-night?
Are you, too, silent?
      [*Dashing his mantle aside, and pointing to his scabbard,*
         which is empty.
                     Ah! this speaks for you!
You 've murdered Henry Mertoun!   Now proceed!
What is it I must pardon?   This and all?
Well, I do pardon you—I think I do.
Thorold, how very wretched you must be!   60
   Tresham. He bade me tell you—
   Mildred.   What I do forbid
Your utterance of!   So much that you may tell
And will not—how you murdered him—but, no!
You 'll tell me that he loved me, never more
Than bleeding out his life there : must I say
' Indeed,' to that?   Enough! I pardon you.
   Tresham. You cannot, Mildred! for the harsh words,
      yes :
Of this last deed Another 's judge ; whose doom
I wait in doubt, despondency, and fear.
   Mildred. Oh, true!   There 's nought for me to pardon!
      True!   70
You loose my soul of all its cares at once.
Death makes me sure of him forever!   You
Tell me his last words?   He shall tell me them,
And take my answer—not in words, but reading
Himself the heart I had to read him late,
Which death—
   Tresham.   Death?   You are dying too?   Well said
Of Guendolen!   I dared not hope you 'd die :
But she was sure of it.

Mildred.   Tell Guendolen
I loved her, and tell Austin—
     Tresham.   Him you loved:
And me?
     Mildred. Ah, Thorold! Was 't not rashly done   80
To quench that blood, on fire with youth and hope
And love of me—whom you loved too, and yet
Suffered to sit here waiting his approach
While you were slaying him? Oh! doubtlessly
You let him speak his poor confused boy's-speech—
Do his poor utmost to disarm your wrath
And respite me!—you let him try to give
The story of our love and ignorance,
And the brief madness and the long despair—
You let him plead all this, because your code   90
Of honor bids you hear before you strike;
But at the end, as he looked up for life
Into your eyes—you struck him down!
     Tresham.   No! no!
Had I but heard him—had I let him speak
Half the truth—less—had I looked long on him
I had desisted! Why, as he lay there,
The moon on his flushed cheek, I gathered all
The story ere he told it; I saw through
The troubled surface of his crime and yours
A depth of purity immovable.   100
Had I but glanced, where all seemed turbidest
Had gleamed some inlet to the calm beneath.
I would not glance: my punishment 's at hand.
There, Mildred, is the truth! and you—say on—
You curse me?
     Mildred.   As I dare approach that Heaven
Which has not bade a living thing despair,
Which needs no code to keep its grace from stain,
But bids the vilest worm that turns on it

Desist and be forgiven,—I—forgive not,
But bless you, Thorold, from my soul of souls !   110
                                        [*Falls on his neck.*
There !   Do not think too much upon the past !
The cloud that 's broke was all the same a cloud
While it stood up between my friend and you ;
You hurt him 'neath its shadow : but is that
So past retrieve ?   I have his heart, you know ;
I may dispose of it : I give it you !
It loves you as mine loves !   Confirm me, Henry !   [*Dies.*
     Tresham. I wish thee joy, beloved ! I am glad
In thy full gladness !
     Guendolen [*without*]. Mildred ! Tresham !
          [*Entering with Austin*]   Thorold,
I could desist no longer.   Ah ! she swoons !   120
That 's well.
     Tresham.   Oh ! better far than that !
     Guendolen.   She 's dead !
Let me unlock her arms !
     Tresham.   She threw them thus
About my neck, and blessed me, and then died :
You 'll let them stay now, Guendolen !
     Austin.   Leave her
And look to him !   What ails you, Thorold ?
     Guendolen.   White
As she, and whiter !   Austin ! quick—this side !
     Austin. A froth is oozing through his clenched teeth ;
Both lips, where they 're not bitten through, are black :
Speak, dearest Thorold !
     Tresham.   Something does weigh down
My neck beside her weight : thanks ; I should fall   130
But for you, Austin, I believe !—there, there,
'T will pass away soon !—ah !—I had forgotten :
I am dying.
     Guendolen.   Thorold—Thorold—why was this ?

Tresham. I said, just as I drank the poison off,
The earth would be no longer earth to me,
The life out of all life was gone from me.
There are blind ways provided, the foredone
Heart-weary player in this pageant-world
Drops out by, letting the main masque defile
By the conspicuous portal: I am through— 140
Just through!

   Guendolen. Don't leave him, Austin! Death is close.

   Tresham. Already Mildred's face is peacefuller.
I see you, Austin—feel you: here's my hand,
Put yours in it—you, Guendolen, yours too!
You 're lord and lady now—you 're Treshams; name
And fame are yours: you hold our 'scutcheon up.—
Austin, no blot on it! You see how blood
Must wash one blot away: the first blot came,
And the first blood came. To the vain world's eye
All 's gules again: no care to the vain world, 150
From whence the red was drawn!

   Austin.   No blot shall come!

   Tresham. I said that; yet it did come. Should it come,
Vengeance is God's, not man's. Remember me! [*Dies.*

   Guendolen [*letting fall the pulseless arm*]. Ah! Thorold! we
      can but—remember you!

COLOMBE'S BIRTHDAY.

A PLAY.

"Ivy and violet, what do ye here
With blossom and shoot in the warm spring-weather,
Hiding the arms of Monchenci and Vere?" —HANMER.

NO ONE LOVES AND HONORS BARRY CORNWALL MORE THAN DOES
ROBERT BROWNING;
WHO, HAVING NOTHING BETTER THAN THIS PLAY TO
GIVE HIM IN PROOF OF IT,
MUST SAY SO.

London, 1844.

COLOMBE'S BIRTHDAY.

ACT I.

Morning. Scene.—*A Corridor leading to the Audience-chamber.*

Gaucelme, Clugnet, Maufroy, *and other* Courtiers, *round* Guibert, *who is silently reading a paper : as he drops it at the end—*

Guibert. That this should be her birthday; and the day
We all invested her, twelve months ago,
As the late Duke's true heiress and our liege ;
And that this also must become the day—
Oh! miserable lady!

1 *Courtier.*   Ay, indeed?

2 *Courtier.* Well, Guibert?

3 *Courtier.*   But your news, my friend, your news !
The sooner, friend, one learns Prince Berthold's pleasure,
The better for us all: how writes the Prince ?
Give me ! I 'll read it for the common good.

Guibert. In time, sir,—but till time comes, pardon me !   10
Our old Duke just disclosed his child's retreat,
Declared her true succession to his rule,
And died : this birthday was the day, last year,
We convoyed her from Castle Ravestein—
That sleeps out trustfully its extreme age
On the Meuse' quiet bank, where she lived queen
Over the water-buds—to Juliers' court
With joy and bustle. Here again we stand ;

Sir Gaucelme's buckle 's constant to his cap :
To-day 's much such another sunny day !   20
    Gaucelme. Come, Guibert, this outgrows a jest, I think !
You 're hardly such a novice as to need
The lesson you pretend.
    Guibert.   What lesson, sir ?
That everybody, if he 'd thrive at court,
Should, first and last of all, look to himself ?
Why, no : and therefore with your good example—
Ho, Master Adolf !—to myself I 'll look.

                Enter ADOLF.

    Guibert. The Prince's letter ; why, of all men else
Comes it to me ?
    Adolf.   By virtue of your place,
Sir Guibert ! 'T was the Prince's express charge,   30
His envoy told us, that the missive there
Should only reach our lady by the hand
Of whosoever held your place.
    Guibert.   Enough !   [*Adolf retires.*
Then, gentles, who 'll accept a certain poor
Indifferently honorable place,
My friends, I make no doubt, have gnashed their teeth
At leisure minutes these half-dozen years
To find me never in the mood to quit ?—
Who asks may have it, with my blessing, and—
This to present our lady. Who 'll accept ?   40
You—you—you ? There it lies, and may, for me !
    Maufroy [*a youth, picking up the paper, reads aloud*].
' Prince Berthold, proved by titles following
Undoubted Lord of Juliers, comes this day
To claim his own, with license from the Pope,
The Emperor, the Kings of Spain and France '—
    Gaucelme. Sufficient ' titles following,' I judge !
Don't read another ! Well—' to claim his own ?'

Maufroy. 'And take possession of the Duchy held
Since twelve months, to the true heir's prejudice,
By '—Colombe, Juliers' mistress, so she thinks,   50
And Ravestein's mere lady, as we find !
Who wants the place and paper?   Guibert 's right.
I hope to climb a little in the world—
I 'd push my fortunes—but, no more than he,
Could tell her on this happy day of days
That, save the nosegay in her hand, perhaps,
There 's nothing left to call her own.—Sir Clugnet,
You famish for promotion ; what say you?

Clugnet [an old man]. To give this letter were a sort, I
     take it,
Of service : services ask recompense :   60
What kind of corner may be Ravestein?

Guibert. The castle ?—Oh ! you 'd share her fortunes?
     Good !
Three walls stand upright, full as good as four,
With no such bad remainder of a roof.

Clugnet. Oh !—but the town ?

Guibert.   Five houses, fifteen huts,
A church whereto was once a spire, 't is judged ;
And half a dyke, except in time of thaw.

Clugnet. Still, there 's some revenue ?

Guibert.   Else Heaven forefend !
You hang a beacon out, should fogs increase ;
So, when the autumn floats of pine-wood steer   70
Safe 'mid the white confusion, thanks to you,
Their grateful raftsman flings a guilder in ;—
That 's if he mean to pass your way next time.

Clugnet. If not?

Guibert.   Hang guilders, then—he blesses you !

Clugnet. What man do you suppose me? Keep your paper !
And, let me say, it shows no handsome spirit
To dally with misfortune : keep your place !

    Gaucelme. Some one must tell her.
    Guibert.   Some one may : you may !
    Gaucelme. Sir Guibert, 't is no trifle turns me sick
Of court-hypocrisy at years like mine,   80
But this goes near it.   Where 's there news at all ?
Who 'll have the face, for instance, to affirm
He never heard, e'en while we crowned the girl,
That Juliers' tenure was by Salic law ;
That one, confessed her father's cousin's child,
And, she away, indisputable heir,
Against our choice protesting and the Duke's,
Claimed Juliers ?—nor, as he preferred his claim,
That first this, then another potentate,
Inclined to its allowance ?—I or you,   90
Or any one except the lady's self ?
Oh ! it had been the direst cruelty
To break the business to her !   Things might change :
At all events, we 'd see next masque at end,
Next mummery over first ; and so the edge
Was taken off sharp tidings as they came,
Till here 's the Prince upon us, and there 's she—
Wreathing her hair, a song between her lips,
With just the faintest notion possible
That some such claimant earns a livelihood   100
About the world, by feigning grievances
Few pay the story of but grudge its price,
And fewer listen to a second time.
Your method proves a failure ; now try mine !
And, since this must be carried—
    Guibert [*snatching the paper from him*]. By your leave !
Your zeal transports you !   'T will not serve the Prince
So much as you expect, this course you 'd take.
If she leaves quietly her palace—well ;
But if she died upon its threshold—no :
He 'd have the trouble of removing her.   110

Come, gentles, we 're all—what the devil knows!
You, Gaucelme, won't lose character, beside—
You broke your father's heart superiorly
To gather his succession—never blush!
You 're from my province, and, be comforted,
They tell of it with wonder to this day.
You can afford to let your talent sleep.
We 'll take the very worst supposed, as true:
There, the old Duke knew, when he hid his child
Among the river flowers at Ravestein,   120
With whom the right lay!   Call the Prince our Duke!
There, she 's no Duchess, she 's no anything
More than a young maid with the bluest eyes:
And now, sirs, we 'll not break this young maid's heart
Coolly as Gaucelme could and would!   No haste!
His talent 's full-blown, ours but in the bud:
We 'll not advance to his perfection yet—
Will we, Sir Maufroy?   See, I 've ruined Maufroy
Forever as a courtier!

    Gaucelme.   Here 's a coil!
And, count us, will you?   Count its residue,   130
This boasted convoy, this day last year's crowd!
A birthday, too, a gratulation-day!
I 'm dumb: bid that keep silence!

    Maufroy and others.   Eh, Sir Guibert?
He 's right: that does say something; that 's bare truth.
Ten—twelve, I make; a perilous dropping off!

    Guibert.   Pooh—is it audience hour?   The vestibule
Swarms too, I wager, with the common sort
That want our privilege of entry here.

    Gaucelme.   Adolf!   [*Re-enter Adolf.*]   Who 's outside?
    Guibert.   Oh! your looks suffice!
Nobody waiting?

    Maufroy [*looking through the door-folds*].   Scarce our num-
    ber!

Guibert.   'Sdeath !   140
Nothing to beg for, to complain about ?
It can't be !   Ill news spreads, but not so fast
As thus to frighten all the world !
        Gaucelme.   The world
Lives out of doors, sir—not with you and me
By presence-chamber porches, state-room stairs,
Wherever warmth 's perpetual ; outside 's free
To every wind from every compass-point,
And who may get nipped needs be weather-wise.
The Prince comes and the lady's people go ;
The snow-goose settles down, the swallows flee—   150
Why should they wait for winter-time ?   'T is instinct :
Don't you feel somewhat chilly ?
        Guibert.   That 's their craft ?
And last year's crowders-round and criers-forth
That strewed the garlands, over-arched the roads,
Lighted the bonfires, sang the loyal songs !
Well 't is my comfort, you could never call me
The People's Friend !   The people keep their word—
I keep my place : don't doubt I 'll entertain
The people when the Prince comes, and the people
Are talked of !   Then, their speeches—no one tongue   160
Found respite, not a pen had holiday—
For they wrote, too, as well as spoke, these knaves !
Now see : we tax and tithe them, pill and poll,
They wince and fret enough, but pay they must—
We manage that—so, pay with a good grace
They might as well, it costs so little more.
But when we 've done with taxes, meet folk next
Outside the toll-booth and the rating-place,
In public—there they have us if they will,
We 're at their mercy after that, you see !   170
For one tax not ten devils could extort—
Over and above necessity, a grace ;

This prompt disbosoming of love, to wit—
Their vine-leaf wrappage of our tribute-penny,
And crowning attestation, all works well.
Yet this precisely do they thrust on us!
These cappings quick, these crook-and-cringings low,
Hand to the heart, and forehead to the knee,
With grin that shuts the eyes and opes the mouth—
So tender they their love ; and, tender made,   180
Go home to curse us, the first doit we ask.
As if their souls were any longer theirs!
As if they had not given ample warrant
To who should clap a collar on their neck,
Rings in their nose, a goad to either flank,
And take them for the brute they boast themselves!—
Stay—there's a bustle at the outer door—
And somebody entreating—that's my name!
Adolf—I heard my name!

   Adolf.   'T was probably
The suitor,

   Guibert.   Oh! there is one?

   Adolf.   With a suit   190
He'd fain enforce in person.

   Guibert.   The good heart—
And the great fool! Just ope the mid-door's fold!
Is that a lappet of his cloak I see?

   Adolf. If it bear plenteous sign of travel—ay,
The very cloak my comrades tore!

   Guibert.   Why tore?

   Adolf. He seeks the Duchess' presence in that trim :
Since daybreak, was he posted hereabouts
Lest he should miss the moment.

   Guibert.   Where's he now?

   Adolf. Gone for a minute possibly, not more ;
They have ado enough to thrust him back.   200

   Guibert. Ay—but my name I caught?

  Adolf.   O sir—he said—
What was it ?—You had known him formerly,
And, he believed, would help him did you guess
He waited now ; you promised him as much :
The old plea ! Faith, he 's back—renews the charge !—
[*Speaking at the door*] So long as the man parleys, peace
    outside—
Nor be too ready with your halberts there !
  Gaucelme. My horse bespattered, as he blocked the path,
A thin sour man, not unlike somebody.
  Adolf. He holds a paper in his breast, whereon 210
He glances when his cheeks flush and his brow
At each repulse—
  Gaucelme.   I noticed he 'd a brow.
  Adolf. So glancing, he grows calmer, leans awhile
Over the balustrade, adjusts his dress,
And presently turns round, quiet again,
With some new pretext for admittance.—Back !—
[*To Guibert*] Sir, he has seen you ?—Now cross halberts !
   Ha !—
Pascal is prostrate—there lies Fabian too !
No passage ! Whither would the madman press ?
Close the doors quick on me !
  Guibert.   Too late ! He 's here. 220

  Enter, hastily and with discomposed dress, VALENCE.
  Valence. Sir Guibert, will you help me ?—Me, that come
Charged by your townsmen, all who starve at Cleves,
To represent their heights and depths of woe
Before our Duchess and obtain relief !
Such errands barricade such doors, it seems ;
But not a common hindrance drives me back
On all the sad yet hopeful faces, lit
With hope for the first time, which sent me forth.
Cleves, speak for me ! Cleves' men and women, speak !

Who followed me—your strongest—many a mile   230
That I might go the fresher from their ranks—
Who sit—your weakest—by the city gates,
To take me fuller of what news I bring
As I return—for I must needs return !—
Can I ? 'T were hard, no listener for their wrongs,
To turn them back upon the old despair—
Harder, Sir Guibert, than imploring thus—
So, I do—any way you please—implore !
If you—but how should you remember Cleves ?
Yet they of Cleves remember you so well !—   240
Ay, comment on each trait of you they keep,
Your words and deeds caught up at second hand—
Proud, I believe, at bottom of their hearts,
O' the very levity and recklessness
Which only prove that you forget their wrongs.
Cleves, the grand town, whose men and women starve,
Is Cleves forgotten ?—Then, remember me !
You promised me that you would help me once
For other purpose : will you keep your word ?
    Guibert. And who may you be, friend ?
    Valence.   Valence of Cleves.
    Guibert. Valence of—not the advocate of Cleves,   251
I owed my whole estate to, three years back ?
Ay, well may you keep silence ! Why, my lords,
You 've heard, I 'm sure, how, Pentecost three years,
I was so nearly ousted of my land
By some knaves'-pretext—eh ? when you refused me
Your ugly daughter, Clugnet !—and you 've heard
How I recovered it by miracle—
When I refused her ! Here 's the very friend—
Valence of Cleves, all parties have to thank !   260
Nay, Valence, this procedure 's vile in you !
I 'm no more grateful than a courtier should,
But politic am I—I bear a brain,

Can cast about a little, might require
Your services a second time.   I tried
To tempt you with advancement here to court—
'No!'—well, for curiosity at least
To view our life here—'No!'—our Duchess, then—
A pretty woman's worth some pains to see,
Nor is she spoiled, I take it, if a crown   270
Complete the forehead pale and tresses pure—
  Valence. Our city trusted me its miseries,
And I am come.
  Guibert.   So much for taste!   But 'come,'
So may you be, for anything I know,
To beg the Pope's cross, or Sir Clugnet's daughter,
And with an equal chance you get all three!
If it was ever worth your while to come,
Was not the proper way worth finding too?
  Valence. Straight to the palace-portal, sir, I came—
  Guibert. And said?—
  Valence.   That I had brought the miseries
Of a whole city to relieve.
  Guibert.   Which saying   281
Won your admittance?   You saw me, indeed,
And here, no doubt, you stand: as certainly,
My intervention, I shall not dispute,
Procures you audience ; which, if I procure—
That paper's closely written—by Saint Paul,
Here flock the Wrongs, follow the Remedies,
Chapter and verse, One, Two, A, B, and C !
Perhaps you'd enter, make a reverence,
And launch these 'miseries' from first to last?   290
  Valence. How should they let me pause or turn aside?
  Gaucelme [*to Valence*]. My worthy sir, one question ! You've
   come straight
From Cleves, you tell us : heard you any talk
At Cleves about our lady?

Valence.   Much.

Gaucelme.   And what?

Valence. Her wish was to redress all wrongs she knew.

Gaucelme. That you believed?

Valence.   You see me, sir!

Gaucelme.   Nor stopped
Upon the road from Cleves to Juliers here,
For any—rumors you might find afloat?

Valence. I had my townsmen's wrongs to busy me.

Gaucelme. This is the lady's birthday, do you know?—
Her day of pleasure?

Valence.   That the great, I know,   301
For pleasure born, should still be on the watch
To exclude pleasure when a duty offers;
Even as, for duty born, the lowly too
May ever snatch a pleasure if in reach:
Both will have plenty of their birthright, sir!

Gaucelme [aside to Guibert]. Sir Guibert, here's your man!
          No scruples now—
You'll never find his like! Time presses hard.
I've seen your drift and Adolf's too, this while,
But you can't keep the hour of audience back   310
Much longer, and at noon the Prince arrives.
[*Pointing to Valence*] Intrust him with it—fool no chance
          away!

Guibert. Him?

Gaucelme.   With the missive! What's the man to
          her?

Guibert. No bad thought!—Yet, 't is yours, who ever played
The tempting serpent; else 't were no bad thought!
I should—and do—mistrust it for your sake,
Or else—

          Enter an Official *who communicates with* ADOLF.

     Adolf. The Duchess will receive the court!

Guibert. Give us a moment, Adolf!   Valence, friend,
I 'll help you!   We of the service, you 're to mark,
Have special entry, while the herd—the folks   320
Outside—get access through our help alone ;—
Well, it is so, was so, and I suppose
So ever will be: your natural lot is, therefore,
To wait your turn and opportunity,
And probably miss both.   Now, I engage
To set you, here and in a minute's space,
Before the lady, with full leave to plead
Chapter and verse, and A, and B, and C,
To heart's content.
  Valence.   I grieve that I must ask—
This being, yourself admit, the custom here—   330
To what the price of such a favor mounts?
 Guibert. Just so!   You 're not without a courtier's tact.
Little at court, as your quick instinct prompts,
Do such as we without a recompense.
  Valence. Yours is?—
  Guibert.   A trifle: here 's a document
'T is some one's duty to present her Grace—
I say, not mine—these say, not theirs—such points
Have weight at court.   Will you relieve us all
And take it?   Just say, ' I am bidden lay
This paper at the Duchess' feet!'
  Valence.   No more?   340
I thank you, sir!
  Adolf.   Her Grace receives the court!
 Guibert [*aside*]. Now, *sursum corda*, quoth the mass-priest!
   Do—
Whoever 's my kind saint, do let alone
These pushings to and fro, and pullings back ;
Peaceably let me hang o' the devil's arm
The downward path, if you can't pluck me off
Completely!   Let me live quite his, or yours!

[*The Courtiers begin to range themselves, and move toward the door.*

After me, Valence! So, our famous Cleves
Lacks bread? Yet don't we gallants buy their lace?
And dear enough—it beggars me, I know,   350
To keep my very gloves fringed properly.
This, Valence, is our Great State Hall you cross;
Yon gray urn's veritable marcasite,
The Pope's gift: and those salvers testify
The Emperor. Presently you 'll set your foot —
But you don't speak, friend Valence!

    Valence.   I shall speak.

    Gaucelme [*aside to Guibert*]. Guibert—it were no such ungraceful thing
If you and I, at first, seemed horror-struck
With the bad news. Look here, what you shall do!
Suppose you, first, clap hand to sword and cry   360
' Yield strangers our allegiance? First I 'll perish
Beside your Grace '—and so give me the cue
To—

    Guibert. Clap your hand to note-book and jot down
That to regale the Prince with? I conceive.—
[*To Valence*] Do, Valence, speak, or I shall half suspect
You 're plotting to supplant us, me the first,
I' the lady's favor! Is 't the grand harangue
You mean to make, that thus engrosses you?—
Which of her virtues you 'll apostrophize?
Or is 't the fashion you aspire to start,   370
Of that close-curled, not unbecoming hair?
Or what else ponder you?

    Valence.   My townsmen's wrongs.

ACT II.

Noon.   SCENE.—*The Presence-chamber.*

The DUCHESS *and* SABYNE.

The Duchess. Announce that I am ready for the court!

Sabyne. 'T is scarcely audience-hour, I think ; your Grace
May best consult your own relief, no doubt,
And shun the crowd : but few can have arrived.

The Duchess. Let those not yet arrived, then, keep away!
'T was me, this day last year at Ravestein,
You hurried.   It has been full time, beside,
This half-hour.   Do you hesitate ?

Sabyne.   Forgive me !

The Duchess. Stay, Sabyne ; let me hasten to make sure
Of one true thanker : here with you begins   10
My audience, claim you first its privilege !
It is my birth's event they celebrate :
You need not wish me more such happy days,
But—ask some favor !   Have you none to ask ?
Has Adolf none, then ? this was far from least
Of much I waited for impatiently,
Assure yourself !   It seemed so natural
Your gift, beside this bunch of river-bells,
Should be the power and leave of doing good
To you, and greater pleasure to myself.   20
You ask my leave to-day to marry Adolf ?
The rest is my concern.

Sabyne.   Your grace is ever
Our lady of dear Ravestein—but, for Adolf—

The Duchess. 'But?' You have not, sure, changed in
    your regard
And purpose towards him?
    Sabyne.   We change?
    The Duchess.   Well then? Well?
    Sabyne. How could we two be happy, and, most like,
Leave Juliers, when—when—but 't is audience-time!
    The Duchess. 'When, if you left me, I were left indeed!'
Would you subjoin that?—Bid the court approach!—
Why should we play thus with each other, Sabyne?   30
Do I not know, if courtiers prove remiss,
If friends detain me, and get blame for it,
There is a cause? Of last year's fervid throng
Scarce one half comes now.
    Sabyne [*aside*].   One half? No, alas!
    The Duchess. So can the mere suspicion of a cloud
Over my fortunes strike each loyal heart.
They 've heard of this Prince Berthold; and, forsooth,
Some foolish arrogant pretence he makes
May grow more foolish and more arrogant,
They please to apprehend! I thank their love.   40
Admit them!
    Sabyne [*aside*]. How much has she really learned?
    The Duchess. Surely, whoever 's absent, Tristan waits?—
Or at least Romuald, whom my father raised
From nothing—come, he 's faithful to me, come!—
Sabyne, I should but be the prouder—yes,
The fitter to comport myself aright—
Not Romuald? Xavier—what said he to that?
For Xavier hates a parasite, I know!—   [*Sabyne goes out.*
Well, sunshine 's everywhere, and summer too.
Next year 't is the old place again, perhaps—   50
The water-breeze again, the birds again.—
It cannot be! It is too late to be!
What part had I, or choice in all of it?
  9

Hither they brought me ; I had not to think
Nor care, concern myself with doing good
Or ill, my task was just—to live—to live,
And, answering ends there was no need explain,
To render Juliers happy—so they said.
All could not have been falsehood ; some was love,
And wonder and obedience.   I did all   60
They looked for : why then cease to do it now?
Yet this is to be calmly set aside,
And—ere next birthday's dawn, for aught I know,
Things change, a claimant may arrive, and I—
It cannot nor it shall not be !   His right?
Well then, he has the right, and I have not—
But who bade all of you surround my life
And close its growth up with your ducal crown
Which, plucked off rudely, leaves me perishing ?
I could have been like one of you—loved, hoped,   70
Feared, lived, and died like one of you—but you
Would take that life away and give me this,
And I will keep this !   I will face you !   Come !

Enter *the* Courtiers *and* VALENCE.

The Courtiers. Many such happy mornings to your Grace !
The Duchess [*aside, as they pay their devoir*]. The same
      words, the same faces—the same love !
I have been over-fearful.   These are few ;
But these, at least, stand firmly ; these are mine.
As many come as may ; and if no more,
'T is that these few suffice—they do suffice !
What succor may not next year bring me ? Plainly,   80
I feared too soon.—[*To the Court*] I thank you, sirs ; all
      thanks !
   Valence [*aside, as the Duchess passes from one group to an-
      other, conversing*]. 'T is she—the vision this day last
      year brought,

When, for a golden moment at our Cleves,
She tarried in her progress hither.   Cleves
Chose me to speak its welcome, and I spoke—
Not that she could have noted the recluse—
Ungainly, old before his time—who gazed.
Well, Heaven's gifts are not wasted, and that gaze
Kept, and shall keep me to the end, her own!
She was above it—but so would not sink   90
My gaze to earth!   The people caught it, hers—
Thenceforward, mine; but thus entirely mine,
Who shall affirm, had she not raised my soul
Ere she retired and left me—them?   She turns—
There's all her wondrous face at once!   The ground
Reels and—[*Suddenly occupying himself with his paper.*]
        These wrongs of theirs I have to plead!
    The Duchess [*to the Court*]. Nay, compliment enough! and
        kindness' self
Should pause before it wish me more such years.
'T was fortunate that thus, ere youth escaped,
I tasted life's pure pleasure—one such, pure,   100
Is worth a thousand, mixed—and youth 's for pleasure:
Mine is received; let my age pay for it.
    Gaucelme. So pay, and pleasure paid for, thinks your
        Grace,
Should never go together?
    Guibert.   How, Sir Gaucelme?
Hurry one's feast down unenjoyingly
At the snatched breathing-intervals of work?
As good you saved it till the dull day's-end
When, stiff and sleepy, appetite is gone.
Eat first, then work upon the strength of food!
    The Duchess. True: you enable me to risk my future,   110
By giving me a past beyond recall.
I lived, a girl, one happy leisure year:
Let me endeavor to be the Duchess now!

And so—what news, Sir Guibert, spoke you of?—
        [*As they advance a little, and Guibert speaks*—
That gentleman?
    Valence [*aside*].   I feel her eyes on me.
    Guibert. [*to Valence*]. The Duchess, sir, inclines to hear
      your suit.
Advance!—He is from Cleves.
    Valence [*coming forward*] [*aside*]. Their wrongs—their
      wrongs!
    The Duchess. And you, sir, are from Cleves? How fresh
      in mind,
The hour or two I passed at queenly Cleves!
She entertained me bravely, but the best   120
Of her good pageant seemed its standers-by
With insuppressive joy on every face!
What says my ancient, famous, happy Cleves?
    Valence. Take the truth, lady—you are made for truth!
So think my friends; nor do they less deserve
The having you to take it, you shall think,
When you know all—nay, when you only know
How, on that day you recollect at Cleves,
When the poor acquiescing multitude
Who thrust themselves with all their woes apart   130
Into unnoticed corners, that the few
Their means sufficed to muster trappings for
Might fill the foreground, occupy your sight
With joyous faces fit to bear away
And boast of as a sample of all Cleves—
How, when to daylight these crept out once more,
Clutching, unconscious, each his empty rags
Whence the scant coin, which had not half bought bread,
That morn he shook forth, counted piece by piece,
And, well-advisedly, on perfumes spent them   140
To burn, or flowers to strew, before your path—
How, when the golden flood of music and bliss

Ebbed, as their moon retreated, and again
Left the sharp black-point rocks of misery bare—
Then I, their friend had only to suggest
' Saw she the horror as she saw the pomp !'
And as one man they cried ' He speaks the truth :
' Show her the horror !   Take from our own mouths
Our wrongs and show them, she will see them too !'
This they cried, lady !   I have brought the wrongs.   150

   The Duchess. Wrongs ?   Cleves has wrongs—apparent
      now and thus ?
I thank you !   In that paper ?   Give it me !

   Valence. There, Cleves !—In this !—What did I promise,
      Cleves ?—
Our weavers, clothiers, spinners are reduced
Since—Oh ! I crave your pardon !   I forget
I buy the privilege of this approach,
And promptly would discharge my debt.   I lay
This paper humbly at the Duchess' feet.

                  [*Presenting Guibert's paper.*

   Guibert. Stay ! for the present—
   The Duchess.   Stay, sir ? I take aught
That teaches me their wrongs with greater pride   160
Than this your ducal circlet.—Thank you, sir !—

      [*The Duchess reads hastily ; then, turning to the Court-
        iers—*
What have I done to you ?   Your deed or mine
Was it, this crowning me ?   I gave myself
No more a title to your homage, no,
Than church-flowers, born this season, wrote the words
In the saint's-book that sanctified them first.
For such a flower, you plucked me ; well, you erred—
Well, 't was a weed ; remove the eyesore quick !
But should you not remember it has lain
Steeped in the candles' glory, palely shrined,   170
Nearer God's Mother than most earthly things ?—

That if 't be faded 't is with prayer's sole breath—
That the one day it boasted was God's day?
Still, I do thank you! Had you used respect,
Here might I dwindle to my last white leaf,
Here lose life's latest freshness, which even yet
May yield some wandering insect rest and food:
So, fling me forth, and—all is best for all!
[*After a pause*] Prince Berthold, who art Juliers' Duke, it
       seems—
The King's choice, and the Emperor's, and the Pope's— 180
Be mine, too! Take this people! Tell not me
Of rescripts, precedents, authorities—
But take them, from a heart that yearns to give!
Find out their love—I could not; find their fear—
I would not; find their like—I never shall,
Among the flowers!   [*Taking off her coronet.*
          Colombe of Ravestein
Thanks God she is no longer Duchess here!
  Valence [*advancing to Guibert*]. Sir Guibert, knight, they
      call you—this of mine
Is the first step I ever set at court.
You dared make me your instrument, I find; 190
For that, so sure as you and I are men,
We reckon to the utmost presently:
But as you are a courtier and I none,
Your knowledge may instruct me. I, already,
Have too far outraged, by my ignorance
Of courtier-ways, this lady, to proceed
A second step and risk addressing her:—
I am degraded—you let me address!
Out of her presence, all is plain enough
What I shall do—but in her presence, too, 200
Surely there's something proper to be done.—
[*To the others*] You, gentles, tell me if I guess aright—
May I not strike this man to earth?

The Courtiers [*as Guibert springs forward, withholding him*].   Let go!—
The clothiers' spokesman, Guibert?   Grace a churl?
    The Duchess [*to Valence*].   Oh! be acquainted with your
        party, sir!
He's of the oldest lineage Juliers boasts;
A lion crests him for a cognizance;
'Scorning to waver'—that's his 'scutcheon's word;
His office with the new Duke—probably
The same in honor as with me; or more,   210
By so much as this gallant turn deserves.
He's now, I dare say, of a thousand times
The rank and influence that remain with her
Whose part you take!   So, lest for taking it
You suffer—
    Valence.   I may strike him then to earth?
    Guibert [*falling on his knee*].   Great and dear lady, pardon
        me!   Hear once!
Believe me and be merciful—be just!
I could not bring myself to give that paper
Without a keener pang than I dared meet—
And so felt Clugnet here, and Maufroy here—   220
No one dared meet it.   Protestation's cheap—
But, if to die for you did any good,
[*To Gaucelme*] Would not I die, sir?   Say your worst of me!
But it does no good, that's the mournful truth.
And since the hint of a resistance, even,
Would just precipitate, on you the first,
A speedier ruin—I shall not deny,
Saving myself indubitable pain,
I thought to give you pleasure—who might say?—
By showing that your only subject found   230
To carry the sad notice was the man
Precisely ignorant of its contents;
A nameless, mere provincial advocate;

One whom 't was like you never saw before,
Never would see again.   All has gone wrong;
But I meant right, God knows, and you, I trust!
    The Duchess. A nameless advocate, this gentleman?—
I pardon you, Sir Guibert!—
    Guibert [*rising, to Valence*]. Sir, and you?—
    Valence. Rejoice that you are lightened of a load.
Now, you have only me to reckon with.   240
    The Duchess. One I have never seen, much less obliged?—
    Valence. Dare I speak, lady?
    The Duchess.   Dare you!   Heard you not
I rule no longer?
    Valence.   Lady, if your rule
Were based alone on such a ground as these
                      [*Pointing to the courtiers.*
Could furnish you—abjure it!   They have hidden
A source of true dominion from your sight.
    The Duchess. You hear them—no such source is left—
    Valence.   Hear Cleves!
Whose haggard craftsmen rose to starve this day,
Starve now, and will lie down at night to starve,
Sure of a like to-morrow—but as sure   250
Of a most unlike morrow-after-that,
Since end things must, end howsoe'er things may.
What curbs the brute-force instinct in its hour?
What makes—instead of rising, all as one,
And teaching fingers, so expert to wield
Their tool, the broadsword's play or carbine's trick—
What makes that there 's an easier help, they think,
For you, whose name so few of them can spell,
Whose face scarce one in every hundred saw—
You simply have to understand their wrongs,   260
And wrongs will vanish—so, still trades are plied,
And swords lie rusting, and myself stand here?
There is a vision in the heart of each

Of justice, mercy, wisdom, tenderness
To wrong and pain, and knowledge of its cure ;
And these embodied in a woman's form
That best transmits them, pure as first received,
From God above her, to mankind below.
Will you derive your rule from such a ground,
Or rather hold it by the suffrage, say,   270
Of this man—this—and this ?

    The Duchess [*after a pause*]. You come from Cleves.
How many are at Cleves of such a mind !

    Valence [*from his paper*]. 'We, all the manufacturers of
        Cleves '—

    The Duchess. Or stay, sir—lest I seem too covetous—
Are you my subject ? such as you describe
Am I to you, though to no other man ?

    Valence [*from his paper*]. 'Valence ordained your Advo-
        cate at Cleves '—

    The Duchess [*replacing the coronet*]. Then I remain Cleves'
        Duchess ! Take you note,
While Cleves but yields one subject of this stamp,
I stand her lady till she waves me off !   280
For her sake, all the Prince claims I withhold ;
Laugh at each menace ; and, his power defying,
Return his missive with its due contempt !

                              [*Casting it away.*

    Guibert [*picking it up*]. Which to the Prince I will deliver,
        lady—
Note it down, Gaucelme—with your message too !

    The Duchess. I think the office is a subject's, sir !—
Either—how style you him ?—my special guarder
The Marshal's—for who knows but violence
May follow the delivery ?—or, perhaps,
My Chancellor's—for law may be to urge   290
On its receipt !—or, even my Chamberlain's—
For I may violate established form !—

[*To Valence*] Sir—for the half-hour till this service ends,
Will you become all these to me?
> *Valence* [*falling on his knee*].   My liege!
> *The Duchess*. Give me!
>   [*The Courtiers present their badges of office.*
>   [*Putting them by*] Whatever was their virtue once,
They need new consecration. [*Raising Valence*] Are you
        mine?—
I will be Duchess yet!   [*She retires.*
> *The Courtiers*.   Our Duchess yet!
A glorious lady! Worthy love and dread!
I 'll stand by her—and I, whate'er betide!
> *Guibert* [*to Valence*]. Well done, well done, sir! I care
>   not who knows,   300
You have done nobly and I envy you—
Tho' I am but unfairly used, I think ;
For when one gets a place like this I hold,
One gets too the remark that its mere wages,
The pay and the preferment, make our prize.
Talk about zeal and faith apart from these,
We 're laughed at—much would zeal and faith subsist
Without these also! Yet, let these be stopped,
Our wages discontinue—then, indeed,
Our zeal and faith—we hear on every side—   310
Are not released—having been pledged away
I wonder for what zeal and faith in turn?
Hard money purchased me my place! No, no—
I 'm right, sir—but your wrong is better still,
If I had time and skill to argue it.
Therefore, I say, I 'll serve you, how you please—
If you like—fight you, as you seem to wish—
The kinder of me that, in sober truth,
I never dreamed I did you any harm—
> *Gaucelme*. Or, kinder still, you 'll introduce, no doubt,   320
His merits to the Prince who 's just at hand,

And let no hint drop he's made Chancellor
And Chamberlain and Heaven knows what beside!
   Clugnet [*to Valence*]. You stare, young sir, and threaten!
      Let me say,
That at your age, when first I came to court,
I was not much above a gentleman ;
While now—
   Valence. You are Head-Lackey? With your office
I have not yet been graced, sir !
   Other Courtiers [*to Clugnet*]. Let him talk !
Fidelity, disinterestedness,
Excuse so much ! Men claim my worship ever   330
Who stanchly and steadfastly—

              Enter ADOLF.

   Adolf.   The Prince arrives.
   Courtiers. Ha ? How ?
   Adolf.   He leaves his guard a stage behind
At Aix, and enters almost by himself.
   1 *Courtier.* The Prince ! This foolish business puts all
      out.
   2 *Courtier.* Let Gaucelme speak first !
   3 *Courtier.*   Better I began
About the state of Juliers : should one say
All's prosperous and inviting him ?
   4 *Courtier.*   Or rather,
All's prostrate and imploring him ?
   5 *Courtier.*   That's best.
Where's the Cleves' paper, by the way ?
   4 *Courtier* [*to Valence*].   Sir—sir—
If you'll but lend that paper—trust it me,   340
I'll warrant—
   5 *Courtier.* Softly, sir—the Marshal's duty !
   Clugnet. Has not the Chamberlain a hearing first
By virtue of his patent ?

Gaucelme.   Patents?—Duties?
All that, my masters, must begin again!
One word composes the whole controversy:
We're simply now—the Prince's!
     The Others.   Ay—the Prince's!

Enter SABYNE.

Sabyne. Adolf! Bid—Oh! no time for ceremony!
Where's whom our lady calls her only subject?
She needs him. Who is here the Duchess's?
     Valence [*starting from his reverie*]. Most gratefully I fol-
          low to her feet.   350

ACT III.

Afternoon. SCENE.—*The Vestibule.*

Enter PRINCE BERTHOLD *and* MELCHIOR.

Berthold. A thriving little burgh this Juliers looks.
[*Half apart*] Keep Juliers, and as good you kept Cologne:
Better try Aix, though!—

Melchior.   Please 't your Highness speak?

Berthold [*as before*]. Aix, Cologne, Frankfort   Milan —
Rome!—

Melchior.   The Grave.—
More weary seems your Highness, I remark,
Than sundry conquerors whose path I 've watched
Through fire and blood to any prize they gain.
I could well wish you, for your proper sake,
Had met some shade of opposition here—
Found a blunt seneschal refuse unlock,   10
Or a scared usher lead your steps astray.
You must not look for next achievement's palm
So easily : this will hurt your conquering.

Berthold. My next?   Ay—as you say, my next and next!
Well, I am tired, that 's truth, and moody too,
This quiet entrance-morning : listen why !
Our little burgh, now, Juliers—'t is indeed
One link, however insignificant,
Of the great chain by which I reach my hope—
A link I must secure ; but otherwise,   20
You 'd wonder I esteem it worth my grasp.
Just see what life is, with its shifts and turns !
It happens now—this very nook—to be

A place that once—not a long while since, neither—
When I lived an ambiguous hanger-on
Of foreign courts, and bore my claims about,
Discarded by one kinsman, and the other
A poor priest merely—then, I say, this place
Shone my ambition's object; to be Duke—
Seemed then what to be Emperor seems now.   30
My rights were far from being judged as plain
In those days as of late, I promise you:
And 't was my day-dream, Lady Colombe here
Might e'en compound the matter, pity me,
Be struck, say, with my chivalry and grace—
I was a boy!—bestow her hand at length,
And make me Duke, in her right if not mine.
Here am I, Duke confessed, at Juliers now.
Hearken: if ever I be Emperor,
Remind me what I felt and said to-day!   40
    Melchior. All this consoles a bookish man like me.—
And so will weariness cling to you.   Wrong,
Wrong!   Had you sought the lady's court yourself—
Faced the redoubtables composing it,
Flattered this, threatened that man, bribed the other—
Pleaded by writ and word and deed your cause—
Conquered a footing inch by painful inch—
And, after long years' struggle, pounced at last
On her for prize—the right life had been lived,
And justice done to divers faculties   50
Shut in that brow.   Yourself were visible
As you stood victor, then; whom now—your pardon!
I am forced narrowly to search and see—
So are you hid by helps—this Pope, your uncle—
Your cousin, the other King!   You are a mind—
They, body: too much of mere legs-and-arms
Obstructs the mind so!   Match these with their like:
Match mind with mind!

Berthold.   And where 's your mind to match?
They show me legs-and-arms to cope withal!
I 'd subjugate this city—where 's its mind?   60

> [*The Courtiers enter slowly.*

Melchior. Got out of sight when you came troops and all!
And in its stead, here greets you flesh-and-blood—
A smug œconomy of both, this first! —

> [*As Clugnet bows obsequiously.*

Well done, gout, all considered!—I may go?
Berthold. Help me receive them!
Melchior.   Oh! they just will say
What yesterday at Aix their fellows said—
At Treves, the day before!—Sir Prince, my friend,
Why do you let your life slip thus?—Meantime,
I have my little Juliers to achieve—
The understanding this tough Platonist,   70
Your holy uncle disinterred, Amelius—
Lend me a company of horse and foot,
To help me through his tractate—gain my Duchy!
Berthold. And Empire, after that is gained, will be—?
Melchior. To help me through your uncle's comment,
        Prince!   [*Goes.*
Berthold. Ah! Well: he o'er-refines—the scholar's fault!
How do I let my life slip? Say, this life,
I lead now, differs from the common life
Of other men in mere degree, not kind,
Of joys and griefs,—still there is such degree—   80
Mere largeness in a life is something, sure—
Enough to care about and struggle for,
In this world: for this world, the size of things;
The sort of things, for that to come, no doubt.
A great is better than a little aim;
And when I wooed Priscilla's rosy mouth
And failed so, under that gray convent wall,
Was I more happy than I should be now

                    [*By this time, the Courtiers are ranged before him.*
If failing of my Empire?   Not a whit.—
Here comes the mind, it once had tasked me sore   90
To baffle, but for my advantages!
All 's best as 't is: these scholars talk and talk.
                                        [*Seats himself.*
   The Courtiers. Welcome our Prince to Juliers!—to his
        heritage!
Our dutifullest service proffer we!
   Clugnet. I, please your Highness, having exercised
The function of Grand Chamberlain at court,
With much acceptance, as men testify—
   Berthold. I cannot greatly thank you, gentlemen!
The Pope declares my claim to the Duchy founded
On strictest justice; if you concede it, therefore,   100
I do not wonder: and the kings my friends
Protesting they will see such claim enforced,
You easily may offer to assist us.
But there 's a slight discretionary power
To serve me in the matter, you 've had long,
Though late you use it.   This is well to say—
But could you not have said it months ago?
I 'm not denied my own Duke's truncheon, true—
'T is flung me—I stoop down, and from the ground
Pick it, with all you placid standers-by—   110
And now I have it, gems and mire at once,
Grace go with it to my soiled hands, you say!
   Guibert. By Paul, the advocate our doughty friend
Cuts the best figure!
   Gaucelme.   If our ignorance
May have offended, sure our loyalty—
   Berthold. Loyalty?   Yours?—Oh!—of yourselves you
        speak!—
I mean the Duchess all this time, I hope!
And since I have been forced repeat my claims

As if they never had been made before,
As I began, so must I end, it seems.   120
The formal answer to the grave demand!
What says the lady?

 Courtiers [one to another]. 1 *Courtier.* Marshal!
         2 *Courtier.*   Orator!

 Guibert. A variation of our mistress' way!
Wipe off his boots' dust, Clugnet!—that he waits!

 1 *Courtier.* Your place!

 2 *Courtier.* Just now it was your own!

 Guibert.   The devil's!

 Berthold [to Guibert]. Come forward, friend—you with
  the paper, there!
Is Juliers the first city I 've obtained?
By this time, I may boast proficiency
In each decorum of the circumstance.   130
Give it me as she gave it—the petition!
Demand, you style it—What 's required, in brief?
What title's reservation, appanage's
Allowance?—I heard all at Treves, last week.

 Gaucelme [to Guibert]. 'Give it him as she gave it!'

 Guibert.   And why not?
[*To Berthold*] The lady crushed your summons thus together,
And bade me, with the very greatest scorn
So fair a frame could hold, inform you—

 Courtiers.   Stop—
Idiot!—

 Guibert. Inform you she denied your claim,
Defied yourself!—I tread upon his heel,   140
The blustering advocate!

 Berthold.   By heaven and earth!
Dare you jest, sir?

 Guibert.   Did they at Treves, last week?

 Berthold [starting up]. Why then, I look much bolder than
  I knew,

 10

And you prove better actors than I thought—
Since, as I live, I took you as you entered
For just so many dearest friends of mine,
Fled from the sinking to the rising power—
The sneaking'st crew, in short, I e'er despised!
Whereas, I am alone here for the moment,
With every soldier left behind at Aix!   150
Silence? That means the worst? I thought as much!
What follows next then?

    Courtiers.   Gracious Prince—he raves!
    Guibert. He asked the truth, and why not get the truth?
    Berthold. Am I a prisoner? Speak, will somebody?—
But why stand paltering with imbeciles?
Let me see her, or—

    Guibert.   Her, without her leave,
Shall no one see: she 's Duchess yet!

    Courtiers [*footsteps without, as they are disputing*]. Good
        chance!
She 's here—the Lady Colombe's self!

    Berthold.   'T is well!
[*Aside*] Array a handful thus against my world?
Not ill done truly! Were not this a mind   160
To match one's mind with? Colombe!—Let us wait!
I failed so, under that gray convent wall!
She comes.

    Guibert. The Duchess! Strangers, range yourselves.
      [*As the Duchess enters in conversation with Valence,*
        Berthold and the Courtiers fall back a little.
    The Duchess. Presagefully it beats, presagefully,
My heart: the right is Berthold's and not mine.
    Valence. Grant that he has the right, dare I mistrust
Your power to acquiesce so patiently
As you believe, in such a dream-like change
Of fortune—change abrupt, profound, complete?
    The Duchess. Ah! the first bitterness is over now!   170

Bitter I may have felt it to confront
The truth, and ascertain those natures' value
I had so counted on ; that was a pang :
But I did bear it, and the worst is over.
Let the Prince take them !—

  Valence.   And take Juliers too ?—
Your people without crosses, wands, and chains—
Only with hearts ?

  The Duchess.   There I feel guilty, sir !
I cannot give up what I never had ;
For I ruled these, not them—these stood between.
Shall I confess, sir ? I have heard by stealth   180
Of Berthold from the first ; more news and more :
Closer and closer swam the thunder-cloud,
But I was safely housed with these, I knew.
At times when to the casement I would turn,
At a bird's passage or a flower-trail's play,
I caught the storm's red glimpses on its edge—
Yet I was sure some one of all these friends
Would interpose : I followed the bird's flight
Or plucked the flower—some one would interpose !

  Valence. Not one thought on the people—and Cleves there !

  The Duchess. Now, sadly conscious my real sway was
    missed,   191
Its shadow goes without so much regret ;
Else could I not again thus calmly bid you
Answer Prince Berthold !

  Valence.   Then you acquiesce ?

  The Duchess. Remember over whom it was I ruled !

  Guibert [*stepping forward*]. Prince Berthold, yonder, craves
    an audience, lady !

  The Duchess [*to Valence*]. I only have to turn, and I shall
    face
Prince Berthold ! Oh ! my very heart is sick !
It is the daughter of a line of Dukes

This scornful, insolent adventurer   200
Will bid depart from my dead father's halls!
I shall not answer him—dispute with him—
But, as he bids, depart!   Prevent it, sir!
Sir—but a mere day's respite!   Urge for me—
What I shall call to mind I should have urged
When time 's gone by—'t will all be mine you urge!
A day—an hour—that I myself may lay
My rule down!   'T is too sudden—must not be!
The world 's to hear of it!   Once done—forever!
How will it read, sir?   How be sung about?   210
Prevent it!
    Berthold [*approaching*].   Your frank indignation, lady,
Cannot escape me.   Overbold I seem ;
But somewhat should be pardoned my surprise
At this reception—this defiance, rather.
And if, for their and your sake, I rejoice
Your virtues could inspire a trusty few
To make such gallant stand in your behalf,
I cannot but be sorry, for my own,
Your friends should force me to retrace my steps :
Since I no longer am permitted speak   220
After the pleasant peaceful course prescribed
No less by courtesy than relationship—
Which I remember, if you once forgot.
But never must attack pass unrepelled.
Suffer that through you I demand of these,
Who controverts my claim to Juliers?—
    The Duchess.   Me,
You say, you do not speak to—
    Berthold.   Of your subjects
I ask, then : whom do you accredit?   Where
Stand those should answer!
    Valence [*advancing*].   The lady is alone!
    Berthold.   Alone, and thus?   So weak and yet so bold?

Valence. I said she was alone—
   Berthold.   And weak, I said.   231
   Valence. When is man strong until he feels alone?
It was some lonely strength at first, be sure,
Created organs, such as those you seek,
By which to give its varied purpose shape—
And, naming the selected ministrants,
Took sword, and shield, and sceptre—each, a man!
That strength performed its work and passed its way:
You see our lady: there the old shapes stand!—
A Marshal, Chamberlain, and Chancellor—   240
' Be helped their way, into their death put life
And find advantage!'—so you counsel us.
But let strength feel alone, seek help itself—
And, as the inland-hatched sea-creature hunts
The sea's breast out—as, littered 'mid the waves,
The desert-brute makes for the desert's joy,
So turns our lady to her true resource,
Passing o'er hollow fictions, worn-out types—
And I am first her instinct fastens on.
And prompt I say, as clear as heart can speak,   250
The people will not have you; nor shall have!
It is not merely I shall go bring Cleves
And fight you to the last—though that does much,
And men and children—ay, and women too,
Fighting for home, are rather to be feared
Than mercenaries fighting for their pay—
But, say you beat us, since such things have been,
And, where this Juliers laughed, you set your foot
Upon a steaming bloody plash—what then?
Stand you the more our lord that there you stand?   260
Lord it o'er troops whose force you concentrate,
A pillared flame whereto all ardors tend—
Lord it 'mid priests whose schemes you amplify,
A cloud of smoke 'neath which all shadows brood—

But never, in this gentle spot of earth,
Can you become our Colombe, our play-queen,
For whom, to furnish lilies for her hair,
We 'd pour our veins forth to enrich the soil!—
Our conqueror? Yes!—Our despot? Yes!—Our Duke!
Know yourself, know us!

    Berthold [*who has been in thought*]. Know your lady, also!
[*Very deferentially*] To whom I needs must exculpate my-
        self   271
For having made a rash demand, at least.
Wherefore to you, sir, who appear to be
Her chief adviser, I submit my claims,   [*Giving papers.*
But, this step taken, take no further step,
Until the Duchess shall pronounce their worth.
Here be our meeting-place, at night its time;
Till when I humbly take the lady's leave!

      [*He withdraws. As the Duchess turns to Valence, the
         Courtiers interchange glances and come forward a little.*

  1 *Courtier.* So, this was their device!
  2 *Courtier.* No bad device!   280
  3 *Courtier.* You 'd say they love each other, Guibert's
    friend
From Cleves, and she the Duchess!—
  4 *Courtier.*   And moreover,
That all Prince Berthold comes for, is to help
Their loves!
  5 *Courtier.* Pray, Guibert, what is next to do?
  Guibert [*advancing*]. I laid my office at the Duchess' foot—
  Others. And I—and I—and I!
  The Duchess.   I took them, sirs.
  Guibert [*apart to Valence*]. And now, sir, I am simple knight
    again—
Guibert, of the great ancient house, as yet
That never bore affront; whate'er your birth,—
As things stand now, I recognize yourself—   290

If you 'll accept experience of some date—
As like to be the leading man o' the time,
Therefore as much above me now, as I
Seemed above you this morning.   Then I offered
To fight you : will you be as generous
And now fight me ?
   Valence.   Ask when my life is mine !
   Guibert. 'T is hers now !
   Clugnet [*apart to Valence, as Guibert turns from him*]. You,
      sir, have insulted me
Grossly—will grant me, too, the selfsame favor
You 've granted him just now, I make no question ?
   Valence. I promise you, as him, sir.
   Clugnet.   Do you so ?   300
Handsomely said !   I hold you to it, sir.
You 'll get me reinstated in my office
As you will Guibert !
   The Duchess.   I would be alone !
      [*They begin to retire slowly ; as Valence is about to fol-
        low—*
Alone, sir—only with my heart : you stay !
   Gaucelme. You hear that ?   Ah ! light breaks upon me !
      Cleves—
It was at Cleves some man harangued us all—
With great effect—so those who listened said,
My thoughts being busy elsewhere : was this he,
Guibert ?—your strange, disinterested man !
Your uncorrupted, if uncourtly friend !   310
The modest worth you mean to patronize !
He cares about no Duchesses, not he—
His sole concern is with the wrongs of Cleves !
What, Guibert ?   What, it breaks on you at last ?
   Guibert. Would this hall's floor were a mine's roof !—I 'd
      back
And in her very face—

    Gaucelme.   Apply the match
That fired the train—and where would you be, pray?
    Guibert. With him!
    Gaucelme.   Stand, rather, safe outside with me!
The mine 's charged—shall I furnish you the match
And place you properly?—To the antechamber!   320
    Guibert. Can you?
    Gaucelme.   Try me!—Your friend 's in fortune!
    Guibert.   Quick—
To the antechamber!—He is pale with bliss!
    Gaucelme. No wonder! Mark her eyes!
    Guibert.   To the antechamber!
                          [*The Courtiers retire.*
    The Duchess. Sir, could you know all you have done for me
You were content! You spoke, and I am saved!
    Valence. Be not too sanguine, lady! Ere you dream,
That transient flush of generosity
Fades off, perchance! The man, beside, is gone—
Him we might bend; but see, the papers here—
Inalterably his requirement stays,   330
And cold, hard words have we to deal with now.
In that large eye there seemed a latent pride,
To self-denial not incompetent,
But very like to hold itself dispensed
From such a grace: however, let us hope!
He is a noble spirit in noble form.
I wish he less had bent that brow to smile
As with the fancy how he could subject
Himself upon occasion to—himself!
From rudeness, violence, you rest secure;   340
But do not think your Duchy rescued yet!
    The Duchess. You—who have opened a new world to me,
Will never take the faded language up
Of that I leave? My Duchy—keeping it,
Or losing it—is that my sole world now?

Valence. Ill have I spoken if you thence despise
Juliers ; although the lowest, on true grounds,
Be worth more than the highest rule on false :
Aspire to rule on the true grounds !

 The Duchess.   Nay, hear—
False I will never—rash I would not be !   350
This is indeed my birthday—soul and body,
Its hours have done on me the work of years.
You hold the requisition : ponder it !
If I have right, my duty 's plain : if he—
Say so, nor ever change a tone of voice !
At night you meet the Prince ; meet me at eve !
Till when, farewell ! This discomposes you ?
Believe in your own nature, and its force
Of renovating mine ! I take my stand
Only as under me the earth is firm :   360
So, prove the first step stable, all will prove.
That first I choose—[*laying her hand on his*] the next to
   take, choose you !   [*She withdraws.*
 Valence [*after a pause*]. What drew down this on me ?—on
   me, dead once,
She thus bids live—since all I hitherto
Thought dead in me, youth's ardors and emprise,
Burst into life before her, as she bids
Who needs them. Whither will this reach, where end ?
Her hand's print burns on mine—Yet she 's above—
So very far above me ! All 's too plain :
I saved her when the others sank away,   370
And she rewards me as such souls reward—
The changed voice, the suffusion of the cheek,
The eye's acceptance, the expressive hand—
Reward, that 's little, in her generous thought,
Though all to me—
      I cannot so disclaim
Heaven's gift, nor call it other than it is !

She loves me!—
[*Looking at the Prince's papers*] Which love these per-
　　　chance forbid.
Can I decide against myself—pronounce
She is the Duchess and no mate for me?—
Cleves, help me!　Teach me—every haggard face—　　380
To sorrow and endure!　I will do right
Whatever be the issue.　Help me, Cleves!

ACT IV.

Evening. Scene.—*An Antechamber.*

Enter the Courtiers.

Maufroy. Now, then, that we may speak—how spring this
    mine?

Gaucelme. Is Guibert ready for its match? He cools!
Not so friend Valence with the Duchess there!
'Stay, Valence! Are not you my better self?'
And her cheek mantled—

Guibert.   Well, she loves him, sir:
And more—since you will have it I grow cool
She's right: he's worth it

Gaucelme.   For his deeds to-day?
Say so!

Guibert. What should I say beside?

Gaucelme.   Not this—
For friendship's sake leave this for me to say—
That we're the dupes of an egregious cheat!
This plain unpractised suitor, who found way
To the Duchess through the merest die's turn-up,
A year ago had seen her and been seen,
Loved and been loved.

Guibert.   Impossible!

Gaucelme.   Nor say—
How sly and exquisite a trick, moreover,
Was this which—taking not their stand on facts
Boldly, for that had been endurable,
But worming on their way by craft, they choose
Resort to, rather—and which you and we,

10

Sheep-like, assist them in the playing off!   20
The Duchess thus parades him as preferred,
Not on the honest ground of preference,
Seeing first, liking more, and there an end—
But as we all had started equally,
And at the close of a fair race he proved
The only valiant, sage, and loyal man.
Herself, too, with the pretty fits and starts—
The careless, winning, candid ignorance
Of what the Prince might challenge or forego—
She had a hero in reserve!   What risk   30
Ran she?   This deferential, easy Prince
Who brings his claims for her to ratify—
He 's just her puppet for the nonce!   You 'll see—
Valence pronounces, as is equitable,
Against him : off goes the confederate :
As equitably, Valence takes her hand !
    The Chancellor. You run too fast : her hand no subject
        takes.
Do not our archives hold her father's will?
That will provides against such accident,
And gives next heir, Prince Berthold, the reversion   40
Of Juliers, which she forfeits, wedding so.
    Gaucelme. I know that, well as you—but does the Prince?
Knows Berthold, think you, that this plan, he helps,
For Valence's ennoblement—would end,
If crowned with the success which seems its due,
In making him the very thing he plays,
The actual Duke of Juliers?   All agree
That Colombe's title waived or set aside,
He is next heir.
    The Chancellor. Incontrovertibly.
    Gaucelme. Guibert, your match, now, to the train !
    Guibert.   Enough !
I 'm with you : selfishness is best again.   51

I thought of turning honest—what a dream!
Let 's wake now!
    Gaucelme.   Selfish, friend, you never were:
'T was but a series of revenges taken
On your unselfishness for prospering ill.
But now that you 're grown wiser, what 's our course?—
    Guibert. Wait, I suppose, till Valence weds our lady,
And then, if we must needs revenge ourselves,
Apprize the Prince.
    Gaucelme.   The Prince, ere then dismissed
With thanks for playing his mock part so well?   60
Tell the Prince now, sir! Ay, this very night—
Ere he accepts his dole and goes his way,
Explain how such a marriage makes him Duke,
Then trust his gratitude for the surprise!
    Guibert. Our lady wedding Valence all the same
As if the penalty were undisclosed?
Good! If she loves, she 'll not disown her love,
Throw Valence up. I wonder you see that.
    Gaucelme. The shame of it—the suddenness and shame!
Within her, the inclining heart—without,   70
A terrible array of witnesses—
And Valence by, to keep her to her word,
With Berthold's indignation or disgust!
We 'll try it!—Not that we can venture much.
Her confidence we 've lost forever; Berthold's
Is all to gain.
    Guibert.   To-night, then, venture we!
Yet—if lost confidence might be renewed?
    Gaucelme. Never in noble natures! With the base
      ones—
Twist off the crab's claw, wait a smarting-while,
And something grows and grows and gets to be   80
A mimic of the lost joint, just so like
As keeps in mind it never, never will

Replace its predecessor! Crabs do that;
But lop the lion's foot—and—
    Guibert.   To the Prince!
    Gaucelme [*aside*]. And come what will to the lion's foot, I
        pay you,
My cat's-paw, as I long have yearned to pay!
[*Aloud*]. Footsteps! Himself! 'T is Valence breaks on us,
Exulting that their scheme succeeds. We'll hence—
And perfect ours! Consult the archives first—
Then, fortified with knowledge, seek the Hall!   90
    Clugnet [*to Gaucelme as they retire*]. You have not smiled
        so since your father died!

     As they retire, enter VALENCE *with papers.*

    Valence. So must it be! I have examined these
With scarce a palpitating heart—so calm,
Keeping her image almost wholly off,
Setting upon myself determined watch,
Repelling to the uttermost his claims,
And the result is—all men would pronounce
And not I, only, the result to be—
Berthold is heir; she has no shade of right
To the distinction which divided us,   100
But, suffered to rule first, I know not why,
Her rule connived at by those Kings and Popes,
To serve some devil's-purpose—now 't is gained,
Whate'er it was, the rule expires as well.—
Valence, this rapture—selfish can it be?
Eject it from your heart, her home!—It stays!
Ah! the brave world that opens on us both!—
Do my poor townsmen so esteem it? Cleves,
I need not your pale faces! This, reward
For service done to you? Too horrible!   110
I never served you; 't was myself I served—
Nay, served not—rather saved from punishment

Which, had I failed you then, would plague me now!
My life continues yours, and your life mine.
But if, to take God's gift, I swerve no step—
Cleves!—If I breathe no prayer for it—if she,

[*Footsteps without.*

Colombe, that comes now, freely gives herself—
Will Cleves require that, turning thus to her,
I—

Enter PRINCE BERTHOLD.

            Pardon, sir! I did not look for you
Till night, i' the Hall; nor have as yet declared   120
My judgment to the lady.
    Berthold.   So I hoped.
    Valence. And yet I scarcely know why that should
        check
The frank disclosure of it first to you—
What her right seems, and what, in consequence,
She will decide on—
    Berthold.   That I need not ask.
    Valence. You need not: I have proved the lady's mind—
And, justice being to do, dare act for her.
    Berthold. Doubtless she has a very noble mind.
    Valence. Oh! never fear but she 'll in each conjuncture
Bear herself bravely! She no whit depends   130
On circumstance; as she adorns a throne,
She had adorned
    Berthold.   A cottage—in what book
Have I read that of every queen that lived?
A throne! You have not been instructed, sure,
To forestall my request?
    Valence.   'T is granted, sir!
My heart instructs me. I have scrutinized
Your claims—
    Berthold. Ah!—claims, you mean, at first preferred?
I come, before the hour appointed me,

To pray you let those claims at present rest,
In favor of a new and stronger one.   140
    Valence. You shall not need a stronger: on the part
O' the lady, all you offer I accept,
Since one clear right suffices: yours is clear.
Propose!
    Berthold. I offer her my hand.
    Valence.   Your hand?
    Berthold. A Duke's, yourself say; and, at no far time,
Something here whispers me—the Emperor's.
The lady's mind is noble; which induced
This seizure of occasion ere my claims
Were—settled, let us amicably say!
    Valence. Your hand!
    Berthold.   He will fall down and kiss it next!—
Sir, this astonishment 's too flattering,   151
Nor must you hold your mistress' worth so cheap.
Enhance it, rather—urge that blood is blood—
The daughter of the Burgraves, Landgraves, Markgraves,
Remains their daughter! I shall scarce gainsay.
Elsewhere or here, the lady needs must rule;
Like the imperial crown's great chrysoprase,
They talk of—somewhat out of keeping there,
And yet no jewel for a meaner cap.
    Valence. You wed the Duchess?
    Berthold.   Cry you mercy, friend!
Will the match also influence fortunes here?   16:
A natural solicitude enough.
Be certain, no bad chance it proves for you!
However high you take your present stand,
There 's prospect of a higher still remove—
For Juliers will not be my resting-place,
And, when I have to choose a substitute
To rule the little burgh, I 'll think of you.
You need not give your mates a character.

And yet I doubt your fitness to supplant   170
The gray, smooth chamberlain : he 'd hesitate
A doubt his lady could demean herself
So low as to accept me.   Courage, sir !
I like your method better : feeling's play
Is franker much, and flatters me beside.
   Valence. I am to say, you love her ?
   Berthold.   Say that too !
Love has no great concernment, thinks the world,
With a Duke's marriage.   How go precedents
In Julier's story—how use Juliers' Dukes ?
I see you have them here in goodly row ;   180
Yon must be Luitpold—ay, a stalwart sire !—
Say, I have been arrested suddenly
In my ambition's course, its rocky course,
By this sweet flower : I fain would gather it
And then proceed—so say and speedily—
Nor stand there like Duke Luitpold's brazen self !—
Enough, sir : you possess my mind, I think.
This is my claim, the others being withdrawn,
And to this be it that, i' the Hall to-night,
Your lady's answer comes ; till when, farewell ! [*He retires.*
   Valence [*after a pause*]. The heavens and earth stay as
      they were ; my heart   191
Beats as it beat : the truth remains the truth.
What falls away, then, if not faith in her ?
Was it my faith that she could estimate
Love's value, and, such faith still guiding me,
Dare I now test her ?   Or grew faith so strong
Solely because no power of test was mine ?

Enter the Duchess.

   The Duchess. My fate, sir !   Ah! you turn away.   All 's
      over.
But you are sorry for me ?   Be not so !
  11

What I might have become, and never was,   200
Regret with me!   What I have merely been,
Rejoice I am no longer!   What I seem
Beginning now, in my new state, to be,
Hope that I am!—for, once my rights proved void,
This heavy roof seems easy to exchange
For the blue sky outside—my lot henceforth.

  Valence. And what a lot is Berthold's!

  The Duchess.   How of him?

  Valence. He gathers earth's whole good into his arms;
Standing, as man now, stately, strong, and wise,
Marching to fortune, not surprised by her.   210
One great aim, like a guiding-star, above—
Which tasks strength, wisdom, stateliness, to lift
His manhood to the height that takes the prize;
A prize not near—lest overlooking earth
He rashly spring to seize it—nor remote,
So that he rest upon his path content:
But day by day, while shimmering grows shine,
And the faint circlet prophesies the orb,
He sees so much as, just evolving these,
The stateliness, the wisdom, and the strength,   220
To due completion, will suffice this life,
And lead him at his grandest to the grave.
After this star, out of a night he springs;
A beggar's cradle for the throne of thrones
He quits; so, mounting, feels each step he mounts,
Nor, as from each to each exultingly
He passes, overleaps one grade of joy.
This, for his own good:—with the world, each gift
Of God and man—reality, tradition,
Fancy and fact—so well environ him,   230
That as a mystic panoply they serve—
Of force, untenanted, to awe mankind,
And work his purpose out with half the world,

While he, their master, dexterously slipt
From such encumbrance, is meantime employed
With his own prowess on the other half.
Thus shall he prosper, every day's success
Adding, to what is he, a solid strength—
An aëry might to what encircles him,
Till at the last, so life's routine lends help,   240
That as the Emperor only breathes and moves,
His shadow shall be watched, his step or stalk
Become a comfort or a portent, how
He trails his ermine take significance—
Till even his power shall cease to be most power,
And men shall dread his weakness more, nor dare
Peril their earth its bravest, first and best,
Its typified invincibility.
Thus shall he go on, greatening, till he ends—
The man of men, the spirit of all flesh,   250
The fiery centre of an earthly world!
    The Duchess. Some such a fortune I had dreamed should
        rise
Out of my own—that is, above my power
Seemed other, greater potencies to stretch—
    Valence. For you?
    The Duchess.   It was not I moved there, I think;
But one I could—though constantly beside,
And aye approaching—still keep distant from,
And so adore.   'T was a man moved there.
    Valence.   Who?
    The Duchess. I felt the spirit, never saw the face.
    Valence. See it! 'T is Berthold's! He enables you   260
To realize your vision.
    The Duchess.   Berthold?
    Valence.   Duke—
Emperor to be: he proffers you his hand.
    The Duchess. Generous and princely!

Valence.   He is all of this.

The Duchess. Thanks, Berthold, for my father's sake.   No hand

Degrades me!

Valence.   You accept the proffered hand?

The Duchess. That he should love me!

Valence.   'Loved' I did not say!

Had that been—love might so incline the Prince

To the world's good, the world that's at his foot—

I do not know, this moment, I should dare

Desire that you refused the world—and Cleves—   270

The sacrifice he asks.

The Duchess.   Not love me, sir?

Valence. He scarce affirmed it.

The Duchess.   May not deeds affirm?

Valence. What does he?—Yes, yes, very much he does!

All the shame saved, he thinks, and sorrow saved—

Immitigable sorrow, so he thinks—

Sorrow that's deeper than we dream, perchance!

The Duchess. Is not this love?

Valence.   So very much he does!

For look, you can descend now gracefully:

All doubts are banished that the world might have,

Or worst, the doubts yourself, in after-time,   280

May call up of your heart's sincereness now.

To such, reply, 'I could have kept my rule—

Increased it to the utmost of my dreams—

Yet I abjured it.'   This he does for you:

It is munificently much.

The Duchess.   Still 'much!'

But why is it not love, sir?   Answer me!

Valence. Because not one of Berthold's words and looks

Had gone with love's presentment of a flower

To the beloved: because bold confidence,

Open superiority, free pride—   290

Love owns not, yet were all that Berthold owned:
Because where reason even finds no flaw,
Unerringly a lover's instinct may.

    The Duchess. You reason, then, and doubt?

    Valence.   I love, and know.

    The Duchess. You love?—How strange! I never cast a
        thought

On that! Just see our selfishness! You seemed
So much my own—I had no ground—and yet,
I never dreamed another might divide
My power with you, much less exceed it.

    Valence.   Lady,

I am yours wholly.

    The Duchess.   Oh! no, no, not mine!   300

'T is not the same now, never more can be.—
Your first love, doubtless. Well, what 's gone from me?
What have I lost in you?

    Valence.   My heart replies—

No loss there! So to Berthold back again:
This offer of his hand he bids me make—
Its obvious magnitude is well to weigh.

    The Duchess. She 's—yes, she must be very fair for you!

    Valence. I am a simple advocate of Cleves.

    The Duchess. You! With the heart and brain that so
        helped me,

I fancied them exclusively my own,   310
Yet find are subject to a stronger sway!
She must be—tell me, is she very fair?

    Valence. Most fair, beyond conception or belief.

    The Duchess. Black eyes?— no matter! Colombe, the
        world leads

Its life without you, whom your friends professed
The only woman—see how true they spoke!
One lived this while, who never saw your face,
Nor heard your voice—unless— Is she from Cleves?

Valence. Cleves knows her well.

The Duchess.   Ah!—just a fancy, now!   320
When you poured forth the wrongs of Cleves—I said—
Thought, that is, afterward—

Valence.   You thought of me?

The Duchess. Of whom else?   Only such great cause, I
       thought,
For such effect: see what true love can do!
Cleves is his love.   I almost fear to ask—
And will not.   This is idling: to our work!
Admit before the Prince, without reserve,
My claims misgrounded; then may follow better—
When you poured out Cleves' wrongs impetuously,
Was she in your mind?

Valence.   All done was done for her—
To humble me!

The Duchess.   She will be proud at least.   330

Valence. She?

The Duchess.   When you tell her.

Valence.   That will never be.

The Duchess. How—are there sweeter things you hope to
       tell?
No, sir!   You counselled me—I counsel you
In the one point I—any woman—can.
Your worth, the first thing; let her own come next—
Say what you did through her, and she through you—
The praises of her beauty afterward!
Will you?

Valence.   I dare not.

The Duchess.   Dare not?

Valence.   She I love
Suspects not such a love in me.

The Duchess.   You jest.

Valence. The lady is above me and away.   340
Not only the brave form, and the bright mind,

And the great heart, combine to press me low—
But all the world calls rank divides us.
     The Duchess.   Rank!
Now grant me patience!   Here 's a man declares
Oracularly in another's case—
Sees the true value and the false, for them—
Nay, bids them see it, and they straight do see.
You called my court's love worthless—so it turned:
I threw away as dross my heap of wealth,
And here you stickle for a piece or two!   350
First—has she seen you?
     Valence.   Yes.
     The Duchess.   She loves you, then.
     Valence. One flash of hope burst, then succeeded night;
And all 's at darkest now.   Impossible!
     The Duchess. We 'll try: you are—so to speak—my sub-
          ject yet?
     Valence. As ever—to the death.
     The Duchess.   Obey me, then!
     Valence. I must.
     The Duchess.   Approach her, and—no! first of all
Get more assurance.   ' My instructress,' say,
' Was great, descended from a line of kings,
And even fair '—wait why I say this folly—
' She said, of all men, none for eloquence,   360
Courage, and—what cast even these to shade—
The heart they sprung from—none deserved like him
Who saved her at her need : if she said this,
What should not one I love, say?'
     Valence.   Heaven—this hope—
O lady, you are filling me with fire!
     The Duchess. Say this!—nor think I bid you cast aside
One touch of all the awe and reverence;
Nay—make her proud for once to heart's content
That all this wealth of heart and soul 's her own!

Think you are all of this—and, thinking it— 370
Obey!

    Valence. I cannot choose.

    The Duchess.   Then, kneel to her—

                            [Valence sinks on his knee.

I dream!

    Valence. Have mercy! Yours, unto the death—
I have obeyed. Despise, and let me die!

    The Duchess. Alas! sir, is it to be ever thus?
Even with you as with the world? I know
This morning's service was no vulgar deed
Whose motive, once it dares avow itself,
Explains all done and infinitely more,
So takes the shelter of a nobler cause.
Your service named its true source—loyalty! 380
The rest's unsaid again. The Duchess bids you,
Rise, sir. The Prince's words were in debate.

    Valence [*rising*]. Rise? Truth, as ever, lady, comes from
        you!
I should rise—I who spoke for Cleves, can speak
For man—yet tremble now, who stood firm then.
I laughed—for 't was past tears—that Cleves should starve
With all hearts beating loud the infamy,
And no tongue daring trust as much to air:
Yet here, where all hearts speak, shall I be mute?
O lady, for your own sake look on me! 390
On all I am, and have, and do—heart, brain,
Body and soul—this Valence and his gifts!
I was proud once: I saw you, and they sank,
So that each, magnified a thousand times,
Were nothing to you—but such nothingness,
Would a crown gild it, or a sceptre prop,
A treasure speed, a laurel-wreath enhance?
What is my own desert? But should your love
Have—there's no language helps here—singled me—

Then—oh! that wild word 'then!'—be just to love, 400
In generosity its attribute!
Love, since you pleased to love! All 's cleared—a stage
For trial of the question kept so long:
Judge you—Is love or vanity the best?
You, solve it for the world's sake—you, speak first
What all will shout one day—you, vindicate
Our earth and be its angel! All is said.
Lady, I offer nothing—I am yours:
But, for the cause' sake, look on me and him,
And speak!
    The Duchess. I have received the Prince's message. 410
Say, I prepare my answer!
    Valence.   Take me, Cleves!
                                    [He withdraws.
    The Duchess. Mournful — that nothing 's what it calls it-
    self!
Devotion, zeal, faith, loyalty—mere love!
And, love in question, what may Berthold's be?
I did ill to mistrust the world so soon:
Already was this Berthold at my side.
The valley-level has its hawks no doubt:
May not the rock-top have its eagles, too?
Yet Valence—let me see his rival then!

ACT V.

Night.   SCENE.—*The Hall.*

Enter BERTHOLD *and* MELCHIOR.

Melchior. And here you wait the matter's issue?
Berthold.   Here.
Melchior. I don't regret I shut Amelius, then.
But tell me, on this grand disclosure—how
Behaved our spokesman with the forehead?
Berthold.   Oh!
Turned out no better than the foreheadless—
Was dazzled not so very soon, that's all!
For my part, this is scarce the hasty, showy,
Chivalrous measure you give me credit of.
Perhaps I had a fancy—but 't is gone.—
Let her commence the unfriended innocent   10
And carry wrongs about from court to court?
No, truly!   The least shake of Fortune's sand—
My uncle-Pope chokes in a coughing fit,
King-cousin takes a fancy to blue eyes—
And wondrously her claims would brighten up;
Forth comes a new gloss on the ancient law,
O'erlooked provisos, o'erpast premises,
Follow in plenty.   No: 't is the safe step.
The hour beneath the convent-wall is lost:
Juliers and she, once mine, are ever mine.   20
Melchior. Which is to say, you, losing heart already,
Elude the adventure.
Berthold.   Not so—or, if so—

Why not confess at once that I advise
None of our kingly craft and guild just now
To lay, one moment, down their privilege
With the notion they can any time at pleasure
Retake it: that may turn out hazardous.
We seem, in Europe, pretty well at end
O' the night, with our great masque : those favored few
Who keep the chamber's top, and honor's chance   30
Of the early evening, may retain their place
And figure as they list till out of breath.
But it is growing late : and I observe
A dim grim kind of tipstaves at the doorway
Not only bar new-comers entering now,
But caution those who left, for any cause,
And would return, that morning draws too near ;
The ball must die off, shut itself up.   We—
I think, may dance lights out and sunshine in,
And sleep off headache on our frippery :   40
But friend the other, who cunningly stole out,
And, after breathing the fresh air outside,
Means to re-enter with a new costume,
Will be advised go back to bed, I fear.
I stick to privilege, on second thoughts.

    Melchior. Yes—you evade the adventure : and, beside,
Give yourself out for colder than you are.
King Philip, only, notes the lady's eyes ?
Don't they come in for somewhat of the motive
With you too?

    Berthold.   Yes—no : I am past that now.   50
Gone 't is : I cannot shut my soul to fact.
Of course, I might by forethought and contrivance
Reason myself into a rapture.   Gone :
And something better come instead, no doubt.

    Melchior. So be it !   Yet, all the same, proceed my way,
Though to your ends ; so shall you prosper best !

The lady—to be won for selfish ends—
Will be won easier my unselfish—call it,
Romantic way.

    Berthold.   Won easier?

    Melchior.   Will not she?

    Berthold. There I profess humility without bound :   60
Ill cannot speed—not I—the Emperor.

    Melchior. And I should think the Emperor best waived,
From your description of her mood and way.
You could look, if it pleased you, into hearts,
But are too indolent and fond of watching
Your own—you know that, for you study it.

    Berthold. Had you but seen the orator her friend,
So bold and voluble an hour before,
Abashed to earth at aspect of the change !
Make her an Empress? Ah ! that changed the case !   70
Oh ! I read hearts ! 'T is for my own behoof,
I court her with my true worth : wait the event !
I learned my final lesson on that head
When years ago—my first and last essay—
Before the priest my uncle could by help
Of his superior raise me from the dirt—
Priscilla left me for a Brabant lord
Whose cheek was like the topaz on his thumb.
I am past illusion on that score.

    Melchior.   Here comes
The lady—

    Berthold. And there you go. But do not ! Give me   80
Another chance to please you ! Hear me plead !

    Melchior. You 'll keep, then, to the lover, to the man ?

Enter the DUCHESS, *followed by* ADOLF *and* SABYNE, *and after an interval by the* Courtiers.

    Berthold. Good auspice to our meeting !

    The Duchess.   May it prove !—
And you, sir, will be Emperor one day ?

Berthold. Ay, that's the point !—I may be Emperor.

The Duchess. 'T is not for my sake only, I am proud
Of this you offer ; I am prouder far
That from the highest state should duly spring
The highest, since most generous, of deeds.

Berthold. Generous—still that !—You underrate yourself.
You are, what I, to be complete, must have—   91
Find now, and may not find, another time.
While I career on all the world for stage,
There needs at home my representative.

The Duchess. Such, rather, would some warrior-woman be—
One dowered with lands and gold, or rich in friends—
One like yourself.

Berthold.   Lady, I am myself,
And have all these: I want what's not myself,
Nor has all these. Why give one hand two swords?
Here's one already ; be a friend's next gift   100
A silk glove, if you will—I have a sword.

The Duchess. You love me, then?

Berthold.   Your lineage I revere,
Honor your virtue, in your truth believe,
Do homage to your intellect, and bow
Before your peerless beauty.

The Duchess.   But, for love—

Berthold. A further love I do not understand.
Our best course is to say these hideous truths,
And see them, once said, grow endurable :
Like waters shuddering from their central bed,
Black with the midnight bowels of the earth,   110
That, once up-spouted by an earthquake's throe,
A portent and a terror—soon subside,
Freshen apace, take gold and rainbow hues
In sunshine, sleep in shadow, and at last
Grow common to the earth as hills or trees—
Accepted by all things they came to scare.

The Duchess.   You cannot love, then?
Berthold.   Charlemagne, perhaps!
Are you not over-curious in love-lore?
The Duchess. I have become so very recently.
It seems, then, I shall best deserve esteem,   120
Respect, and all your candor promises,
By putting on a calculating mood—
Asking the terms of my becoming yours?
Berthold. Let me not do myself injustice, neither.
Because I will not condescend to fictions
That promise what my soul can ne'er acquit,
It does not follow that my guarded phrase
May not include far more of what you seek
Than wide profession of less scrupulous men.
You will be Empress, once for all; with me   130
The Pope disputes supremacy—you stand,
And none gainsays, the earth's first woman.
The Duchess.   That—
Or simple Lady of Ravestein again?
Berthold.   The matter's not in my arbitrament:
Now I have my claims—which I regret—
Cede one, cede all.
The Duchess.   This claim, then, you enforce?
Berthold. The world looks on.
The Duchess.   And when must I decide?
Berthold. When, lady? Have I said thus much so promptly
For nothing?—poured out, with such pains, at once
What I might else have suffered to ooze forth   140
Droplet by droplet in a lifetime long—
For aught less than as prompt an answer, too?
All 's fairly told now: who can teach you more?
The Duchess. I do not see him.
Berthold.   I shall ne'er deceive.
This offer should be made befittingly,
Did time allow the better setting forth

The good of it, with what is not so good,
Advantage, and disparagement as well ;
But, as it is, the sum of both must serve.
I am already weary of this place ;   150
My thoughts are next stage on to Rome.   Decide !
The Empire—or—not even Juliers now !
Hail to the Empress—farewell to the Duchess !—

> [*The Courtiers, who have been drawing nearer and near-
> er, interpose.*

    Gaucelme. 'Farewell,' Prince? when we break in at our
    risk—
    Clugnet. Almost upon court-license trespassing—
    Gaucelme. To point out how your claims are valid yet !
You know not, by the Duke her father's will,
The lady, if she weds beneath her rank,
Forfeits her Duchy in the next heir's favor—
So 't is expressly stipulate.   And if   160
It can be shown 't is her intent to wed
A subject, then yourself, next heir, by right
Succeed to Juliers.
    Berthold.   What insanity !—
    Guibert. Sir, there 's one Valence, the pale fiery man
You saw and heard this morning—thought, no doubt,
Was of considerable standing here :
I put it to your penetration, Prince,
If aught save love, the truest love for her
Could make him serve the lady as he did !
He 's simply a poor advocate of Cleves—   170
Creeps here with difficulty, finds a place
With danger, gets in by a miracle,
And for the first time meets the lady's face—
So runs the story : is that credible ?
For, first—no sooner in, than he 's apprised
Fortunes have changed ; you are all-powerful here,
The lady as powerless : he stands fast by her !

The Duchess [*aside*]. And do such deeds spring up from
    love alone?

Guibert. But here occurs the question, does the lady
Love him again?   I say, how else can she?   180
Can she forget how he stood singly forth
In her defence, dared outrage all of us,
Insult yourself—for what, save love's reward?

The Duchess [*aside*]. And is love then the sole reward of
    love?

Guibert. But, love him as she may and must—you ask,
Means she to wed him?   'Yes,' both natures answer!
Both, in their pride, point out the sole result;
Nought less would he accept nor she propose.
For each conjuncture was she great enough—
Will be for this.

Clugnet.   Though, now that this is known,   190
Policy, doubtless, urges she deny—

The Duchess. What, sir, and wherefore?—since I am not
    sure
That all is any other than you say!
You take this Valence, hold him close to me,
Him with his actions: can I choose but look?
I am not sure love trulier shows itself
Than in this man you hate and would degrade,
Yet, with your worst abatement, show me thus.
Nor am I—thus made look within myself
Ere I had dared—now that the look is dared—   200
Sure that I do not love him!

Guibert.   Hear you, Prince?

Berthold. And what, sirs, please you, may this prattle mean,
Unless to prove with what alacrity
You give your lady's secrets to the world?
How much indebted, for discovering
That quality, you make me, will be found
When there's a keeper for my own to seek.

Courtiers. 'Our lady?'—

Berthold.   She assuredly remains.

The Duchess. Ah, Prince!—and you too can be generous?
You could renounce your power, if this were so,   210
And let me, as these phrase it, wed my love
Yet keep my Duchy?   You perhaps exceed
Him even in disinterestedness!

Berthold. How, lady, should all this affect my purpose?
Your will and choice are still, as ever, free.
Say, you have known a worthier than myself
In mind and heart, of happier form and face—
Others must have their birthright: I have gifts,
To balance theirs, not blot them out of sight.
Against a hundred alien qualities,   220
I lay the prize I offer.   I am nothing:
Wed you the Empire?

The Duchess.   And my heart away?

Berthold. When have I made pretension to your heart?
I give none.   I shall keep your honor safe;
With mine I trust you, as the sculptor trusts
Yon marble woman with the marble rose,
Loose on her hand, she never will let fall,
In graceful, slight, silent security.
You will be proud of my world-wide career,
And I content in you the fair and good.   230
What were the use of planting a few seeds
The thankless climate never would mature—
Affections all repelled by circumstance?
Enough: to these no credit I attach—
To what you own find nothing to object.
Write simply on my requisition's face
What shall content my friends—that you admit,
As Colombe of Ravestein, the claims therein,
Or never need admit them, as my wife—
And either way, all 's ended!

12

The Duchess.   Let all end!   240
Berthold. The requisition!—
Guibert.   Valence holds, of course!
Berthold. Desire his presence!   [*Adolf goes out.*
Courtiers [*to each other*].   Out it all comes yet;
He 'll have his word against the bargain yet:
He 's not the man to tamely acquiesce.
One passionate appeal—upbraiding even,
May turn the tide again.   Despair not yet!
                              [*They retire a little.*
Berthold [*to Melchior*]. The Empire has its old success, my
      friend!
Melchior. You 've had your way: before the spokesman
      speaks,
Let me but this once work a problem out,
And ever more be dumb!   The Empire wins?   250
To better purpose have I read my books!

Enter VALENCE.

Melchior [*to the Courtiers*]. Apart, my masters!
                    [*To Valence*] Sir, one word with you!
I am a poor dependant of the Prince's—
Pitched on to speak, as of slight consequence.
You are no higher, I find; in other words,
We two, as probably the wisest here,
Need not hold diplomatic talk like fools.
Suppose I speak, divesting the plain fact
Of all their tortuous phrases, fit for them?
Do you reply so, and what trouble saved!   260
The Prince, then—an embroiled strange heap of news
This moment reaches him—if true or false,
All dignity forbids he should inquire
In person or by worthier deputy,
Yet somehow must inquire, lest slander come;
And so 't is I am pitched on.   You have heard
His offer to your lady?

Valence.   Yes.

Melchior.   Conceive
Her joy thereat?

  Valence.   I cannot.

  Melchior.   No one can :
All draws to a conclusion, therefore.

   Valence [*aside*].   So !
No after-judgment—no first thought revised—   270
Her first and last decision !—me she leaves,
Takes him ; a simple heart is flung aside,
The ermine o'er a heartless breast embraced.
O Heaven, this mockery has been played too oft !
Once, to surprise the angels—twice, that fiends,
Recording, might be proud they chose not so—
Thrice, many thousand times, to teach the world
All men should pause, misdoubt their strength, since men
Can have such chance yet fail so signally—
But ever, ever this farewell to Heaven,   280
Welcome to earth —this taking death for life—
This spurning love and kneeling to the world—
O Heaven, it is too often and too old !

  Melchior. Well, on this point, what but an absurd rumor
Arises—these, its source—its subject, you !
Your faith and loyalty misconstruing,
They say your service claims the lady's hand !
Of course, nor Prince nor lady can respond :
Yet something must be said ; for, were it true
You made such claim, the Prince would—

  Valence.   Well, sir—would ?—

  Melchior. Not only probably withdraw his suit,   291
But, very like, the lady might be forced
Accept your own.   Oh ! there are reasons why !
But you 'll excuse at present all save one—
I think so.   What we want is your own witness
For or against—her good or yours : decide !

Valence [*aside*].   Be it her good if she accounts it so!—
[*After a contest*] For what am I but hers, to choose as
    she?
Who knows how far, beside, the light from her
May reach, and dwell with, what she looks upon?   300
    Melchior [*to the Prince*]. Now to him, you!
    Berthold [*to Valence*].   My friend acquaints you, sir,
The noise runs—
    Valence.   Prince, how fortunate you are,
Wedding her as you will, in spite of noise,
To show belief in love!   Let her but love you,
All else you disregard!   What else can be?
You know how love is incompatible
With falsehood—purifies, assimilates
All other passions to itself.
    Melchior.   Ay, sir :
But softly!   Where, in the object we select,
Such love is, perchance, wanting?
    Valence.   Then indeed,   310
What is it you can take?
    Melchior.   Nay, ask the world!
Youth, beauty, virtue, an illustrious name,
An influence o'er mankind.
    Valence.   When man perceives—
Ah! I can only speak as for myself!
    The Duchess. Speak for yourself!
    Valence.   May I?—no, I have spoken,
And time 's gone by.   Had I seen such an one,
As I loved her—weighing thoroughly that word—
So should my task be to evolve her love ;
If for myself!—if for another—well.
    Berthold. Heroic, truly!   And your sole reward—   320
The secret pride in yielding up love's right?
    Valence. Who thought upon reward?   And yet how much
Comes after—oh! what amplest recompense!

Is the knowledge of her nought? the memory nought?—
Lady, should such an one have looked on you,
Ne'er wrong yourself so far as quote the world
And say love can go unrequited here!
You will have blessed him to his whole life's end—
Low passions hindered, baser cares kept back,
All goodness cherished where you dwelt—and dwell.   330
What would he have? He holds you—you, both form
And mind, in his—where self-love makes such room
For love of you, he would not serve you now
The vulgar way—repulse your enemies,
Win you new realms, or best, in saving old
Die blissfully—that's past so long ago!
He wishes you no need, thought, care of him—
Your good, by any means, himself unseen,
Away, forgotten!—He gives that life's task up,
As it were—but this charge which I return—   340
          [*Offers the requisition, which she takes*
Wishing your good.

    The Duchess [*having subscribed it*]. And opportunely, sir—
Since at a birthday's close, like this of mine,
Good wishes gentle deeds reciprocate.
Most on a wedding-day, as mine is too,
Should gifts be thought of: yours comes first by right.
Ask of me!

    Berthold. He shall have whate'er he asks,
For your sake and his own.

    Valence [*aside*]. If I should ask—
The withered bunch of flowers she wears—perhaps,
One last touch of her hand, I never more
Shall see!— [*After a pause, presenting his paper to the Prince.*
      Cleves' Prince, redress the wrongs of Cleves!   350

    Berthold. I will, sir.

    The Duchess [*as Valence prepares to retire*]. Nay, do out
    your duty first!

You bore this paper; I have registered
My answer to it: read it and have done!   [*Valence reads it.*
I take him—give up Juliers and the world.
This is my Birthday.

    Melchior.   Berthold, my one hero
Of the world she gives up, one friend worth my books,
Sole man I think it pays the pains to watch—
Speak, for I know you through your Popes and Kings!

        Berthold [*after a pause*]. Lady, well rewarded! Sir, as
           well deserved!

I could not imitate—I hardly envy—   360
I do admire you.   All is for the best.
Too costly a flower were this, I see it now,
To pluck and set upon my barren helm
To wither—any garish plume will do.
I 'll not insult you and refuse your Duchy—
You can so well afford to yield it me,
And I were left, without it, sadly off.
As it is—for me—if that will flatter you,
A somewhat wearier life seems to remain
Than I thought possible where—   Faith, their life   370
Begins already!   They 're too occupied
To listen; and few words content me best.—
[*Abruptly to the Courtiers*] I am your Duke, though!   Who
        obey me here?

    The Duchess. Adolf and Sabyne, follow us—

    Guibert [*starting from the Courtiers*].   And I?
Do I not follow them, if I may n't you?
Shall not I get some little duties up
At Ravestein and emulate the rest?
God save you, Gaucelme!   'T is my Birthday; too!

    Berthold. You happy handful that remain with me—
That is, with Dietrich the black Barnabite   380
I shall leave over you—will earn your wages,
Or Dietrich has forgot to ply his trade!

Meantime—go copy me the precedents
Of every installation, proper styles
And pedigrees of all your Juliers' Dukes—
While I prepare to plod on my old way,
And somewhat wearily, I must confess!

 The Duchess [*with a light joyous laugh as she turns from
  them*]. Come, Valence, to our friends, God's earth—
Valence [*as she falls into his arms*].   And thee!

A SOUL'S TRAGEDY.

ACT FIRST,
BEING WHAT WAS CALLED THE POETRY OF CHIAPPINO'S LIFE;
AND ACT SECOND, ITS PROSE.

London, 1846.

PERSONS.

LUITOLFO and EULALIA, betrothed lovers.
CHIAPPINO, their friend.
OGNIBEN, the Pope's Legate.
Citizens of Faenza.

PLACE, *Faenza.*

TIME, 15—.

A SOUL'S TRAGEDY.

ACT I.

Inside Luitolfo's house. CHIAPPINO, EULALIA.

Eulalia. What is it keeps Luitolfo? Night's fast falling,
And 't was scarce sunset—had the ave-bell
Sounded before he sought the Provost's house?
I think not: all he had to say would take
Few minutes, such a very few, to say!
How do you think, Chiappino? If our lord
The Provost were less friendly to your friend
Than everybody here professes him,
I should begin to tremble—should not you?
Why are you silent when so many times   10
I turn and speak to you?
   Chiappino.   That 's good!
   Eulalia.   You laugh?
   Chiappino. Yes. I had fancied nothing that bears price
In the whole world was left to call my own;
And, may be, felt a little pride thereat.
Up to a single man's or woman's love,
Down to the right in my own flesh and blood,
There's nothing mine, I fancied—till you spoke;—
Counting, you see, as 'nothing' the permission
To study this peculiar lot of mine
In silence: well, go silence with the rest   20
Of the world's good! What can I say, shall serve?

 Eulalia. This—lest you, even more than needs, embitter
Our parting : say your wrongs have cast, for once,
A cloud across your spirit !
 Chiappino.   How a cloud?
 Eulalia. No man nor woman loves you, did you say?
 Chiappino. My God, were 't not for thee !
 Eulalia.   Ay, God remains,
Even did men forsake you.
 Chiappino.   Oh, not so !
Were 't not for God, I mean, what hope of truth—
Speaking truth, hearing truth, would stay with man ?
I now—the homeless, friendless, penniless,   30
Proscribed, and exiled wretch who speak to you—
Ought to speak truth, yet could not, for my death—
The thing that tempts me most—help speaking lies
About your friendship and Luitolfo's courage
And all our townsfolk's equanimity—
Through sheer incompetence to rid myself
Of the old, miserable, lying trick
Caught from the liars I have lived with—God,
Did I not turn to thee ! It is thy prompting
I dare to be ashamed of, and thy counsel   40
Would die along my coward lip, I know.
But I do turn to thee. This craven tongue,
These features which refuse the soul its way,
Reclaim thou ! Give me truth—truth, power to speak—
And after be sole present to approve
The spoken truth ! Or, stay, that spoken truth,
Who knows but you too may approve ?
 Eulalia.   Ah, well—
Keep silence then, Chiappino !
 Chiappino.   You would hear,
You shall now—why the thing we please to style
My gratitude to you and all your friends   50
For service done me, is just gratitude

So much as yours was service—and no more.
I was born here, so was Luitolfo; both
At one time, much with the same circumstance
Of rank and wealth; and both, up to this night
Of parting company, have side by side
Still fared, he in the sunshine—I the shadow.
' Why?' asks the world.   ' Because,' replies the world
To its complacent self, ' these playfellows,
Who took at church the holy water drop   60
Each from the other's finger, and so forth,
Were of two moods : Luitolfo was the proper
Friend-making, everywhere friend-finding soul,
Fit for the sunshine, so it followed him.
A happy-tempered bringer of the best
Out of the worst ; who bears with what 's past cure,
And puts so good a face on 't—wisely passive
Where action 's fruitless, while he remedies
In silence what the foolish rail against ;
A man to smooth such natures as parade   70
Of opposition must exasperate ;
No general gauntlet-gatherer for the weak
Against the strong, yet over-scrupulous
At lucky junctures ; one who won't forego
The after-battle work of binding wounds,
Because, forsooth, he 'd have to bring himself
To side with wound-inflictors for their leave !'—
Why do you gaze, nor help me to repeat
What comes so glibly from the common mouth,
About Luitolfo and his so-styled friend ?   80
    Eulalia. Because that friend's sense is obscured—
    Chiappino.   I thought
You would be readier with the other half
Of the world's story, my half!   Yet, 't is true,
For all the world does say it.   Say your worst !
True, I thank God, I ever said ' you sin,'

When a man did sin : if I could not say it,
I glared it at him ; if I could not glare it,
I prayed against him ; then my part seemed over.
God's may begin yet : so it will, I trust.
    Eulalia. If the world outraged you, did we?
    Chiappino.   What's 'me'
That you use well or ill?   It 's man, in me,   91
All your successes are an outrage to,
You all, whom sunshine follows, as you say !
Here 's our Faenza birthplace ; they send here
A provost from Ravenna : how he rules,
You can at times be eloquent about.
' Then, end his rule !'—' Ah, yes, one stroke does that !
But patience under wrong works slow and sure.
Must violence still bring peace forth?   He, beside,
Returns so blandly one's obeisance ! ah !—   100
Some latent virtue may be lingering yet,
Some human sympathy which, once excite,
And all the lump were leavened quietly :
So, no more talk of striking, for this time !'
But I, as one of those he rules, won't bear
These pretty takings-up and layings-down
Our cause, just as you think occasion suits.
Enough of earnest, is there?   You 'll play, will you?
Diversify your tactics, give submission,
Obsequiousness, and flattery a turn,   110
While we die in our misery patient deaths?
We all are outraged then, and I the first :
I, for mankind, resent each shrug and smirk,
Each beck and bend, each—all you do and are,
I hate !
    Eulalia. We share a common censure, then.
'T is well you have not poor Luitolfo's part
Nor mine to point out in the wide offence.
    Chiappino. Oh ! shall I let you so escape me, lady?

Come, on your own ground, lady—from yourself—
Leaving the people's wrong, which most is mine—   120
What have I got to be so grateful for?
These three last fines, no doubt, one on the other
Paid by Luitolfo?

    Eulalia.   Shame, Chiappino!
    Chiappino.   Shame
Fall presently on who deserves it most!—
Which is to see. He paid my fines—my friend,
Your prosperous smooth lover presently,
Then, scarce your wooer—soon, your husband: well—
I loved you.

    Eulalia.   Hold!
    Chiappino.   You knew it, years ago.
When my voice faltered and my eye grew dim
Because you gave me your silk mask to hold—   130
My voice that greatens when there 's need to curse
The people's Provost to their heart's content —
My eye, the Provost, who bears all men's eyes,
Banishes now because he cannot bear—
You knew—but you do your parts—my part, I:
So be it! You flourish, I decay: all 's well.

    Eulalia. I hear this for the first time.
    Chiappino.   The fault 's there?
Then my days spoke not, and my nights of fire
Were voiceless? Then the very heart may burst,
Yet all prove nought, because no mincing speech   140
Tells leisurely that thus it is and thus?
Eulalia, truce with toying for this once!
A banished fool, who troubles you to-night
For the last time—why, what 's to fear from me?
You knew I loved you!

    Eulalia.   Not so, on my faith!
You were my now-affianced lover's friend—
Came in, went out with him, could speak as he.

All praise your ready parts and pregnant wit;
See how your words come from you in a crowd!
Luitolfo's first to place you o'er himself   150
In all that challenges respect and love,
Yet you were silent then, who blame me now.
I say all this by fascination, sure:
I am all but wed to one I love, yet listen!
It must be, you are wronged, and that the wrongs
Luitolfo pities—
        Chiappino.   You too pity? Do!
But hear first what my wrongs are; so began
This talk and so shall end this talk. I say,
Was 't not enough that I must strive—I saw—
To grow so far familiar with your charms   160
As next contrive some way to win them—which
To do, an age seemed far too little—for, see!
We all aspire to heaven; and there is heaven
Above us: go there! Dare we go? no, surely!
How dare we go without a reverent pause,
A growing less unfit for heaven? Even so,
I dared not speak: the greater fool, it seems!
Was 't not enough to struggle with such folly,
But I must have, beside, the very man
Whose slight, free, loose, and incapacious soul   170
Gave his tongue scope to say whate'er he would—
Must have him load me with his benefits
For fortune's fiercest stroke?
        Eulalia.   Justice to him
That 's now entreating, at his risk perhaps,
Justice for you!   Did he once call those acts
Of simple friendship—bounties, benefits?
        Chiappino. No: the straight course had been to call them so.
Then, I had flung them back, and kept myself
Unhampered, free as he to win the prize
We both sought.   But ' the gold was dross,' he said: 180

'He loved me, and I loved him not : why spurn
A trifle out of superfluity ?
He had forgotten he had done as much.'
So had not I !   Henceforth, try as I could
To take him at his word, there stood by you
My benefactor ; who might speak and laugh
And urge his nothings, even banter me
Before you—but my tongue was tied.   A dream !
Let 's wake : your husband—how you shake at that !
Good—my revenge !

 Eulalia.   Why should I shake ? What forced 190
Or forces me to be Luitolfo's bride ?

 Chiappino. There 's my revenge, that nothing forces you.
No gratitude, no liking of the eye
Nor longing of the heart, but the poor bond
Of habit—here so many times he came,
So much he spoke—all these compose the tie
That pulls you from me.   Well, he paid my fines,
Nor missed a cloak from wardrobe, dish from table ;
He spoke a good word to the Provost here,
Held me up when my fortunes fell away—   200
It had not looked so well to let me drop—
Men take pains to preserve a tree-stump, even,
Whose boughs they played beneath—much more a friend.
But one grows tired of seeing, after the first,
Pains spent upon impracticable stuff
Like me.   I could not change : you know the rest.
I 've spoke my mind too fully out, by chance,
This morning to our Provost ; so ere night
I leave the city on pain of death.   And now
On my account there 's gallant intercession   210
Goes forward—that 's so graceful ; and anon
He 'll noisily come back : 'the intercession
Was made and fails ; all 's over for us both ;
'T is vain contending ; I would better go.'

13

And I do go—and straight to you he turns
Light of a load ; and ease of that permits
His visage to repair the natural bland
Œconomy, sore broken late to suit
My discontent.   Thus, all are pleased—you with him,
He with himself, and all of you with me—   220
'Who,' say the citizens, 'had done far better
In letting people sleep upon their woes,
If not possessed with talent to relieve them
When once awake ; but then I had,' they 'll say,
'Doubtless some unknown compensating pride
In what I did ; and as I seem content
With ruining myself, why, so should they be.'
And so they are, and so be with his prize
The devil, when he gets them speedily !
Why does not your Luitolfo come ?   I long   230
To don this cloak and take the Lugo path.
It seems you never loved me, then ?
    Eulalia.   Chiappino !
    Chiappino.   Never ?
    Eulalia.   Never.
    Chiappino.   That 's sad.   Say what I might,
There was no help from being sure this while
You loved me.   Love like mine must have return,
I thought : no river starts but to some sea.
And had you loved me, I could soon devise
Some specious reason why you stifled love,
Some fancied self-denial on your part,
Which made you choose Luitolfo ; so excepting   240
From the wide condemnation of all here
One woman.   Well, the other dream may break !
If I knew any heart, as mine loved you,
Loved me, though in the vilest breast 't were lodged,
I should, I think, be forced to love again :
Else there 's no right nor reason in the world.

Eulalia. 'If you knew,' say·you—but I did not know.
That's where you're blind, Chiappino !—a disease
Which if I may remove, I'll not repent
The listening to.   You cannot, will not, see   250
How, place you but in every circumstance
Of us you are just now indignant at,
You'd be as we.
Chiappino.   I should be ?—that again !
I, to my friend, my country, and my love,
Be as Luitolfo and these Faentines ?
Eulalia. As we.
Chiappino.   Now, I'll say something to remember !
I trust in nature for the stable laws
Of beauty and utility—Spring shall plant,
And Autumn garner to the end of time :
I trust in God—the right shall be the right   260
And other than the wrong, while he endures :
I trust in my own soul, that can perceive
The outward and the inward, nature's good
And God's : so, seeing these men and myself,
Having a right to speak, thus do I speak.—
I'll not curse—God bears with them, well may I—
But I—protest against their claiming me.
I simply say, if that's allowable,
I would not—broadly—do as they have done.
God curse this townful of born slaves, bred slaves,   270
Branded into the blood and bone, slaves !   Curse
Whoever loves, above his liberty,
House, land, or life ! and —[*a knocking without*] bless my
        hero-friend,
Luitolfo !
Eulalia. How he knocks !
Chiappino.   The peril, lady !
'Chiappino, I have run a risk—a risk !
For when I prayed the Provost—he's my friend—

To grant you a week's respite of the sentence
That confiscates your goods, exiles yourself,
He shrugged his shoulder—I say, shrugged it! Yes,
And fright of that drove all else from my head.   280
Here's a good purse of *scudi:* off with you,
Lest of that shrug come what God only knows!
The *scudi*—friend, they're trash—no thanks, I beg!
Take the north gate—for San Vitale's suburb,
Whose double taxes you appealed against,
In discomposure at your ill-success
Is apt to stone you: there, there—only go!
Beside, Eulalia here looks sleepily.
Shake—oh! you hurt me, so you squeeze my wrist!'—
Is it not thus you'll speak, adventurous friend?   290

    [*As he opens the door, Luitolfo rushes in, his garments
       disordered.*

    Eulalia. Luitolfo! Blood?
    Luitolfo.   There's more—and more of it!
Eulalia—take the garment! No—you, friend!
You take it and the blood from me—you dare!
    Eulalia. Oh! who has hurt you? where's the wound?
    Chiappino.   'Who,' say you?
The man with many a touch of virtue yet!
The Provost's friend has proved too frank of speech,
And this comes of it. Miserable hound!
This comes of temporizing, as I said!
Here's fruit of your smooth speeches and soft looks!
Now see my way! As God lives, I go straight   300
To the palace and do justice, once for all!
    Luitolfo. What says he?
    Chiappino.   I'll do justice on him.
    Luitolfo.   Him?
    Chiappino. The Provost.
    Luitolfo.   I've just killed him.
    Eulalia.   Oh! my God!

 Luitolfo. My friend, they 're on my trace ; they 'll have
  me—now !
They 're round him, busy with him : soon they 'll find
He 's past their help, and then they 'll be on me !
Chiappino, save Eulalia ! I forget—
Were you not bound for—
  Chiappino.   Lugo ?
  Luitolfo.   Ah !—yes—yes !
That was the point I prayed of him to change.
Well, go—be happy ! Is Eulalia safe ?   310
They 're on me !
  Chiappino. 'T is through me they reach you, then !
Friend, seem the man you are ! Lock arms — that 's
  right !
Now tell me what you 've done ; explain how you
That still professed forbearance, still preached peace,
Could bring yourself—
  Luitolfo. What was peace for, Chiappino ?
I tried peace : did that promise, when peace failed,
Strife should not follow ? All my peaceful days
Were just the prelude to a day like this.
I cried 'You call me "friend :" save my true friend !
Save him, or lose me !'
  Chiappino.   But you never said   320
You meant to tell the Provost thus and thus.
  Luitolfo. Why should I say it ? What else did I mean ?
  Chiappino. Well ? He persisted ?—
  Luitolfo.   'Would so order it
You should not trouble him too soon again.'
I saw a meaning in his eye and lip ;
I poured my heart's store of indignant words
Out on him ; then—I know not ! He retorted,
And I—some staff lay there to hand—I think
He bade his servants thrust me out—I struck—
Ah, they come ! Fly you, save yourselves, you two ! 330

The dead back-weight of the beheading axe!
The glowing trip-hook, thumbscrews, and the gadge!
  Eulalia. They do come! Torches in the place! Farewell,
Chiappino! You can work no good to us—
Much to yourself; believe not, all the world
Must needs be cursed henceforth!
    Chiappino.   And you?
    Eulalia.   I stay.
    Chiappino. Ha, ha! Now, listen! I am master here!
This was my coarse disguise; this paper shows
My path of flight and place of refuge—see—
Lugo, Argenta, past San Nicolo,   340
Ferrara, then to Venice and all 's safe!
Put on the cloak! His people have to fetch
A compass round about. There 's time enough
Ere they can reach us, so you straightway make
For Lugo—nay, he hears not! On with it—
The cloak, Luitolfo, do you hear me? See—
He obeys he knows not how. Then, if I must—
Answer me! Do you know the Lugo gate?
  Eulalia. The northwest gate, over the bridge?
  Luitolfo.   I know.
  Chiappino. Well, there—you are not frightened? all my
      route   350
Is traced in that; at Venice you escape
Their power.—Eulalia, I am master here!
      [*Shouts from without. He pushes out Luitolfo, who*
        complies mechanically.
In time! Nay, help me with him—so! He 's gone.
  Eulalia. What have you done? On you, perchance, all
    know
The Provost's hater, will men's vengeance fall
As our accomplice.
    Chiappino.   Mere accomplice? See!
                         [*Putting on Luitolfo's vest.*

Now, lady, am I true to my profession,
Or one of these?
    Eulalia.   You take Luitolfo's place?
    Chiappino. Die for him.
    Eulalia.   Well done!   [*Shouts increase.*
    Chiappino.   How the people tarry!
I can't be silent: I must speak; or sing—   360
How natural to sing now!
    Eulalia.   Hush and pray!
We are to die; but even I perceive
'T is not a very hard thing so to die.
My cousin of the pale-blue tearful eyes,
Poor Cesca, suffers more from one day's life
With the stern husband; Tisbe's heart goes forth
Each evening after that wild son of hers,
To track his thoughtless footstep through the streets:
How easy for them both to die like this!
I am not sure that I could live as they.   370
    Chiappino. Here they come, crowds. They pass the gate?
        Yes!—No!
One torch is in the courtyard. Here flock all.
    Eulalia. At least Luitolfo has escaped. What cries!
    Chiappino. If they would drag one to the market-place,
One might speak there!
    Eulalia.   List, list!
    Chiappino.   They mount the steps.

Enter the Populace.

    Chiappino. I killed the Provost!
    The Populace [*speaking together*]. 'T was Chiappino, friends!
Our saviour! The best man at last as first!
He who first made us feel what chains we wore,
He also strikes the blow that shatters them,
He at last saves us—our best citizen!—   380
Oh! have you only courage to speak now?

My eldest son was christened a year since
'Cino' to keep Chiappino's name in mind—
Cino, for shortness merely, you observe!
The city 's in our hands.   The guards are fled.
Do you, the cause of all, come down—come up—
Come out to counsel us, our chief, our king,
Whate'er rewards you!   Choose your own reward!
The peril over, its reward begins!
Come and harangue us in the market-place!   390
   Eulalia. Chiappino?
   Chiappino.   Yes—I understand your eyes!
You think I should have promptlier disowned
This deed with its strange unforeseen success,
In favor of Luitolfo.   But the peril,
So far from ended, hardly seems begun.
To-morrow, rather, when a calm succeeds,
We easily shall make him full amends;
And meantime—if we save them as they pray,
And justify the deed by its effects?
   Eulalia. You would, for worlds, you had denied at once.   400
   Chiappino. I know my own intention, be assured!
All 's well.—Precede us, fellow-citizens!

ACT II.

The Market-place. LUITOLFO *in disguise mingling with the* Populace *assembled opposite the* Provost's *Palace.*

1 *Bystander* (*to Luitolfo*). You, a friend of Luitolfo's? Then, your friend is vanished—in all probability killed on the night that his patron the tyrannical Provost was loyally suppressed here, exactly a month ago, by our illustrious fellow-citizen, thrice-noble saviour, and new Provost that is like to be, this very morning—Chiappino !

Luitolfo. He the new Provost?

2 *Bystander.* Up those steps will he go, and beneath yonder pillar stand, while Ogniben, the Pope's Legate from Ravenna, reads the new dignitary's title to the people, according to established custom ; for which reason, there is the assemblage you inquire about. 12

Luitolfo. Chiappino—the late Provost's successor? Impossible ! But tell me of that presently. What I would know first of all is, wherefore Luitolfo must so necessarily have been killed on that memorable night?

3 *Bystander.* You were Luitolfo's friend? So was I. Never, if you will credit me, did there exist so poor-spirited a milksop. He, with all the opportunities in the world furnished by daily converse with our oppressor, would not stir a finger to help us ; and when Chiappino rose in solitary majesty and—how does one go on saying?—dealt the godlike blow—this Luitolfo, not unreasonably fearing the indignation of an aroused and liberated people, fled precipitately. He may have got trodden to death in the press at the southeast

gate, when the Provost's guards fled through it to Ravenna with their wounded master—if he did not rather hang himself under some hedge.   28

Luitolfo. Or why not simply have lain perdue in some quiet corner—such as San Cassiano, where his estate was—receiving daily intelligence from some sure friend, meanwhile, as to the turn matters were taking here—how, for instance, the Provost was not dead, after all, only wounded—or, as to-day's news would seem to prove, how Chiappino was not Brutus the Elder, after all, only the new Provost—and thus Luitolfo be enabled to watch a favorable opportunity for returning?   Might it not have been so?   37

3 Bystander. Why, he may have taken that care of himself, certainly, for he came of a cautious stock.   I 'll tell you how his uncle, just such another gingerly treader on tiptoes with finger on lip—how he met his death in the great plague-year: *dico vobis!*   Hearing that the seventeenth house in a certain street was infected, he calculates to pass it in safety by taking plentiful breath, say, when he shall arrive at the eleventh house ; then scouring by, holding that breath, till he be got so far on the other side as number twenty-three, and thus elude the danger.—And so did he begin ; but, as he arrived at thirteen, we will say—thinking to improve on his precaution by putting up a little prayer to St. Nepomucene of Prague, this exhausted so much of his lungs' reserve, that at sixteen it was clean spent—consequently at the fatal seventeen he inhaled with a vigor and persistence enough to suck you any latent venom out of the heart of a stone—Ha, ha!   54

Luitolfo [*aside*]. If I had not lent that man the money he wanted last spring, I should fear this bitterness was attributable to me.—Luitolfo is dead then, one may conclude?

3 Bystander. Why, he had a house here, and a woman to whom he was affianced ; and as they both pass naturally to the new Provost, his friend and heir—

Luitolfo. Ah! I suspected you of imposing on me with your pleasantry! I know Chiappino better.   62

1 *Bystander* [*aside*]. Our friend has the bile! After all, I do not dislike finding somebody vary a little this general gape of admiration at Chiappino's glorious qualities.—Pray, how much may you know of what has taken place in Faenza since that memorable night?

Luitolfo. It is most to the purpose that I know Chiappino to have been by profession a hater of that very office of Provost you now charge him with proposing to accept.   70

1 *Bystander.* Sir, I 'll tell you. That night was indeed memorable. Up we rose, a mass of us, men, women, children; out fled the guards with the body of the tyrant; we were to defy the world: but, next gray morning, 'What will Rome say?' began everybody. You know we are governed by Ravenna, which is governed by Rome. And quietly into the town, by the Ravenna road, comes on mule back a portly personage, Ogniben by name, with the quality of Pontifical Legate; trots briskly through the streets humming a '*Cur fremuere gentes,*' and makes directly for the Provost's Palace—there it faces you. 'One Messer Chiappino is your leader? I have known three-and-twenty leaders of revolts!' —laughing gently to himself—'Give me the help of your arm from my mule to yonder steps under the pillar—So! And now, my revolters and good friends, what do you want? The guards burst into Ravenna last night bearing your wounded Provost; and, having had a little talk with him, I take on myself to come and try appease the disorderliness, before Rome, hearing of it, resort to another method: 't is I come, and not another, from a certain love I confess to, of composing differences. So, do you understand, you are about to experience this unheard-of tyranny from me, that there shall be no heading nor hanging, no confiscation nor exile: I insist on your simply pleasing yourselves. And now, pray, what does please you? To live without any government at all?

Or having decided for one, to see its minister murdered by
the first of your body that chooses to find himself wronged,
or disposed for reverting to first principles and a justice an-
terior to all institutions—and so will you carry matters that
the rest of the world must at length unite and put down such
a den of wild beasts?   As for vengeance on what has just
taken place—once for all, the wounded man assures me he
cannot conjecture who struck him ; and this so earnestly
that one may be sure he knows perfectly well what intimate
acquaintance could find admission to speak with him late
last evening.   I come not for vengeance therefore, but from
pure curiosity to hear what you will do next.'   And thus he
ran on, on, easily and volubly, till he seemed to arrive quite
naturally at the praise of law, order, and paternal government
by somebody from rather a distance.   All our citizens were
in the snare, and about to be friends with so congenial an
adviser ; but that Chiappino suddenly stood forth, spoke out
indignantly, and set things right again.   113

   Luitolfo. Do you see?   I recognize him there !

   3 *Bystander.* Ay, but, mark you, at the end of Chiappino's
longest period in praise of a pure republic—' And by whom
do I desire such a government should be administered, perhaps, but by one like yourself?'—returns the Legate ; there-
upon speaking for a quarter of an hour together, on the natural and only legitimate government by the best and wisest.
And it should seem there was soon discovered to be no such
vast discrepancy at bottom between this and Chiappino's
theory, place but each in its proper light.   ' Oh ! are you
there?' quoth Chiappino : ' Ay, in that, I agree,' returns Chiappino : and so on.   125

   Luitolfo. But did Chiappino cede at once to this?

   1 *Bystander.* Why, not altogether at once.   For instance,
he said that the difference between him and all his fellows
was, that they seemed all wishing to be kings in one or another way—' whereas what right,' asked he, ' has any man to

wish to be superior to another?'—whereat, 'Ah, sir,' answers
the Legate, 'this is the death of me, so often as I expect
something is really going to be revealed to us by you clearer-
seers, deeper-thinkers—this—that your right-hand—to speak
by a figure—should be found taking up the weapon it dis-
played so ostentatiously, not to destroy any dragon in our
path, as was prophesied, but simply to cut off its own fellow
left-hand; yourself set about attacking yourself. For see
now! Here are you who, I make sure, glory exceedingly in
knowing the noble nature of the soul, its divine impulses,
and so forth; and with such a knowledge you stand, as it
were, armed to encounter the natural doubts and fears as to
that same inherent nobility which are apt to waylay us, the
weaker ones, in the road of life. And when we look eagerly
to see them fall before you, lo, round you wheel, only the left-
hand gets the blow; one proof of the soul's nobility destroys
simply another proof, quite as good, of the same, for you are
found delivering an opinion like this! Why, what is this
perpetual yearning to exceed, to subdue, to be better than,
and a king over, one's fellows—all that you so disclaim—but
the very tendency yourself are most proud of, and under another form, would oppose to it—only in a lower stage of man-
ifestation? You don't want to be vulgarly superior to your
fellows after their poor fashion—to have me hold solemnly
up your gown's tail, or hand you an express of the last importance from the Pope, with all these bystanders noticing
how unconcerned you look the while; but neither does our
gaping friend, the burgess yonder, want the other kind of
kingship, that consists in understanding better than his fellows this and similar points of human nature, nor to roll under his tongue this sweeter morsel still—the feeling that,
through immense philosophy, he does *not* feel, he rather
thinks, above you and me!' And so chatting, they glided
off arm-in-arm.

Luitolfo. And the result is—

1 *Bystander.* Why that, a month having gone by, the indomitable Chiappino, marrying as he will Luitolfo's love—at all events succeeding to Luitolfo's wealth—becomes the first inhabitant of Faenza, and a proper aspirant to the Provostship; which we assemble here to see conferred on him this morning. The Legate's Guard to clear the way! He will follow presently.

Luitolfo [*withdrawing a little*]. I understand the drift of Eulalia's communications less than ever. Yet she surely said, in so many words, that Chiappino was in urgent danger: wherefore, disregarding her injunction to continue in my retreat and await the result of, what she called, some experiment yet in process—I hastened here without her leave or knowledge: what could I else? But if this they say be true —if it were for such a purpose, she and Chiappino kept me away— Oh, no, no! I must confront him and her before I believe this of them. And at the word, see!   181

Enter CHIAPPINO *and* EULALIA.

Eulalia. We part here, then? The change in your principles would seem to be complete.

Chiappino. Now, why refuse to see that in my present course I change no principles, only re-adapt them and more adroitly? I had despaired of what you may call the material instrumentality of life, of ever being able to rightly operate on mankind through such a deranged machinery as the existing modes of government; but now, if I suddenly discover how to inform these perverted institutions with fresh purpose, bring the functionary limbs once more into immediate communication with, and subjection to, the soul I am about to bestow on them—do you see? Why should one desire to invent, as long as it remains possible to renew and transform? When all further hope of the old organization shall be extinct, then, I grant you, it may be time to try and create another.   197

Eulalia. And there being discoverable some hope yet in

the hitherto much-abused old system of absolute government by a Provost here, you mean to take your time about endeavoring to realize those visions of a perfect State we once heard of? ²⁰²

Chiappino. Say, I would fain realize my conception of a palace, for instance, and that there is, abstractedly, but a single way of erecting one perfectly. Here, in the market-place is my allotted building-ground ; here I stand without a stone to lay, or a laborer to help me—stand, too, during a short day of life, close on which the night comes. On the other hand, circumstances suddenly offer me—turn and see it—the old Provost's house to experiment upon — ruinous, if you please, wrongly constructed at the beginning, and ready to tumble now. But materials abound, a crowd of workmen offer their services ; here exists yet a hall of audience of originally noble proportions, there a guest-chamber of symmetrical design enough : and I may restore, enlarge, abolish, or unite these to heart's content. Ought I not make the best of such an opportunity, rather than continue to gaze disconsolately with folded arms on the flat pavement here, while the sun goes slowly down, never to rise again? Since you cannot understand this nor me, it is better we should part as you desire. ²²¹

Eulalia. So, the love breaks away too !

Chiappino. No, rather my soul's capacity for love widens— needs more than one object to content it—and, being better instructed, will not persist in seeing all the component parts of love in what is only a single part—nor in finding that so many and so various loves are all united in the love of a woman—manifold uses in one instrument, as the savage has his sword, sceptre, and idol, all in one club-stick. Love is a very compound thing. The intellectual part of my love I shall give to men, the mighty dead or the illustrious living, and determine to call a mere sensual instinct by as few fine names as possible. What do I lose? ²³³

Eulalia. Nay, I only think, what do I lose? and, one more word—which shall complete my instruction—does friendship go too? What of Luitolfo, the author of your present pros̗, perity?

Chiappino. How the author?

Eulalia. That blow now called yours—   239

Chiappino. Struck without principle or purpose, as by a blind natural operation; yet to which all my thought and life directly and advisedly tended. I would have struck it, and could not; he would have done his utmost to avoid striking it, yet did so. I dispute his right to that deed of mine—a final action with him, from the first effect of which he fled away—a mere first step with me, on which I base a whole mighty superstructure of good to follow. Could he get good from it?

Eulalia. So we profess, so we perform!

Enter OGNIBEN. EULALIA *stands apart.*

Ogniben. I have seen three-and-twenty leaders of revolts! By your leave, sir! Perform? What does the lady say of performing?   252

Chiappino. Only the trite saying, that we must not trust profession, only performance.

Ogniben. She'll not say that, sir, when she knows you longer; you'll instruct her better. Ever judge of men by their professions! For though the bright moment of promising is but a moment and cannot be prolonged, yet, if sincere in its moment's extravagant goodness, why, trust it and know the man by it, I say—not by his performance; which is half the world's work, interfere as the world needs must, with its accidents and circumstances: the profession was purely the man's own. I judge people by what they might be—not are, nor will be.   264

Chiappino. But have there not been found, too, performing natures, not merely promising?

Ogniben. Plenty.   Little Bindo of our town, for instance, promised his friend, great ugly Masaccio, once, ' I will repay you !'—for a favor done him.   So, when his father came to die, and Bindo succeeded to the inheritance, he sends straightway for Masaccio and shares all with him—gives him half the land, half the money, half the kegs of wine in the cellar. ' Good ' say you ; and it is good.   But had little Bindo found himself possessor of all this wealth some five years before— on the happy night when Masaccio procured him that interview in the garden with his pretty cousin Lisa — instead of being the beggar he then was   I am bound to believe that in the warm moment of promise he would have given away all the wine-kegs and all the money and all the land, and only reserved to himself some hut on a hill-top hard by, whence he might spend his life in looking and seeing his friend enjoy himself : he meant fully that much, but the world interfered.—To our business !   Did I understand you just now within-doors ?   You are not going to marry your old friend's love, after all ?   285

Chiappino. I must have a woman that can sympathize with and appreciate me, I told you.

Ogniben. Oh, I remember ! you, the greater nature, needs must have a lesser one—avowedly lesser—contest with you on that score would never do—such a nature must comprehend you, as the phrase is, accompany and testify of your greatness from point to point onward.   Why, that were being not merely as great as yourself, but greater considerably !   Meantime, might not the more bounded nature as reasonably count on your appreciation of it, rather ? — on your keeping close by it, so far as you both go together, and then going on by yourself as far as you please ?   Thus God serves us.   298

Chiappino. And yet a woman that could understand the whole of me, to whom I could reveal alike the strength and the weakness —

Ogniben. Ah! my friend, wish for nothing so foolish! Worship your love, give her the best of you to see; be to her like the western lands—they bring us such strange news of —to the Spanish Court; send her only your lumps of gold, fans of feathers, your spirit-like birds and fruits and gems! So shall you, what is unseen of you, be supposed altogether a paradise by her—as these western lands by Spain: though I warrant there is filth, red baboons, ugly reptiles, and squalor enough, which they bring Spain as few samples of as possible. Do you want your mistress to respect your body generally? Offer her your mouth to kiss; don't strip off your boot and put your foot to her lips! You understand my humor by this time! I help men to carry out their own principles: if they please to say two and two make five, I assent, so they will but go on and say four and four make ten.   316

Chiappino. But these are my private affairs; what I desire you to occupy yourself about, is my public appearance presently: for when the people hear that I am appointed Provost, though you and I may thoroughly discern — and easily, too—the right principle at bottom of such a movement, and how my republicanism remains thoroughly unaltered, only takes a form of expression hitherto commonly judged—and heretofore by myself—incompatible with its existence—when thus I reconcile myself to an old form of government instead of proposing a new one—   326

Ogniben. Why, you must deal with people broadly. Begin at a distance from this matter and say — New truths, old truths! sirs, there is nothing new possible to be revealed to us in the moral world; we know all we shall ever know: and it is for simply reminding us, by their various respective expedients, how we do know this and the other matter, that men get called prophets, poets, and the like. A philosopher's life is spent in discovering that, of the half-dozen truths he knew when a child, such an one is a lie, as the world states it in set terms; and then, after a weary lapse of years, and plenty of hard-thinking, it becomes a truth again after all, as he happens to newly consider it and view it in a different relation with the others : and so he restates it, to the confusion of somebody else in good time. As for adding to the original stock of truths—impossible ! Thus, you see the expression of them is the grand business :—you have got a truth in your head about the right way of governing people, and you took a mode of expressing it which now you confess to be imperfect. But what then? There is truth in falsehood, falsehood in truth. No man ever told one great truth, that I know, without the help of a good dozen of lies at least, generally unconscious ones. And as when a child comes in breathlessly and relates a strange story, you try to conjecture from the very falsities in it what the reality was—do not conclude that he saw nothing in the sky, because he assuredly did not see a flying horse there as he says — so, through the contradictory expression, do you see, men should look painfully for, and trust to arrive eventually at, what you call the true principle at bottom. Ah, what an answer is there ! to what will it not prove applicable?— 'Contradictions? Of course there were,' say you !

Chiappino. Still, the world at large may call it inconsistency, and what shall I urge in reply? 359

Ogniben. Why, look you, when they tax you with tergiversation or duplicity, you may answer—you begin to perceive that, when all 's done and said, both great parties in the State, the advocators of change in the present system of things, and the opponents of it, patriot and anti-patriot, are found working together for the common good; and that in the midst of their efforts for and against its progress, the world somehow or other still advances : to which result they contribute in equal proportions, those who spend their life in pushing it onward, as those who give theirs to the business of pulling it back. Now, if you found the world stand still between the opposite forces, and were glad, I should

conceive you; but it steadily advances, you rejoice to see!
By the side of such a rejoicer, the man who only winks as he
keeps cunning and quiet, and says, 'Let yonder hot-headed
fellow fight out my battle! I, for one, shall win in the end
by the blows he gives, and which I ought to be giving'—
even he seems graceful in his avowal, when one considers
that he might say, 'I shall win quite as much by the blows
our antagonist gives him, blows from which he saves me—I
thank the antagonist equally!' Moreover, you may enlarge
on the loss of the edge of party-animosity with age and experience—   382

Chiappino. And naturally time must wear off such asperi-
ties: the bitterest adversaries get to discover certain points
of similarity between each other, common sympathies—do
they not?

Ogniben. Ay, had the young David but sat first to dine
on his cheeses with the Philistine, he had soon discovered
an abundance of such common sympathies. He of Gath, it
is recorded, was born of a father and mother, had brothers
and sisters like another man — they, no more than the sons
of Jesse, were used to eat each other. But, for the sake of
one broad antipathy that had existed from the beginning,
David slung the stone, cut off the giant's head, made a spoil
of it, and after ate his cheeses alone, with the better appetite,
for all I can learn. My friend, as you, with a quickened eyesight, go on discovering much good on the worse side, remember that the same process should proportionably mag-
nify and demonstrate to you the much more good on the
better side! And when I profess no sympathy for the Goli-
aths of our time, and you object that a large nature should
sympathize with every form of intelligence, and see the good
in it, however limited—I answer, 'So I do; but preserve the
proportions of my sympathy, however finelier or widelier I
may extend its action.' I desire to be able, with a quickened eyesight, to descry beauty in corruption where others

see foulness only ; but I hope I shall also continue to see a redoubled beauty in the higher forms of matter, where already everybody sees no foulness at all.   I must retain, too, my old power of selection, and choice of appropriation, to apply to such new gifts ; else they only dazzle instead of enlightening me.   God has his archangels and consorts with them ; though he made too, and intimately sees what is good in, the worm.   Observe, I speak only as you profess to think and so ought to speak ; I do justice to your own principles, that is all.

416

Chiappino. But you very well know that the two parties do, on occasion, assume each other's characteristics.   What more disgusting, for instance, than to see how promptly the newly emancipated slave will adopt, in his own favor, the very measures of precaution which pressed soreliest on himself as institutions of the tyranny he has just escaped from ? Do the classes, hitherto without opinion, get leave to express it ? there follows a confederacy immediately, from which— exercise your individual right and dissent, and woe be to you !

Ogniben. And a journey over the sea to you !   That is the generous way.   Cry—' Emancipated slaves, the first excess, and off I go !'   The first time a poor devil, who has been bastinadoed steadily his whole life long, finds himself let alone and able to legislate, so, begins pettishly, while he rubs his soles, ' Woe be to whoever brings anything in the shape of a stick this way !'—you, rather than give up the very innocent pleasure of carrying one to switch flies with—you go away, to everybody's sorrow.   Yet you were quite reconciled to staying at home while the governors used to pass, every now and then, some such edict as ' Let no man indulge in owning a stick which is not thick enough to chastise our slaves, if need require !'   Well, there are preordained hierarchies among us, and a profane vulgar subjected to a different law altogether ; yet I am rather sorry you should see it so clearly: for, do you know what is to—all but save you at the Day of Judgment, all you men of genius? It is this? that, while you generally began by pulling down God, and went on to the end of your life in one effort at setting up your own genius in his place—still, the last, bitterest concession, wrung with the utmost unwillingness from the experience of the very loftiest of you, was invariably—would one think it?—that the rest of mankind, down to the lowest of the mass, stood not, nor ever could stand, just on a level and equality with yourselves. That will be a point in the favor of all such, I hope and believe.   451

Chiappino. Why, men of genius are generally charged, I think, with doing just the reverse ; and at once acknowledging the natural inequality of mankind, by themselves participating in the universal craving after, and deference to, the civil distinctions which represent it. You wonder they pay such undue respect to titles and badges of superior rank.

Ogniben. Not I—always on your own ground and showing, be it noted! Who doubts that, with a weapon to brandish, a man is the more formidable? Titles and badges are exercised as such a weapon, to which you and I look up wistfully. We could pin lions with it moreover, while in its present owner's hands it hardly prods rats. Nay, better than a mere weapon of easy mastery and obvious use, it is a mysterious divining-rod that may serve us in undreamed-of ways. Beauty, strength, intellect — men often have none of these, and yet conceive pretty accurately what kind of advantages they would bestow · on the possessor. We know at least what it is we make up our mind to forego, and so can apply the fittest substitute in our power. Wanting beauty, we cultivate good-humor ; missing wit, we get riches : but the mystic unimaginable operation of that gold collar and string of Latin names which suddenly turned poor, stupid, little, peevish Cecco of our town into natural lord of the best of us—a Duke he is now—there indeed is a virtue to be reverenced!

Chiappino. Ay, by the vulgar ; not by Messere Stiatta the poet, who pays more assiduous court to him than anybody.

Ogniben. What else should Stiatta pay court to? He has talent, not honor and riches : men naturally covet what they have not.

Chiappino. No, or Cecco would covet talent, which he has not, whereas he covets more riches, of which he has plenty already.   484

Ogniben. Because a purse added to a purse makes the holder twice as rich ; but just such another talent as Stiatta's, added to what he now possesses, what would that profit him ? Give the talent a purse indeed, to do something with ! But lo, how we keep the good people waiting ! I only desired to do justice to the noble sentiments which animate you, and which you are too modest to duly enforce. Come, to our main business : shall we ascend the steps? I am going to propose you for Provost to the people ; they know your antecedents, and will accept you with a joyful unanimity : whereon I confirm their choice. Rouse up ! Are you nerving yourself to an effort? Beware the disaster of Messere Stiatta we were talking of—who, determining to keep an equal mind and constant face on whatever might be the fortune of his last new poem with our townsmen, heard too plainly 'hiss, hiss, hiss,' increase every moment ; till at last the man fell senseless—not perceiving that the portentous sounds had all the while been issuing from between his own nobly clenched teeth and nostrils narrowed by resolve.   503

Chiappino. Do you begin to throw off the mask?—to jest with me, having got me effectually into your trap?

Ogniben. Where is the trap, my friend? You hear what I engage to do, for my part ; you, for yours, have only to fulfil your promise made just now within doors, of professing unlimited obedience to Rome's authority in my person. And I shall authorize no more than the simple re-establishment of the Provostship and the conferment of its privileges upon

yourself; the only novel stipulation being a birth of the peculiar circumstances of the time.

Chiappino. And that stipulation?

Ogniben. Just the obvious one—that in the event of the
discovery of the actual assailant of the late Provost—

Chiappino. Ha!

Ogniben. Why, he shall suffer the proper penalty, of course;
what did you expect?

Chiappino. Who heard of this?   520

Ogniben. Rather, who needed to hear of this?

Chiappino. Can it be, the popular rumor never reached
you—

Ogniben. Many more such rumors reach me, friend, than
I choose to receive; those which wait longest have best
chance. Has the present one sufficiently waited? Now is
its time for entry with effect. See the good people crowding
about yonder palace-steps—which we may not have to ascend, after all! My good friends!—nay, two or three of you
will answer every purpose—who was it fell upon and proved
nearly the death of your late Provost? His successor desires
to hear, that his day of inauguration may be graced by the
act of prompt, bare justice we all anticipate. Who dealt
the blow that night, does anybody know?

Luitolfo [*coming forward*]. I!   535

All. Luitolfo!

Luitolfo. I avow the deed, justify and approve it, and
stand forth now, to relieve my friend of an unearned responsibility. Having taken thought, I am grown stronger;
I shall shrink from nothing that awaits me. Nay, Chiappino—we are friends still: I dare say there is some proof of
your superior nature in this starting aside, strange as it
seemed at first. So, they tell me, my horse is of the right
stock, because a shadow in the path frightens him into
a frenzy, makes him dash my brains out. I understand
only the dull mule's way of standing stockishly, plodding

soberly, suffering on occasion a blow or two with due patience.

Eulalia. I was determined to justify my choice, Chiappino; to let Luitolfo's nature vindicate itself. Henceforth we are undivided, whatever be our fortune.

551

Ogniben. Now, in these last ten minutes of silence, what have I been doing, deem you? Putting the finishing stroke to a homily of mine, I have long taken thought to perfect, on the text, 'Let whoso thinketh he standeth, take heed lest he fall.' To your house, Luitolfo! Still silent, my patriotic friend? Well, that is a good sign, however. And you will go aside for a time? That is better still. I understand: it would be easy for you to die of remorse here on the spot and shock us all, but you mean to live and grow worthy of coming back to us one day. There, I will tell everybody; and you only do right to believe you must get better as you get older. All men do so: they are worst in childhood, improve in manhood, and get ready in old age for another world. Youth, with its beauty and grace, would seem bestowed on us for some such reason as to make us partly endurable till we have time for really becoming so of ourselves, without their aid, when they leave us. The sweetest child we all smile on for his pleasant want of the whole world to break up, or suck in his mouth, seeing no other good in it—would be rudely handled by that world's inhabitants, if he retained those angelic infantine desires when he had grown six feet high, black and bearded. But, little by little, he sees fit to forego claim after claim on the world, puts up with a less and less share of its good as his proper portion; and when the octogenarian asks barely a sup of gruel and a fire of dry sticks, and thanks you as for his full allowance and right in the common good of life—hoping nobody may murder him—he who began by asking and expecting the whole of us to bow down in worship to him—why, I say he is advanced, far onward, very far, nearly out of sight like our friend Chiappino yonder. And now—ay, good-bye to you! He turns round the northwest gate : going to Lugo again? Good-bye!—And now give thanks to God, the keys of the Provost's palace to me, and yourselves to profitable medita-tion at home! I have known *four*-and-twenty leaders of revolts. 587

NOTES.

ABBREVIATIONS USED IN THE NOTES.

Cf (*confer*), compare.
Fol., following.
Id. (*idem*), the same.
New Eng. Dict., the Philological Society's *New English Dictionary*, edited by Murray (Oxford, 1885).
Prol., prologue.
Skeat, Rev. W. W. Skeat's *Etymological Dictionary* (London, 1881).
Wb., Webster's Dictionary (revised quarto ed.).

The abbreviations of the names of Shakespeare's plays will be readily understood. The line-numbers are those of the "Globe" ed.

NOTES.

A BLOT IN THE 'SCUTCHEON.

A Blot in the 'Scutcheon was first published in 1843 as No. V. of *Bells and Pomegranates.* It was written in five days, and has been but slightly modified in the more recent editions. The alterations are given in the notes below.

The play has had three great presentations on the stage. The first was in February, 1843, at the Drury Lane Theatre in London, when it ran about a week. Mr. Phelps played the part of Tresham, Miss Helen Faucit that of Mildred, and Mr. Anderson that of Mertoun. The *Examiner* declares all the characters to have been underacted. This is easily conceivable, considering the key in which the piece is set. On November 27, 1848, Mr. Phelps revived the play at Sadler's Wells. The cast this time included Mr. Phelps, Miss Cooper, and Mr. Dickinson as the principal trio, and Miss Huldart and Mr. Graham as Guendolen and Gerard. The piece had a run of two weeks, and is said to have been excellently mounted and well acted.

But the production which will have most interest for American readers is that by Mr. Lawrence Barrett at Washington in the winter of 1885. His version of the play opens with the second scene. The first scene among the retainers seems quite in Shakespeare's manner, but the modern audience brooks no delay in getting at the plot. So Mr. Barrett takes us at once to the formal reception of Mertoun. For the assumption of the leading rôles, see p. 14 above. Mr. Barrett himself took the part of Tresham. The "cuts" and other alterations will be indicated in the notes.

No one who has seen the play under Mr. Barrett's management but must confess that it has some fine acting qualities. The great stage point is, however, the device of Mr. Barrett rather than of Mr. Browning. See on iii. 2. 56 below.

ACT I.

SCENE I.—In the stage-direction, the 1st ed. has "GERARD, *the Warrener, sitting alone, his back,*" etc.

4. *Poursuivant.* Herald or messenger; also spelt *pursuivant.* Cf.

Shakespeare, 1 *Hen. VI.* ii. 5. 5 : "these grey locks, the pursuivants of death," etc.

13. *Bravery.* Finery ; the familiar old sense. Cf. Shakespeare, *T. of S.* iv. 3. 57 : " With scarfs and fans and double change of bravery," etc. See also p. 237 below, note on 341.

29. *Your hawks.* This allusion to falconry would tend to fix the time of the play in the first quarter of the 18th century. The ancient art, after declining in the 17th, was revived in the early part of the 18th, but was given up about 1725.

42. *Holidays.* The 1st ed. has " holy days."

44. *Cast of hawks.* Couple of hawks. *Cast* is used in this sense only in the language of falconry.

45. *Leash of greyhounds.* That is, three of them. The *leash* was properly the thong or line by which the hounds were led. Cf. *Coriolanus,* i. 6. 38 :

> " Holding Corioli in the name of Rome,
> Even like a fawning greyhound in the leash,
> To let him slip at will."

On the use of the word in the text, cf. 1 *Hen. IV.* ii. 4. 7 : " I am sworn brother to a leash of drawers, and can call them all by their Christen names, as Tom, Dick, and Francis " (there being *three* of them).

46. *Supporter.* In the heraldic sense.

48. *Crab.* Alluding to the crab-apple, of course, whence *crabbed ;* as illustrated by *Winter's Tale,* i. 2, 102 : " Three crabbed months had sour'd themselves to death."

59. *Proper.* In the old sense of comely. Cf. *Tempest,* ii. 2. 63 (Stephano's speech) : "as proper a man as ever went on four legs," etc. See also *Heb.* xi. 23.

61. *A starrier eye.* Cf. i. 2. 48 below.

93. *No herald more.* Alluding to the officer whose business it is to marshal and order royal cavalcades, ceremonies at coronations and other state occasions, etc. He must, of course, be familiar with all the *niceties* of court usage and etiquette.

SCENE II.—16. *He 's the king's.* That is, he is in the army. Cf. ii. 326 below.

27. *As calmly 't is denied.* The 1st ed. has "as quietly denied ;" and in 31, "thank you, for, Lord Tresham," etc.

34. *The world thinks me.* The 1st ed. italicizes *me* here and also two lines below ; so with *is* in 39.

59. *Thicks.* Thickets ; as in Spenser and other writers of that day. Cf. Drayton, *Polyolbion,* xiii. :

> " And through the cumb'rous thicks as fearfully he makes,
> He with his branched head the tender saplings shakes."

60. *Eyass.* Young hawk. Cf. Spenser, *F. Q.* i. 11. 34 :

> " Like Eyas hauke up mounts unto the skies,
> His newly-budded pineons to assay."

72. *She has never known,* etc. Cf. i. 3. 237 below.

110. *I 'd not think.* The *I* is italicized in 1st ed., as in 114 below.

128. *The mercy - stroke.* The death - stroke, as putting an end to torture.

133. *Mildred is fourteen.* In this extraordinary statement seems to be the chief dramatic blemish of the play. It taxes our credulity to believe that Juliet was only fourteen ; but with her we could at least fall back upon the theory that girls develop more rapidly in southern countries than in northern, and that they are married proportionally early. Here we are asked to credit the amazing statement that a conservative English lord deliberately and indeed eagerly arranges the betrothal of his sister at the time-honored Juliet age. It is interesting to note how completely Browning ignores his own limitation as to years. For instance, in 79 above Tresham speaks of Mildred as "imbued with lore," etc. If the English girl of the last century reached that point of culture at fourteen, what must she have been at forty ? It is impossible to believe that Browning ever actually pictured Mildred as fourteen, though we see in the next scene why he wants to represent her as young as possible.

139. *Harangue.* The 1st ed. has "harangues."

152. *You golden creature.* The English ed. (1865) misprints "Yon golden creature."

SCENE III.—There is no change of scene in Barrett's version. The "chamber" adjoins the "saloon," and looks out upon the park.

In the 1st ed. the stage-direction has "*A painted window in the background.*"

27. *The bow-hand.* The hand which holds the bow, or the left hand ; the *arrow-hand* being the right. Cf. Shakespeare, *L. L. L.* iv. I. 135 : "Wide o' the bow-hand ! i' faith, your hand is out ;" that is, far to the left of the mark.

36. *Would die for him.* Cf. ii. 69 below.

67. *That fair dame,* etc. The Countess of Salisbury. The story of the Order of the Garter is too familiar to be retold here.

81. *There 's a woman,* etc. Mr. Barrett was forced to omit this song from the acted play, although he speaks of it as one of the most delightful poems in the world. The dramatic situation was too long delayed by the pause which the song makes. Archdeacon Farrar, in his American lecture on Browning, cited this as the most beautiful song to a woman in the English tongue.

90. *Who am mad to lay my spirit prostrate palpably before her.* For this same expression used from the other side, cf. *In a Gondola :*

> " This woman's heart and soul and brain
> Are mine as much as this gold chain
> She bids me wear ; which—say again—
> I choose to make by cherishing
> A precious thing, or choose to fling
> Over the boat-side, ring by ring."

116. *Expressless.* The word is not in the dictionaries, and is probably Browning's own.

128. *Come what come will,* etc. Cf. *Confessions :*

> " We loved, sir—used to meet:
> How sad and bad and mad it was,
> But then, how it was sweet !"

and *In a Gondola:*

> " but I
> Have lived indeed, and so—yet one more kiss !—can die."

151. *That should spirt water*, etc. Cf. Calpurnia's dream in *Julius Cæsar*, ii. 2. 76 :

> " She dream'd to-night she saw my statua
> Which, like a fountain with an hundred spouts,
> Did run pure blood," etc.

160. *To-morrow!* That is, do it to-morrow. The 1st ed. has " To-morrow ?"

187. *Diamond scales.* That is, sensitive scales, like those used in weighing precious stones.

203. *Bower.* In the old sense of chamber.

217. *My fight-mark.* The compound is apparently Browning's own. The reference is to a knight's wearing his lady's favor in his helmet in tourney or combat. Cf. *Rich. II.* v. 3. 15 :

> " His answer was,—he would unto the stews,
> And from the common'st creature pluck a glove,
> And wear it as a favour; and with that
> He would unhorse the lustiest challenger."

237. *I was so young*, etc. See p. 43 above.

ACT II.

Mr. Barrett was asked what he thought of Dickens's suggestion that Gerard should be made to tell his story for the first time on the stage, and should meet and conquer Tresham's wrath, extending perhaps even to the point of the master's attacking the servant. Mr. Barrett at once declared that such a scene would be impossible in its difficulty. The fact that Tresham has already half grasped the horrible idea makes his anger and grief representable. It is worth remembering in this connection, perhaps, that Charlotte Cushman and Mrs. Kemble believed Lady Macbeth to have read the fatal letter from her husband before she reads it to the audience.

28. *To merely have.* Browning often puts an adverb inside the infinitive in this way. Cf. 216 and 335 below.

31. *I' the midst.* The 1st ed. has " in the midst." Tennyson, on the other hand, has given up sundry contractions of the sort that appear in his early eds. ; as " i' the pane " and " up an' away " in *Mariana*, etc.

35. *A small dark-blue pane.* Cf. i. 3. 48, 63 above, and iii. 1. 43 below.

101. *Settle.* The 1st ed. has " settles ;" and in the stage-direction below " *above him* " for *above his head.*

178. *Her soul.* The *Her* is italicized in 1st ed.

193. *Or, no.* The 1st ed. has " Oh, no ;" and in 195 "silk-slight " for *silk-like.*

235. *I'll hide your shame . . . every eye.* Mr. Barrett omits the rest of this scene except the following lines (241, 284–287) :

> " We too will somehow wear this one day out.
> What were it silently to waste away
> And see thee waste away from this day forth,
> Two scathed things with leisure to repent
> And grow acquainted with the grave and die?"

245. *I have dispatched last night.* The grammars forbid this use of the present perfect, or whatever the tense may be called, with reference to time wholly past.

252. *The Earl!* Italicized in 1st ed.

265. *O' the lattice.* The 1st ed. has " Of the lattice." See on 31 above.

267. *Bacchant.* Evidently an Anglicizing of *Bacchante*, a priestess or votaress of Bacchus, though most of the dictionaries do not recognize this feminine use of the form in the text.

283. *Would scatter.* The 1st ed. has " Had scattered."

289. *It were not.* The 1st ed. has "This were not ;" and in 295 " Invite" for *Invites*.

303. *Losels.* Worthless fellows. Cf. Verstegan, *Restitution*, etc., 1605 : " a Losel is one that hath lost, neglected, or cast off his owne good and welfare, and so is become lewde and careless of credit and honesty ;" and Spenser, *F. Q.* ii. 3. 4 :

> " The whyles a losell wandring by the way,
> One that to bountie never cast his mynd,
> Ne thought of honour ever did assay
> His baser brest," etc.

308. *Such poor outcasts.* The 1st ed. has " these poor outcasts ;" in 314 " safelier " for *surelier ;* and in 320 "where 's" for *where.*

333. *Who said.* The 1st ed. has " Who 've said."

335. *To only signify.* See on 28 above.

351. *Your face.* The 1st ed. has " your sight ;" in 353 " hootings " for *hooting ;* and in 358 " don't believe one half " for *does not believe half.*

356. *Next.* Nearest. Cf. *Winter's Tale*, iii. 3. 129: " home, home, the next way . . . come, good boy, the next way home."

373. *Has Thorold gone*, etc. The 1st ed. has " left " for *gone.*

397. *He is your lover ?* The 1st ed. italicizes *is.*

424. *Thorold 's gone*, etc. Mr. Barrett begins the third act here. Guendolen, Austin, and Mildred pass across the scene with these few words, and disappear within the house. Then Tresham comes back, speaks his soliloquy, and conceals himself among the trees. Mildred's chamber opens by a bow-window and small balcony upon the park.

———

ACT III.

Scene I.—24. *Wimple.* A kind of veil. Cf. *F. Q.* i. 12. 22 :

> " For she had layd her mournefull stole aside,
> And widow-like sad wimple thrown away."

Hence the verb (= plaited or folded like a veil) ; as in *F. Q.* i. 1. 4 : " Under a vele, that wimpled was full low ;" and Shakespeare, *L. L. L.* iii. 1. 181 : " This wimpled, whining, purblind, wayward boy;" that is, the veiled or hoodwinked Cupid.   In the present passage, the English ed. (1885) prints " whimple," a form which, though recognized by the dictionaries for the verb, is inconsistent with the derivation of the word.   It is *wimple* in the 1st ed.

33. *I' the chapel.* The 1st ed. has " In the chapel." See on ii. 31 above.

36. *To watch.* The 1st ed. has " to see."

55. *That was mild.* The 1st ed. italicizes *that ;* and the stage-direction at next line reads : " *They advance to the front of the stage.*"

76. *Seem what you seem.* The 1st ed. has " are what you are ;" and in 81 " will keep " for *retain.*

113. *Were the giving.* The 1st ed. has " had been giving ;" and in 133 " passion's " for *passion.*

152. *Was yours.* The 1st ed. has " have you ;" and in 156 it italicizes *you* in *Never you sin.*

163. *Lowers me down,* etc. Cf. Tennyson, *Dream of Fair Women,* 211 :

> " Lower'd softly with a threefold cord of love
> Down to a silent grave."

170. *Shall have.* The 1st ed. has " to have."

183. *Lift you the body.* The 1st ed. has " Lift you the body, Gerard ;" which makes the line a foot too long.

196. *The boy.* The 1st ed. has " these boys ;" in 211 " this night " for *his breast ;* and in 212 " willingly " for *carelessly.* In 214 it italicizes *I.*

217. *To set the neck to.* Guendolen, in Mr. Barrett's reproduction, makes her exit here, and Tresham at the close of his next speech disappears among the trees. Mildred shortly appears at the window and begins her soliloquy. At iii. 2. 9 she comes out into the park.

220. *A Fury leading thus.* The 1st ed. has " a Fury free to lead."

SCENE II.—4. *Diffused.* Accented on the first syllable ; as similar dissyllabic adjectives and participles often are in Shakespeare when they precede the noun. Cf. *despised,* for instance, in *Hamlet,* iii. 1. 72 : " The pangs of despised love, the law's delay."

37. *Those water-lilies.* The 1st ed. has " the water-lilies." In 56 it italicizes *you* in *Are you, too, silent?* and in 62 *may* in *you may tell.*

56. *Ah! this speaks for you.* During this scene, on Mr. Barrett's stage, Mildred has walked half unconsciously through the trees, and has approached the spot where Mertoun's cloak and hat lie, as he threw them off before the struggle with Tresham. At this instant she catches sight of them. They tell their own story, and she cries " You 've murdered Henry Mertoun !" It will be readily seen how easy it would be on the stage to miss the force of the empty scabbard ; but there is a terrible thrill over the discovery of the cloak unclasped but an instant before by the hands now dead.

Literature does not match the pathos and the helplessness of Mildred's situation.   Desdemona in her chamber singing the weird song wrings the heart; but though she has lost her father and her husband, she has kept her innocence.   Juliet has love and hope even at the worst.   Hermione is sustained by a lofty sense of the justice of her cause.   Ophelia's frenzy comes to assuage her pain and ours.   Marguerite, in *Faust*, is the only woman who can claim kinship with Mildred by virtue of an equal agony.   Even she suffers less, because hers is a less intellectual nature. While it feels most keenly, it does not think so untiringly.   Thought is torture.   Mildred has lost her own self-respect, her brother's love (as she supposes), and her lover.   There is no further depth of misery for her to sound.

71. *You loose.*   The 1st ed. has "You loosed."   In 72 it italicizes *You*, and in 73 *He.*

82. *And love of me,* etc.   The 1st ed. has "And love of me, *you* loved I think, and yet," etc.   In 88 it has "loves" for *love.*

100. *Immovable.*   The English ed. (1885) confuses the sense by the misprint of a comma instead of a period at the end of this line.   The 1st ed. has an exclamation-point.

102. *Had gleamed some inlet.*   Of course *inlet* is the subject of *had gleamed.*

137. *Foredone.*   Exhausted.   Cf. Shakespeare, *M. N. D.* v. 1 381 :

> "Whilst the heavy ploughman snores,
>   All with weary task fordone."

Fordone is the spelling of the early eds. of Shakespeare, and accords with the etymology of the word, the first syllable being the intensive *for*, not *fore.*

138. *This pageant-world.*   This world which is but "a stage where every man must play a part" (*M. of V.* i. 1. 77).   *Pageant* in Shakespeare commonly means a theatrical exhibition, literal or figurative.   Cf. *T. G. of V.* iv. 4. 164: "When all our pageants of delight were play'd;" *A. Y. L.* ii. 7. 138 :

> "This wide and universal theatre
>   Presents more woeful pageants than the scene
>   Wherein we play in ;"

Id. iii. 4. 55 : "If you will see a pageant truly play'd," etc.

139. *Masque.*   Throng of actors.

150. *Gules.*   The heraldic term for red.   Cf. *Hamlet,* ii. 2. 479 :

> "head to foot
>   Now is he total gules; horridly trick'd
>   With blood of fathers, mothers, daughters, sons ;"

and *T. of A.* iv. 3. 59 : "With man's blood paint the ground, gules, gules."   See also the description of the painted window in Keats's *Eve of St. Agnes,* in which "A shielded scutcheon blush'd with blood of queens and kings," and the moon, shining through it, "threw warm gules on Madeline's fair breast," as she knelt in prayer.

COLOMBE'S BIRTHDAY.

This play was first published in 1844 as No. VI. of *Bells and Pomegranates*. It was performed at the Haymarket Theatre in London, April 25, 1853, Miss Helen Faucit taking the part of Colombe ; also, with Miss Alma Murray as Colombe, at St. George's Hall, London, November 19, 1885, under the auspices of the Browning Society. Cf. p. 47 above. The performance referred to by Mr. Conway (p. 46 above) was at the Howard Athenæum in Boston. Feb. 16, 1854.

The action of the play takes place between morning and evening of a single day—the *birthday* of the heroine.

———

ACT I.

1. *That this should be her birthday.* It is often necessary that Browning's sentences and also his situations should be read by the aid of what follows as well as of what precedes. In this respect he differs radically from Shakespeare, who always explains as he goes along ; indeed, *before* he goes along. Here, for example, one must read the scene half through before the real situation reveals itself. The student will find Symons's argument of the play (p. 44 above) very useful. Of course this tendency on the part of Browning is seen fully developed in the dramatic monologues, where the reader must grasp the whole situation before the first line becomes intelligible to him. As illustrations witness *The Soliloquy of the Spanish Cloister*, *The Confessional*, etc. Often the title of the poem gives the needed clue to the action, as in *Mesmerism, Misconceptions, Time's Revenges.* This is worth mention because there is scarcely another poet who depends to any considerable extent upon his titles as keys to his poems. Be it virtue or fault, it is a fact that Browning writes to the highest intelligence and the quickest intuition of his readers.

14. *Ravestein.* The small town of Ravestein, or Ravenstein, is on the Meuse, in the Dutch province of North Brabant. It has about eight hundred inhabitants and an old castle. It is thirty miles west of Cleves.

15. *Extreme.* Accented on the first syllable. See on *Blot*, iii. 2. 4. above, and cf. *express* in 30 below.

16. *Where she lived queen.* The 1st ed. has " where queen she lived." It will be seen that many of the alterations in the text are made, like this, merely to get rid of needless inversions.

17. *Juliers.* A fortified town in Rhenish Prussia, twenty miles northeast of Aix-la-Chapelle. It has now some three thousand inhabitants.

21. *Outgrows.* The 1st ed. has "outgoes."

28. *Of all men else.* An old "confusion of construction." Cf. *Macbeth*, v. 8. 4 : " Of all men else I have avoided thee."

40. *This to present.* The 1st ed. italicizes *This*.

70. *The autumn floats of pine-wood.* The rafts coming down the river.

84. *Salic law.* According to which females were excluded from the succession. Cf. *Hen. V.* i. 2. 35:

> "There is no bar
> To make against your highness' claim to France
> But this, which they produce from Pharamond,—
> 'In terram Salicam mulieres ne succedant':
> No woman shall succeed in Salique land," etc.

85. *That one.* The 1st ed. has "And one."

95. *Mummery.* In the old sense of a theatrical show, like *masque*.

113. *You broke your father's heart*, etc. Cf. iv. 91 below.

118. *We'll take*, etc. This line, and 120 below, are not in the 1st ed.

121. *Call the Prince our Duke.* The 1st ed. reads "Let the Prince be Duke;" and in 125 "So coolly as he could and would."

128. *I've ruined Maufroy*, etc. Maufroy is the youngest of this interesting assembly. He has, as is becoming, the smallest part in the discussion, both here and in act IV. But from what he has to say it would appear that Guibert's cynicism could not much harm him.

129. *Coil.* Ado. Cf. Shakespeare, *R. and J.* ii. 5. 67: "here's such a coil!" *T. of A.* i. 2. 236: "What a coil's here!" etc.

130. *Count its residue*, etc. A good example of the sentences requiring the backward look mentioned in note on 1 above.

133. *Bid that keep silence.* The 1st ed. italicizes *that*.

149. *And the lady's people go.* The 1st ed. has "and the people go; 't is instinct."

151. *Why should they wait*, etc. This line is not in the 1st ed.

155. *Lighted.* The 1st ed. has "Lit up."

163. *Pill and poll.* Plunder and strip; a common alliterative phrase in Elizabethan writers.

174. *Their vine-leaf wrappage*, etc. The enforced tribute being adorned like a voluntary offering.

175. *Crowning.* The reading of the 1st ed. The ed. of 1885 has "crowding," which, as Mr. Browning writes us, is a "vile misprint."

177. *Cappings.* Taking off their caps. Cf. the similar use of *bonneted* in *Coriolanus*, ii. 2. 30: "those who, having been supple and courteous to the people, bonneted, without any further deed to have them at all into their estimation and report." Cotgrave defines the Fr. *bonneter* by "To put off his cap vnto." For *these crook-and-cringings* the 1st ed. has "and crook-and-cringings."

190. *Oh! there is one?* Suitors were doubtless numerous enough last year. It is useless to beg favors of a falling house.

195. *Comrades.* The 1st ed. has "comrade;" and in 202 "What said he?"

220. *Close the doors*, etc. Adolf, who has already had one tussle with the suitor, means to go again into the vestibule and to prevent the entrance of Valence; but he is not quick enough.

222. *Cleves.* A town of Rhenish Prussia, near the Rhine, about seventy miles below Cologne. It is the ancient capital of the Duchy of Cleves, which was long a disputed possession of the house of Prussia. The

Schwanenburg, the old castle which was formerly the ducal residence, still stands on a height in the centre of the town. It derives its name from the tradition of the strange knight who appeared to a Duchess of Cleves in a vessel drawn by a swan, and whom she afterwards married. The story is the subject of a poem by Southey and of the opera of *Lohengrin.* In 1882 the " Lohengrin Monument " was erected in the market-place to commemorate the legend. If the good people of the town are going to do honor to its poetic associations in this way, they should some day set up a memorial to Colombe and Valence, whose fame will outlive the whole line of their ancient dukes. Cleves is only a few miles from the Dutch frontier, and is a favorite summer resort. It has a population of about ten thousand.

244. *O' the.* The 1st ed. has " Of the ;" and in the next line "yourself" for *that you.*

263. *I bear a brain.* Have a brain, that is, am not a fool. Cf. Shakespeare, *R. and J.* i. 3. 29 : " Nay, I do bear a brain,' etc.

There is a frank charm about Guibert's cynicism. Even he himself does not escape its stinging lash.

285. *Which, if I procure.* The 1st ed. has " but if so I do."

291. *How should they let me pause,* etc. *They* refers to *miseries* in the preceding line.

297. *From Cleves to Juliers.* About sixty miles.

312. *Intrust him.* The 1st ed. italicizes *him.*

330, 331. *This being,* etc. The 1st ed. reads :

> " From this yourself admit the custom here,
> What will the price of such a favor be?"

342. *Sursum corda.* Let us lift up our hearts, take courage. The phrase occurs in the mass just before the consecration of the Host.

349. *Lace.* The manufactures of Cleves nowadays are chiefly silk and woollen fabrics, hosiery, hats, leather, etc.

353. *Marcasite.* A crystallized bisulphide of iron.

ACT II.

A curious liberty is here taken of going back in point of time to show us what has passed for the Duchess during the previous act.

4. *But few can have arrived.* The 1st ed. reads : " but if there's few arrived."

17. *It seemed so natural.* The 1st ed. has " so natural it seemed ;" and in 19 " leave to do you good." It does not contain 20. In 25 it italicizes *We.*

32. *If friends detain me.* Sabyne has just been delaying the audience in the vain hope that more subjects might arrive.

38. *Some foolish.* The 1st ed. has " Each foolish ;" and in the next line " More foolish and more arrogant may grow."

65. *It cannot nor it shall not be.* The double negative is archaic. Cf.

Hamlet, i. 2. 158 : " It is not nor it cannot come to good."   In iv. 325 below the double negative of the 1st ed. has been altered.

66. *And I have not.*   The 1st ed. has " I have it not."

80. *Plainly, I feared too soon.*   The youth of the Duchess is illustrated by the fact that one smiling compliment (74) suffices to dispel her fears. Suspicion is almost impossible to her young, pure heart.

82. *The vision this day last year brought.*   This is our first hint that Valence has seen Colombe before.   It is highly characteristic that he should not have mentioned her in his interview with the courtiers.

90. *She was above it,* etc.   The passage is intended to be incoherent, with its wandering pronouns expressive of the intense excitement of the speaker.   This is a free paraphrase of it : " Colombe made me hers at the instant when I cast one look upon her.   Her spirit stood higher than I could see ; but, having had ever so faint a glimpse of her, I could not bend my eyes lower to the earth again.   The people caught her generous gaze, and I among them.   Henceforth she was mine—by the same right by which the worshipper possesses his god.   But perchance she had not been so entirely mine had she not raised my soul before she vanished to feel more keenly the people's needs, bequeathing them to me as a sacred trust."   One can but remember in connection with this fine poetic expression of the way in which love for one entails love for all the scene in which Christ said to Peter, " Lovest thou me ?"

109. *Eat first,* etc.   This line is not in the 1st ed.

112. *I lived,* etc.   The 1st ed. reads : " A girl one happy leisure year I lived."   In 113 it omits *the* before *Duchess;* in 120 it has " us " for *me; in* 125 " nor less do they deserve ;" and in 140 it omits *them.*

151. *Apparent now and thus ?*   The 1st ed. has " which now and thus I know ?"

165. *Church-flowers.*   Lilies and other flowers of religious symbolism used in the decoration of churches.   The 1st ed. has " gave " for *wrote.*

171. *God's Mother.*   The image of the Virgin, whose shrine the flower is supposed to adorn.

174. *Still, I do thank you.*   The 1st ed. has " But " for *Still,* and " the " for *my* in the next line.

176. *Here lose,* etc.   The 1st ed. reads : " Till losing the poor relic which even yet," etc.   In 180 it transposes *King's* and *Pope's ;* and in 185 it has " never will " for *never shall.*

202. *Gentles.*   Cf. *Hen. V.* prol. 8 : " But pardon, gentles all," etc.   It is used in this way only in the plural.

207. *A lion crests him,* etc.   That is, forms the crest of his coat-of-arms, or *'scutcheon;* the motto being *Scorning to waver.*

223. *Say your worst of me !*   That is, to Berthold when he comes.   Cf. i. 363 above.

229. *Give you pleasure.*   The 1st ed. has " get " for *give.*

249. *Starve now,* etc.   In the 1st ed. the line is : " Are starving now, and will lie down at night."

253. *What curbs,* etc.   This line is not in the 1st ed.

259. *In every hundred.*   The 1st ed. has " for every hundred ;" and the next line reads : " That you have simply to receive their wrongs."

263–268. *There is a vision . . . mankind below.* These six lines are not in the 1st ed.

271. *Of this man*, etc. The 1st ed. has "Of this—and this—and this?"

288. *The Marshal's*, etc. The three offices were probably held by the three principal courtiers. The *Chamberlain*, who regulates court etiquette, may well have been the smooth Clugnet.

296. *Thy need.* The 1st ed. has "There needs."

309. *Our wages*, etc. The line is not in the 1st ed. In 312 it has "with what zeal," and in 313 "'T was money" for *Hard money.*

330. *Claim.* The 1st ed. has "claimed;" and in 340 "give" for *lend.*

ACT III.

3. *Aix.* That is, Aix-la-Chapelle.

10. *Seneschal.* The high steward or chief official of a castle or barony.

21. *Esteem.* The 1st ed. has "esteemed;" in 24 "but a short" for *not a long;* and in 31 "apparent" for *as plain.*

27. *The other*, etc. This other kinsman has now become Pope. Cf. 54 below.

40. *Remind me*, etc. In the 1st ed. the line reads: "Will you remind me this I feel and say?"

44. *Faced the redoubtables*, etc. The line is not in the 1st ed. The next there reads: "Flattered this, threatened that, and bribed the other."

47. *Conquered a footing*, etc. The 1st ed. has "Conquered yourself a footing inch by inch." In 51 it has "Safe" for *Shut;* in 52 "you whom" for *then; whom;* in 53 "Narrowly am I forced to search;" in 54 "So by your uncle are you hid, this Pope;" and in 58 "But" for *Match.*

56. *Too much of mere legs-and-arms*, etc. Cf. *Rabbi Ben Ezra*, viii. :

> "What is he but a brute
> Whose flesh hath soul to suit,
> Whose spirit works lest arms and legs want play?
> To man propose this test—
> The body at its best,
> How far can that project thy soul in its lone way?"

63. *Œconomy.* The old etymological spelling of *economy.*

67. *The day before.* Not to be taken literally, as *Treves* is some eighty miles from *Aix* in a direct line. Cf. 134 below.

68. *Why do you let your life slip thus?* An interesting bit of psychology is found in the fact that Browning makes Melchior, a student, the champion of action in preference to diplomacy.

71. *Amelius.* An Italian philosopher of the Neo-Platonic school, who flourished in the latter half of the 3d century.

76. *Ah! Well*, etc. Our dramatic credulity is somewhat taxed in allowing Berthold an argument and a soliloquy after the entrance of the courtiers before he makes the slightest sign of observing their presence.

80. *Of joys*, etc. The 1st ed. reads: "Of joys and sorrows—such degree there is." It does not have the next line. In 91 it reads: "To baffle, let advantages alone;" and in 95 "please 't" for *please.*

108. *Truncheon.* Staff of office, sceptre.

113. *By Paul, the advocate*, etc. Valence is at least consistent.

120. *So must I end, it seems.* The 1st ed. has "so probably I end."

130. *In each decorum*, etc. In the etiquette of such negotiations.

142. *Did they*, etc. The 1st ed. has "Did he," etc. ; and in 153 "have" for *get*.

162. *Under that gray convent wall.* Cf. 86 above.

In this passage may there not be a hint of the Hamlet-nature in Berthold, unable to act except under the supreme stress of a half-accidental emergency.

176. *Your people*, etc. Not only these hollow courtiers, but the people also, who may worship you as do those of Cleves.

179. *I ruled these.* The 1st ed. has "these I ruled ;" in 187 "some one of those about me ;" in 191 "So" for *Now ;* and in 204 "but a day's sole respite."

214. *At this reception*, etc. The line is not in the 1st ed. ; and the same is true of 219 and 221. In 215 we find there "sakes" for *sake*, and in 222 "of" for *by*.

223-225. *Which I remember*, etc. The 1st ed. reads :

> "If you forgot once, I remember now !
> But, unrepelled, attack must never pass.
> Suffer, through you, your subjects I demand," etc.

232. *When is man strong*, etc. There is no finer line in the play, and no profounder truth in poetry.

247, 248. *So turns our lady*, etc. These two lines are not in the 1st ed. In 249 it has "So I am first ;" in 250 "so clear ;" in 260 "as there ;" and in 263 "'mongst priests."

262. *A pillared flame*, etc. Cf. *Exod.* xiii. 21, *Numb.* xiv. 14, etc.

267. *For whom.* The 1st ed. has "Whom we ;" in next line "Would" for *We'd ;* and in 274 "The chief" for *Her chief.*

281. *You'd say*, etc. The 1st ed. reads : "They love each other, Guibert's friend and she !" The 4th Courtier replies "Plainly !" and the 5th Courtier goes on with "Pray, Guibert, what is next to do ?" The rest of the text between 281 and 284 does not appear in the 1st ed.

285. *I laid.* The 1st ed. has "I lay ;" and in 287 "And now, sir, simple knight again am I."

305-314. *You hear that ? . . . at last.* This speech of Gaucelme's is not in the 1st ed.

317. *That fired*, etc. The 1st ed. has "That fires," and "will" for *would*.

326. *Ere you dream.* The 1st ed. has "Ere now, even ;" and in 328 "The man and mood are gone." It does not contain 229. In 332 it has "was" for *seemed*.

349. *Aspire to rule.* The 1st ed. has "Aspire to that ;" and in 356 "At night the Prince you meet."

351. *Soul and body*, etc. It is a common experience, both in fiction and in fact, that a great emotion quickens all the faculties to a mature life. Juliet, for instance, ceases to be a child in the very moment of her joy.

365. *Emprise.* Enterprise, adventurousness. The dictionaries do not recognize this abstract sense of the word, and we do not remember meeting with it elsewhere.

372, 373. *The changed voice*, etc. These two lines are not in the 1st ed. There the next line reads: "Reward, that's little, that is nought to her."

377. *Perchance, forbid.* The 1st ed. has "forbid, perchance."

ACT IV.

1. *How spring this mine?* Cf. iii. 315-319 above and 50 below.

14. *Loved and been loved.* That Valence had loved Colombe is plainly enough said in act iii.; but there is but one line so far (ii. 237) to intimate the truth of the other half of the assertion.

16. *Their stand.* The 1st ed. has "his stand;" in 18 "in his way by craft, he chose;" and in 20 "assist him."

21. *The Duchess*, etc. The 1st ed. reads: "The fruit is, she prefers him to ourselves;" in 22 "the simple ground;" in 23 "First seeing, liking more, and so an end;" in 27 "And she" for *Herself;* in 32 "That" for *Who;* and in 39 "Against such accident that will provides."

24. *But as we all*, etc. Prof. Corson, in his admirable essay on "Browning's Obscurity," mentions the poet's frequent habit of omission. Here the prose construction would be "As *if* we all had started," etc. The ellipsis is a common one in Shakespeare. Cf. *Macbeth*, i. 4. 11 :

> "To throw away the dearest thing he owed,
> As 't were a careless trifle," etc.

It may be doubted whether Browning is much more elliptical than Shakespeare, though he is more so than Tennyson.

42-48. *I know that . . . set aside.* These seven lines are not in the 1st ed. Line 49 is made a question: "He is next heir?"

55. *On your*, etc. The 1st ed. reads: "Upon unselfishness that prospered ill."

57-77. *Wait, I suppose . . . renewed?* The additions and alterations in this portion of the text are so many that we give it in full as it stands in the 1st ed. :

> "*Guibert.* Wait, I suppose, till Valence weds our lady,
> And then apprize the Prince—
>   *Gaucelme.*   Ere then, retired?
> Tell the Prince now, sir! Ay, this very night—
> Ere he accepts his dole and goes his way,
> Tell what has been, declare what's like to be,
> And really makes him all he feigned himself;
> Then trust his gratitude for the surprise!
>   *Guibert.* Good! I am sure she'll not disown her love,
> Throw Valence up—I wonder you see that!
>   *Gaucelme.* The shame of it—the suddenness and shame!
> With Valence there to keep her to her word,
> And Berthold's own reproaches or disgust—
> We'll try it!—Not that we can venture much!

> Her confidence we 've lost forever—his
> Must be to gain!
>   *Guibert.*   To-night, then, venture we!
> Yet—may a lost love never be renewed?"

64. *Than trust his gratitude,* etc. The said gratitude naturally to be shown by rewarding the bearers of the pleasant surprise.

68. *I wonder you see that.* Gaucelme and Guibert never are willing to allow a virtue or a delicacy to each other. This line has a scornful emphasis on *you.*

78. *Smarting - while.* Cf. *breathing - while* (*Rich. III.* i. 3. 60, etc.) and similar compounds.

81. *A mimic,* etc. The 1st ed. has "A mimic of the joint, and just so like."

88–90. *Exulting that,* etc. For these three lines the 1st ed. has:

> " Waits here to boast their scheme succeeds!—We 'll hence—
> And perfect ours! To the Archives and the Hall!"

91. *You have not smiled,* etc. Cf. i. 113 above.

101–104. *But, suffered . . . as well.* For these four lines the 1st ed. has;

> " But, suffered rule first by these Kings and Popes
> To serve some devil's-purpose,—now 'tis gained,
> To serve some devil's-purpose must withdraw!"

107. *On us.* The 1st ed. has "to us;" in 110 and 111 "them" for *you;* in 116 "If no prayer breathe;" and in 119 "I had not looked for you."

122–125. *And yet . . . decide on—.* The 1st ed. reads:

> " *Valence.* And yet I scarce know wherefore that prevents
> Disclosing it to you— disclosing even
> What she determines—"

132. *A cottage.* The 1st ed. has "a hovel."

137. *At first.* The 1st ed. has "I first;" and in the next line "Before our late appointment, sir, I come." In 142 it has "Of the lady."

150. *Your hand!* A bewildered repetition of his former speech (144).

154. *Burgraves, Landgraves, Markgraves.* German titles of nobility (*Burggraf, Landgraf, Markgraf*), the last being commonly Anglicized as *Margrave.*

157. *Chrysoprase.* A precious variety of chalcedony, of an apple-green color in the finest specimens.

158. *Talk of.* The 1st ed. has "tell me;" in 161 "The match will influence many fortunes here?" and in 162 "A natural enough solicitude."

168. *To rule,* etc. This line is not in the 1st ed.

171. *Gray.* The 1st ed. has "grew," which was undoubtedly a misprint for "grey." It cannot be = *grewsome.*

172. *Demean herself.* Degrade herself. Skeat is doubtless right in regarding this *demean* as the *demean* = conduct (cf. *demeanour*) "altered in sense owing to an obvious (but absurd) popular etymology which allied the word to the English *mean*, base;" but it is used by not a few good writers of our day. Wb. cites an example of it from Shakespeare (*C. of E.* iv. 3. 83):

> " Now, out of doubt Antipholus is mad,
>   Else would he never so demean himself ;"

but there, as elsewhere in the plays, it clearly has the other meaning.

180. *I see you have them*, etc. The line is not in the 1st ed. ; neither is 188 below. In 183 that ed. has " In my ambition's course — say, rocky course."

186. *Duke Luitpold's brazen self.* His bronze statue.

189. *And to this*, etc. The 1st ed. reads : " To this claim be it, in the Hall to-night ;" in 193 " What falls away, if not my faith in her ?" and in 196 " Dare I to test her now,—or had I faith."

202-204. *What I seem*, etc. The 1st ed. reads :

> " What I now
> Begin, a simple woman now, to be,
> Hope that I am,—for, now my rights are void," etc.

208. *He gathers*, etc. The line is not in the 1st ed., where the speech begins thus :

> " *Valence.* He stands, a man, now ; stately, strong, and wise—
> One great aim, like a guiding-star, before—
> Which tasks strength, wisdom, stateliness to follow,
> As, not its substance, but its shine he tracks,
> Nor dreams of more than, just evolving these
> To fulness, will suffice him to life's end.
> After this star," etc.

In this lofty speech are " some things hard to be understood ; " but on the whole it seems best not to attempt a paraphrase of it. If one keeps in mind how high is Berthold's ambition, it may be followed, with a little patience.

227. *Grade.* The word is etymologically equivalent to *step*.

236. *On the other half.* The 1st ed. has " with " for *on ;* in the next line " So shall he go on, every day's success ;" in 239 " airy " for *aëry ;* and in 240 " shall grow " for *lends help.*

242. *His step or stalk.* His friendly or his hostile approach.

245-249. *Till even . . . he ends.* For these five lines the 1st ed. has :

> " Till even his power shall cease his power to be,
> And most his weakness men shall fear, nor vanquish
> Their typified invincibility.
> So shall he go on, so at last shall end." etc.

The first four lines of the passage as it now stands are most subtle. A moment's reflection shows, however, how true they are. For example, Germany does not tremble half so much to-day at the strong rule of Bismarck as she trembles at the thought of his possible illness and death. " Men shall dread his weakness more." The subject of *dare* is *their earth ;* that is, " man's earth dares not put in peril its bravest, first and best." If this *typified invincibility* should fail, there would be no safety else.

251. *The fiery centre*, etc. Alluding to the theory that the central parts of our earth are in a state of fiery fusion.

258. *'T was a man.* The 1st ed. has " A man 't was ;" in 267 " so might love " for *love might so ;* in 270 " Give counsel " for *Desire that ;* and in 272 " say more " for *affirm.*

264. *Thanks, Berthold*, etc. Colombe alludes to the provision of her father's will (see 39 above), which gives the kingdom to the next of right, should she wed beneath her rank. Berthold's hand will not degrade her —at least technically, according to the terms of the late Duke's will.

282. *I could have kept my rule.* The 1st ed. has "my rule I could have kept;" in 284 "Yet abjured all. This Berthold does for you;" and in 291 "and" for *yet*.

288. *Had gone with love's presentment*, etc. The words and looks with which Berthold offered this most serious of gifts had not so much grace in them as would have gone with the most trifling service from a real lover.

304. *So to Berthold back again.* The 1st ed. has "So of Berthold's proposition;" in 310 "both" for *them*; in 316 "single" for *only*, and "were" for *spoke*; in 322 "a cause" for *great cause*; and in 325 "Nor will not" (cf. ii. 65 above) for *And will not*.

340. *Away.* Used figuratively of course, like *above*.

341. *Brave.* In the old sense of beautiful, admirable. Cf. what Miranda says at the first view of Ferdinand (*Tempest*, i. 2. 400): "It carries a brave form. But 't is a spirit."

354. *So to speak.* The 1st ed. has "somehow;" and in 367 "that awe" for *the awe*.

357. *Assurance.* Not from the unknown lady, but from himself; a hint to be bolder.

379. *A nobler cause.* The 1st ed. has "a meaner cause," and adds the line "Whence rising, its effects may amply show." In 384 and 385 it has "that" for *who*.

381. *The rest's unsaid again.* Not so easily, as Valence makes appear in his next speech.

387, 388. *With all hearts*, etc. All feeling it most thrillingly, but none daring to speak of it.

396. *Would a crown gild it*, etc. The 1st ed. has "What would a crown gild," etc.

402. *Love since*, etc. The 1st ed. has "Love as you pleased love! All is cleared—a stage." There is no pause at the end of the next line, and 404 begins "For you." In 405 *speak* is "say."

ACT V.

2. *Amelius.* See on iii. 71 above.

3. *This grand disclosure.* The offer of his hand to Colombe. Cf. iv. 144 fol. above.

4. *Oh!* The 1st ed. has "Oh!—he," etc. On *spokesman with the forehead*, cf. i. 212 above.

9. *Perhaps I had*, etc. This line is not in the 1st ed.; neither is 19 below.

Browning does not mean us to forget that, with all his manly qualities, Berthold has committed the poet's unpardonable sin. He has de-

nied the right of that internal voice which counsels love. For a brief
perfect illustration of Browning's contempt for this especial weakness,
see *Youth and Art* (our *Select Poems*, p. 85), and *Dis Aliter Visum:*

> " Let the mere starfish in his vault
>   Crawl in a wash of weed, indeed,
> Rose-jacynth to the finger-tips:
>   He, whole in body and soul, outstrips
> Man, found with either in default.
>
> But what 's whole can increase no more,
>   Is dwarfed and dies, since here 's its sphere.
> The devil laughed at you in his sleeve !
>   You knew not? That I will believe ;
> Or you had saved two souls—nay, four."

10. *The unfriended.* The 1st ed. omits *the.* Line 13 reads : " My uncle
chokes in his next coughing-fit ;" in 14 we find " King Philip " for *King-
cousin ;* in 17 "past o'er " for *o'erpast ;* in 18 "safer " for *safe.*

22. *Elude the adventure.* Melchior likes as little this easy way out of
the difficulty by the device of marriage as he liked the submission of Juliers without a struggle. He has set his heart upon some situation which
shall tax and develop and demonstrate the powers of Berthold.

28. *We seem, in Europe,* etc. A free-and-easy but very shrewd reference to revolutionary tendencies in Europe and the possible results for
hereditary rulers. The figure of the masquerade is capitally carried out,
and is withal in admirable keeping with Berthold's character. The critics who find him lacking in intellectual power, or a mere foil to Valence,
are commended to the study of this speech.

42. *And, after breathing,* etc. This line is not in the 1st ed. ; and the
next has " And thinks " for *Means to.*

49. *For somewhat.* The 1st ed. omits *for*—apparently an accident. In
51 it has "eyes" for *soul ;* in 54 "better 's " for *better ;* in 55 "So be it !
Yet, proceed my way the same ;" and in 56 "end " for *ends.*

68. *So bold,* etc. This line is not in the 1st ed. ; and the same is true
of 70. In 71 that ed. has "And " for *'T is ;* in 72 "see " for *wait ;* in 75
" Before my uncle could obtain the ear ;" in 76 "superior, help me," etc. ;
and in 82 "gallant " for *lover.*

72. *My true worth.* From a worldly point of view.

77. *Priscilla.* Cf. iii. 86 above.

104. *To your intellect.* The 1st ed. has "to intelligence ;" in the next
line "a " for *your ;* and in 114 " Under the sun and in the air,—at last,"
etc.

109-116. *Like waters,* etc. There could not be a better description of
certain lakes in Italy which owe their origin to earthquakes or volcanic
action. Even Lake Avernus, the ancient gateway of hell, is now a very
gem of placid loveliness.

129. *Profession.* The 1st ed. has "professions ;" in 138 "at first " for
so promptly ; in 145 "more leisurely " for *befittingly ;* and in 146 " Would "
for *Did,* and " off " for *forth.*

147. *The good,* etc. This line is not in the 1st ed.

151-153. *Decide ! . . . the Duchess !* The 1st ed. reads thus:

> " Now either
> Hail to the Empress—farewell to the Lady !"

155 *Almost upon court-license trespassing.*   See on ii. 288 above.

162. *Then yourself*, etc.   The 1st ed. ends the speech with " then yourself—" Berthold breaking in with " What insolence !"   In 169 below it
has " Had made " for *Could make.*

189. *For each conjuncture.*   The reading of the 1st ed., for which the
ed. of 1885 misprints " For each conjecture."

195. *Actions.*   The 1st ed. has " action ;" in 205 " But how " for *How
much ;* in 207 " When next a keeper for my own 's to seek ;" in 211 " argue " for *phrase it ;* and in 220 " other " for *alien.*

205. *How much indebted*, etc.   One of the most frequent causes of
Browning's obscurity is the peculiar inversion which he practises.   Order
of arrangement in a sentence seems less important to him than to other
English writers.   Perhaps his wide linguistic knowledge may be partly
accountable for this.   Shakespeare had a certain advantage in knowing
" small Latin and less Greek."   In the present passage the sense is simply this : " How much I am indebted to you for revealing your true abil-
ity in the way of keeping secrets will be discovered to you when I have
myself secrets to keep."

233. *Affections all repelled*, etc.   A man of affairs so large will have no
time for the nurture of the affections, even were he foolishly to plant them
now.

241. *Valence holds, of course !*   In the 1st ed. this speech is given to
" *Courtiers.*"   In 243 that ed. has " still " for *yet ;* and in 248 " comes "
for *speaks.*

244. *To tamely acquiesce.*   See on *Blot*, ii. 28.

253. *Prince's.*   The 1st ed. has " Prince ;" in 258 " So I shall speak ;"
and in 260 " trouble's " for *trouble.*

275. *Once, to surprise the angels.*   Cf. Shakespeare, *M. for M.* ii. 2. 121:

> " but man, proud man,
>
> *   *   *   *   *
>
> Plays such fantastic tricks before high heaven
> As make the angels weep, who, with our spleens,
> Would all themselves laugh mortal."

276. *Recording*, etc.   The 1st ed. has " Might record, hug themselves
they chose not so ;" and in 279 " Could have the " for *Can have such.*

287. *They say*, etc.   The 1st ed. has " The lady's hand your service
claims, they say ;" in 294 " this " for *one ;* in 303 " it " for *noise ;* and in
321 " your own " for *love's right.*

331, 332. *He holds you*, etc.   The 1st ed. reads :

> " He has you—you, the form,
> And you, the mind, where self-love made such room," etc.

In 335 it has " you " for *old ;* and in 347 " For his sake and for yours."

349, 350. *One last touch*, etc.   The 1st ed. has :

> " One last touch of—
> [*After a pause, presenting his paper to the Prince.*
> Redress the wrongs of Cleves !"

362. *Too costly a flower*, etc.　Cf. iv. 184 above.　The 1st ed. has "were you" for *were this*; and in 365 "rule" for *Duchy.*

380. *Barnabite.*　A monk of the order of St. Barnabas—an unwelcome substitute for the Duke.

386. *Plod.*　The 1st ed. has "go."

A SOUL'S TRAGEDY.

This drama, was first published in 1846 (with *Luria*) as No. VIII. of *Bells and Pomegranates.*　The number had the following dedication : *

I DEDICATE

THESE LAST ATTEMPTS FOR THE PRESENT AT DRAMATIC POETRY

𝕿𝖔 𝖆 𝕲𝖗𝖊𝖆𝖙 𝕯𝖗𝖆𝖒𝖆𝖙𝖎𝖈 𝕻𝖔𝖊𝖙;

"WISHING WHAT I WRITE MAY BE READ BY HIS LIGHT"—

IF A PHRASE ORIGINALLY ADDRESSED, BY NOT THE LEAST WORTHY OF HIS CONTEMPORARIES,

TO SHAKESPEARE,

MAY BE APPLIED HERE, BY ONE WHOSE SOLE PRIVILEGE IS A GRATE-FUL AMBITION,

TO WALTER SAVAGE LANDOR.

March 29, 1846.

In a letter, acknowledging the dedication, Landor said :

"Accept my thanks for the richest of Easter offerings made to any one for many years.　I stayed at home last evening on purpose to read *Luria*, and if I lost my good music (as I certainly did) I was well compensated in kind.　To-day I intend to devote two rainy hours entirely to *A Soul's Tragedy.*　I wonder whether I shall find it as excellent as *Luria !*　You have conferred too high a distinction on me in your graceful inscription. I am more of a dramatist in prose than in poetry. . . . Go on and pass *us* poor devils !　If you do not go far ahead of me, I will crack my whip at you and make you spring forward.　So, to use a phrase of Queen Eliza-beth,　　　Yours as you demean yourself,　　　W. LANDOR."

No. VIII. of *Bells and Pomegranates* contained also the following preface :

"Here ends my first series of *Bells and Pomegranates :* and I take the opportunity of explaining, in reply to inquiries, that I only meant by that title to indicate an endeavor towards something like an alternation, or mixture, of music with discoursing, sound with sense, poetry with thought; which looks too ambitious, thus expressed, so the symbol was preferred.

---

* This was afterwards made the dedication to *Luria*, "these last attempts" being changed to "this last attempt," as stated on p. 9 above.

It is little to the purpose, that such is actually one of the most familiar of the many Rabbinical (and Patristic) acceptations of the phrase ; because I confess that, letting authority alone, I supposed the bare words, in such juxtaposition, would sufficiently convey the desired meaning. 'Faith and good works' is another fancy, for instance, and perhaps no easier to arrive at : yet Giotto placed a pomegranate-fruit in the hand of Dante, and Raffaelle crowned his Theology (in the *Camera della Segnatura*) with blossoms of the same ; as if the Bellari and Vasari would be sure to come after, and explain that it was merely '*simbolo delle buone opere—il qual Pomogranato fu però usato nelle vesti del Pontefice appresso gli Ebrei.*' R. B."

On the title of *A Soul's Tragedy*, see p. 55 above, and compare what Browning says in the dedication of *Sordello* to M. Milsand, written in 1863, or twenty-three years after it was published : "The historical decoration was purposely of no more importance than a background requires; and my stress lay on the incidents in the development of a soul : *little else is worth study ; I at least always thought so.*"

ACT I.

The heading in the 1st ed. is "Part 1." The alterations in more recent eds. are few compared with those in the *Blot* and *Colombe*.

2. *The ave-bell.* Rung about half an hour after sunset as a signal to the people to repeat the *Ave-Maria*.

49. *We please.* The 1st ed. has "we 're pleased."

60. *At church.* That is, when christened.

61. *Each.* The 1st ed. has "One."

72. *Gauntlet-gatherer.* Champion ; taking up in their behalf the *gauntlets* thrown down by their enemies.

77. *Wound-inflictors.* The 1st ed. has "their inflictors."

94. *Faenza.* A town in Italy (the ancient *Faventia*), twenty miles to the southwest of Ravenna. It was annexed to the States of the Church in 1509 by Pope Julius II. In the 15th century it was the seat of important ceramic manufactures (recently revived), whence the French name *faïence* for certain wares in that line. The population is now about twenty thousand.

117. *Nor mine.* The 1st ed. has "Or mine."

126, 127. *Your prosperous smooth lover*, etc. The 1st ed. reads thus :

> "Your prosperous smooth husband presently,
> Then, scarce your wooer—now, your lover : well—"

129. *My eye grew dim.* The 1st ed. has "eyes," and also in 133 below.

137. *The fault 's there?* The 1st ed. has "Oh, the fault was there ?" which makes the line a foot too long (cf. note on *Blot*, iii. 1. 183). In 144 it has "oh " for *why.*

153. *By fascination.* In spite of myself, as if under the influence of some *fascination*, or enchantment.

161. *As next.* The 1st ed. has "As to ;" and in 181 "to spurn" for *why spurn.*

198. *Nor missed a cloak*, etc.   That is, had to make no sacrifices in doing it.

207. *By chance.*   The 1st ed. has "for once."

214. *I would better.*   The 1st ed. has "I had better," which good old English idiom it had been better to retain.   Cf. our *Select Poems of Browning*, p. 194, note on 78.

217. *The natural.*   The 1st ed. has "its natural;" in 219 "So" for *Thus;* and in 224 "they woke" for *awake.*

231. *The Lugo path.*   The road to Lugo, a town about ten miles north of Faenza and twenty west of Ravenna.   It takes its name from the ancient *Lucus Dianæ*, the site of which it is supposed to occupy.

234. *Help from.*   The 1st ed. has "helping."

258. *Spring shall plant*, etc.   Cf. *Gen.* viii. 22.

272. *Loves.*   The 1st ed. has "loved;" in 275 "I have run a risk—my God!" in 276 "How" for *For;* in 277 "his sentence;" and in 278 "and exiles you" for *exiles yourself.*

286. *Ill-success.*   Cf. *Rich. III.* iv. 4. 236: "dangerous success;" Sidney, *Arcadia:* "my heart misgave me some evil successe," etc.   The original meaning of the word was issue or result—that which *succeeds* in point of time.   Bacon (*Adv. of L.* ii. 4. 2) speaks of "the successes and issues of actions."

316. *Promise.*   The 1st ed. has "say that."

332. *The glowing trip-hook, thumbscrews, and the gadge.*   The *trip-hook* and the *gadge* are obviously instruments of torture, like the *thumbscrews*, but neither word is to be found in the dictionaries.

338. *My coarse disguise.*   Referring to the *cloak* he has on.

340. *Argenta.*   A small town eighteen miles southeast of *Ferrara*, or about half-way between *Lugo* and that city.   The only *San Nicolo* that we can find in that part of Italy is a village on the road from Faenza to Bologna, twenty miles or more directly *west* of Lugo, while Argenta is almost directly *north.*   Cf. the inconsistencies in the famous ride from Ghent to Aix as noted in our *Select Poems of Browning*, p. 164.

351. *You escape.*   The 1st ed. has "you'll escape."

386. *Come up.*   The 1st ed. repeats "come down;" and in the next line it has "come forth" for *come out.*

ACT II.

7. *He the new Provost?*   The 1st ed. italicizes *He;* in 11 it has "usage" for *custom;* in 13 "old" for *late;* and in 21 "so when" for *and when.*

30. *San Cassiano.*   There is a village of this name south of Lake Garda, not far from Solferino.

35. *Brutus the Elder.*   Who drove the Tarquins from Rome, but did *not* make himself king in their stead.

42. *Dico vobis.*   I tell you.

49. *St. Nepomucene.*   St. John Nepomuc, as he was called from his birthplace (a small town in Bohemia), the patron saint of his native

country, and especially honored in Prague the capital. Cf. Longfellow, *Golden Legend*, i. :

> " Like Saint John Nepomuck in stone
> Looking down into a stream."

63. *I do not dislike finding somebody*, etc.   Like the man who was tired of hearing Aristides called the Just.

79. *Cur fremuere gentes?*   The beginning of the second Psalm in the Vulgate.

89. *Resort.*   The 1st ed. has "resorts."

93. *Heading nor hanging.*   Cf. Shakespeare, *M. for M.* ii. 1. 250 : "it is but heading and hanging," etc.

103. *And this so earnestly*, etc.   The Provost does not wish to expose Luitolfo.

105. *Late last evening.*   The 1st ed. has "so late that evening ;" and just below "And thus ran he on, easily and volubly," etc.

124. *Ay, in that I agree.*   The 1st ed. omits *Ay.*

143. *Which are apt.*   The 1st ed. has "that are apt ;" and in 147 it omits *for*, putting a dash in its place.

168. *Luitolfo's wealth.*   The 1st ed. has "goods" for *wealth ;* in 175 "injunctions" for *injunction ;* and in 178 "Yet if what" for *But if this.*

174. *In urgent danger.*   She did not mean *bodily* danger, as Luitolfo supposed.

216. *Ought I not make*, etc.   The 1st ed. has "Ought I not rather make," omitting the *rather* in next line ; in 219 it has "But" for *Since*, with a colon instead of the comma in the next line ; in 226 fol. "nor in finding the so many and so various loves united in the love of a woman—finding all uses in one instrument," etc. ; and in 230 " I shall give the intellectual part of my love to men, the mighty dead or illustrious living," etc.

234. *Nay I only think, what do I lose?*   The 1st ed. has "love" for *lose*, apparently a misprint ; and in 241 "and to which" for *yet to which.*

297. *Thus God serves us.*   The 1st ed. has " So God," etc.

304. *The western lands.*   The recently discovered America.   It will be borne in mind that the time is the 16th century.

314. *Principles.*   The 1st ed. has "principle ;" and in 329 "why" for *sirs.*

338. *To newly consider.*   See on *Blot*, ii. 28 above.   Cf. 491 below.

341. *Thus, you see.*   The 1st ed. has " So, you see."

363. *Advocators.*   A word to be found in none of the dictionaries except the *New Eng. Dict.* where this is the only passage quoted for this meaning.   It was used in the 15th century in the sense of intercessor, patron (saint).

368. *Spend their life.*   The 1st ed. has "spent" for *spend*, and "gave" for *give* in next line.

380. *May enlarge.*   The 1st ed. has "must enlarge."

388. *His cheeses.*   See 1 Sam. xvii. 18.

395. *After.*   Cf. *Tempest*, ii. 2. 10 : "And after bite me," etc.

408. *Higher forms of matter*.   The 1st ed. omits *of matter ;* and in 424 it has " there is " for *there follows.*

439. *Profane vulgar.* The "profanum vulgus" of Horace (*Od.* iii. I. I).

452. *Generally.* The 1st ed. has "usually ;" and in 465–471 it has the second person for the first—"you" for *us* and *we*, and "your" for *our*.

491. *To duly enforce.* See on 338 above.

495. *Are you*, etc. The 1st ed. has "You are," etc.

555. *Let whoso thinketh*, etc. See 1 *Cor.* x. 12.

562. *You must get better.* The 1st ed. has "will" for *must ;* in 565 "would really seem" for *would seem ;* and in 577 "will thank" for *thanks*.

581. *Nearly out of sight, like our friend Chiappino yonder.* The vital importance of critical moments is Browning's favorite theme. The character must be prepared by long, patient training for "the stress and strain" of an unforeseen and half-unrecognized occasion. The power to judge of the real ethical value of any given act is strengthened if not positively created by years of careful study of the relations of conduct and of people. This observation must be unselfish as well as keen. No better example can be found of all these general considerations than the character of Chiappino in *A Soul's Tragedy.* He is equal to one lofty choice. He takes upon himself the act of Luitolfo when he supposes that to do so is to meet death in one of its most hideous forms. He bears the test of torturing adversity. But at the next step he falters. The importance of truth—where an instant before a lie has been the truest heroism—he does not see. This time the moment does not seem to him important—

> "To-morrow . . .
> We easily shall make him full amends."

One is reminded of the line in Lowell's great *Present Crisis:* "Never shows the choice momentous till the judgment hath passed by."

So by the one treacherous casting, fixed only half-consciously in its place, the whole structure of character is made unsafe, and presently topples to destruction. Browning, like Shakespeare, seldom shows us a veritable tragedy—a soul lost beyond the possibility of recall. Even Guido (in *The Ring and the Book*) has one chance given him by the stern merciful justice of the Pope. But Chiappino slinks out of sight, the victim of his own treachery, and we realize that for him there is no hope.

ADDENDA.

"COLOMBE'S BIRTHDAY" AT BOSTON IN 1854.—Since the above pages were in type we have had the pleasure of an interview with Mrs. Lander (*née* Davenport), who took the part of the heroine in the performance of *Colombe's Birthday* at the Howard Athenæum in Boston, on the 16th of February, 1854. As it was the last night of her engagement, the play was given only once. It was also given once during Miss Davenport's engagement in Philadelphia, on the 31st of March, 1854.

Mrs. Lander has kindly marked for us the "cuts" in the play as performed in 1854. They were as follows :

ACT I.—Omit lines 15, 16 ("That . . . bank"); 36–38 ; 46, 47 ; 68–74 ; 86 ; 88–90 ("nor, as . . . allowance"); 93–96 ("Things . . . came"); 112–

117 ; 144–186 (" The world . . . themselves "); 194 ; 197–200 ; 208–216 ; 225–228 ; 230–238 ; 241, 242 ; 309–311 ; 342–347 ; 352–355 ; 357–364 ; 365–367 (" or I shall . . . favor "). After 220 add : *"Valence (outside).* Give place ! I must, I will have audience !"

ACT II.—Omit lines 90–94 (" She was . . . them ?"); 99–111 ; 138–141 ; 148–150 (" Take . . . lady !"); 169–173 ; 199–201 ; 220–227 ; 238–240 (" Sir, and you . . . with "); 250–252 ; 257–262 ; 302–313 ; 328–331 (" Let him . . . steadfastly"); 337.

ACT III.—Omit lines 68–75 (" Meantime . . . Prince !"); 77–84 (" Say . . . no doubt !"), 108–112 ; 124 ; 129, 130 ; 220–224 ; 227 (" Me . . . speak to—"); 233–246 ; 258, 259 (" And, where . . . plash"); 262 ; 264 ; 284–303 (" Pray . . . Guibert !"); 305–310 (" Ah, light . . . friend"); 315–321 ; 326–328 (" Ere you . . . perchance "); 330 ; 332–339 ; 369–376.

ACT IV.—Omit lines 1–91 ; 106 ; 109–113 ; 141–144 (" You shall . . . Propose !"); 157–159 ; 162 ; 164–169 ; 171–173 (" He'd hesitate . . . accept me "); 178–181 (" How go . . . sire !"); 186 ; 209 ; 212–???; 224, 225 (" A beggar's . . . quits "); 226–237 (" nor . . . prosper"); 242–248 (" his step . . . invincibility ") ; 365 ; 386–389 ; 402–404 (" All 's cleared . . . Judge you "). Lines 406–410 are modified thus :

> " What all will shout one day.—All is said.
> Look on me and him Decide
> Between the emperor and the man —and speak !"

ACT V.—Omit lines 2 ; 5 ; 9 ; 16–20 ; 33–44 ; 64–66 ; 69 ; 71–76 (" And for . . . dirt"); 107–116 ; 126–129 ; 139–141 ; 144–149 (" I shall . . . serve "); 187–190 (" Both . . . for this !"); 205–207 ; 209–213 ; 217, 218 (" In mind . . . birthright"); 219–221 (" not blot . . . offer "); 224–233 ; 235 ; 242–246 (" Out . . . not yet !"); 248–250 (" You've . . . dumb "); 258–266 (" Suppose . . . lady ?"); 270 ; 275–281 ; 283 ; 298–300 ; 305–308 (" What . . . itself "); 322, 323 (" And yet . . . recompense !"); 330–336 (*retaining* " For love of you."); 356 ; 380–383 (" That is . . . Meantime "). After 353 add : " I let the emperor go, and take the man."

The above includes all the omissions and alterations worth noting. A few changes in a word or two are passed by.

The representation of the play occupied two hours, including the usual intervals between acts.

INDEX OF WORDS AND PHRASES EXPLAINED.

Webster's School Dictionaries

REVISED EDITIONS

WEBSTER'S SCHOOL DICTIONARIES in their revised form constitute a progressive series, carefully graded and especially adapted for Primary Schools, Common Schools, High Schools, Academies, and private students. These Dictionaries have all been thoroughly revised, entirely reset, and made to conform in all essential respects to that great standard authority in English—Webster's International Dictionary.

WEBSTER'S PRIMARY SCHOOL DICTIONARY . . . $0.48

Containing over 20,000 words and meanings, with over 400 illustrations.

WEBSTER'S COMMON SCHOOL DICTIONARY . $0.72

Containing over 25,000 words and meanings, with over 500 illustrations.

WEBSTER'S HIGH SCHOOL DICTIONARY . . . $0.98

Containing about 37,000 words and definitions, and an appendix giving a pronouncing vocabulary of Biblical, Classical, Mythological, Historical, and Geographical proper names, with over 800 illustrations.

WEBSTER'S ACADEMIC DICTIONARY. Cloth, $1.50 ; Indexed, $1.80

The Same . . . Half Calf, $2.75 ; Indexed, $3.00

Abridged directly from the International Dictionary, and giving the orthography, pronunciations, definitions, and synonyms of the large vocabulary of words in common use, with an appendix containing various useful tables, with over 800 illustrations.

SPECIAL EDITIONS

Webster's Countinghouse Dictionary . Sheep, Indexed,	$2.40
Webster's Condensed Dictionary . Cloth, $1.44 ; Indexed,	1 75
The Same . . . Half Calf, $2.75 ; Indexed,	3.00
Webster's Handy Dictionary	.15
Webster's Pocket Dictionary. Cloth	.57
The Same. Roan Flexible	.69
The Same. Roan Tucks	.78
The Same. Morocco, Indexed	.90
Webster's American People's Dictionary and Manual .	.48
Webster's Practical Dictionary	.80

Copies of any of Webster's Dictionaries will be sent, prepaid, to any address on receipt of the price by the Publishers:

American Book Company

New York   Cincinnati   Chicago

(S. S. 104)

Rolfe's English Classics

DESIGNED FOR USE IN HIGH SCHOOLS AND OTHER SECONDARY SCHOOLS

Edited by WILLIAM J. ROLFE, Litt.D.

Formerly Head Master, High School, Cambridge, Mass.

Bound in uniform flexible cloth, 12mo.   Illustrated.   Each 56 cents

---

BROWNING'S SELECT POEMS

Containing Twenty Selected Poems with Introduction, Sketch of the Life of Browning, Chronological Table of his works, a list of the books most useful in the Study of his works, Critical Comments, and Notes.

BROWNING'S DRAMAS

Containing the following selections : "A Blot in the 'Scutcheon," "Colcombe's Birthday," and "A Soul's Tragedy"—with Introduction, Critical Comments, and Notes.

GOLDSMITH'S SELECT POEMS

Three Poems, with copious critical and explanatory Notes, Biography of Goldsmith, and selections from memoirs of the poet by Thackeray, Coleman the Younger, Campbell, Forster, and Irving.

GRAY'S SELECT POEMS

Seven Poems, with the history of each and copious Notes. The Introduction contains Robert Carruther's Life of Gray and William Howitt's description of Stoke-Pogis.

MILTON'S MINOR POEMS

Containing all of Milton's Minor Poems except the Translation, with biographical and critical Introductions, and historical and explanatory Notes.

MACAULAY'S LAYS OF ANCIENT ROME

The Introduction includes the Author's Preface, John Stuart Mill's Review, and Professor Henry Morley's Introduction to the "Lays."

WORDWORTH'S SELECT POEMS

Containing Eleven Poems, with full Notes. Illustrated by Abbey, Parsons, and other famous artists.

Copies will be sent, prepaid, on receipt of the price.

American Book Company

New York   Cincinnati   -   Chicago

(S. S. 96)

A History of English Literature

By REUBEN POST HALLECK, M.A. (Yale)

Cloth, 12mo, 499 pages.   With numerous illustrations.   Price $1.25.

Halleck's History of English Literature is a concise and interesting text-book of the history and development of English literature from the earliest times to the present.   While this work is sufficiently simple to be readily comprehended by high school students, the treatment is not only philosophic, but also stimulating and suggestive, and will naturally lead to original thinking.

The book is a history of literature and not a mere collection of biographical sketches.   Only enough of the facts of an author's life are given to make students interested in him as a personality, and to show how his environment affected his work.   The author's productions, their relation to the age, and the reasons why they hold a position in literature, receive treatment commensurate with their importance.

One of the most striking features of the work consists in the way in which literary movements are clearly outlined at the beginning of each of the chapters.   Special attention is given to the essential qualities which differentiate one period from another, and to the animating spirit of each age.   The author shows that each period has contributed something definite to the literature of England, either in laying characteristic foundations, in presenting new ideals, in improving literary form, or in widening the circle of human thought.

At the end of each chapter a carefully prepared list of books is given to direct the student in studying the original works of the authors treated.   He is told not only what to read, but also where to find it at the least cost.

The book contains as a frontispiece a Literary Map of England in colors, showing the counties, the birthplaces, the homes, and the haunts of the chief authors, specially prepared for this work.

Copies of Halleck's History of English Literature will be sent, prepaid, to any address on receipt of price.

American Book Company

New York   •   Cincinnati   •   Chicago

(S. S. 90)

IMPORTANT TEXT=BOOKS IN RHETORIC

BY ADAMS SHERMAN HILL

Boylston Professor of Rhetoric and Oratory in Harvard University

---

BEGINNINGS OF RHETORIC AND COMPOSITION . $1.25

This book is designed primarily to meet the needs of pupils in secondary schools who are learning to express themselves with the pen ; at the same time it contains so much information that is new in presentation and permanent in value that it is well adapted to more mature minds. It aims to stimulate the pupils to put their natural selves into all that they write. It shows the young writer how to present what he has to say in the best English within his reach and in a form best adapted to his purpose. No supplement with exercises is required in connection with this work, as the book is complete in itself. Nearly two hundred exercises are introduced to aid the pupil in the most practical way.

FOUNDATIONS OF RHETORIC $1.00

The object of this book is to train boys and girls to say in written language, correctly, clearly, and effectively, what they have to say. It takes cognizance of faults such as those who are to use it are likely to commit, either from ignorance or from imitation of bad models, and of merits such as are within their reach. It gives a minimum of space to technicalities and a maximum of space to essentials. In language singularly direct and simple it sets forth fundamental principles of correct speaking, and accompanies each rule with abundant illustrations and examples.

PRINCIPLES OF RHETORIC $1.20

This popular work has been almost wholly rewritten, and is enlarged by much new material. The treatment is based on the principle that the function of rhetoric is not to provide the student of composition with materials for thought, nor yet to lead him to cultivate style for style's sake, but to stimulate and train his powers of expression—to enable him to say what he has to say in appropriate language. Deficiencies that time has disclosed have been supplied, the treatment of each topic adapted to present needs, and the book in its revised form has been made more serviceable.

AMERICAN BOOK COMPANY

(S.S. 87)

Text-Books in Grammar for Advanced Grades

BASKERVILL AND SEWELL'S ENGLISH GRAMMAR . 90 cents

An advanced grammar for use in High School, Academy and College classes. It combines in a remarkable degree a clear and concise statement of the facts of the language, based on its reputable use in literature, with rational methods for teaching and applying the same. The treatment includes Parts of Speech, Analysis, and Syntax, each part separate and distinct, but so articulated into the others as to make a complete, systematic, and harmonious whole.

LYTE'S ADVANCED GRAMMAR AND COMPOSITION . 75 cents

For use in High Schools, Normal Schools, and other Preparatory Schools. Based on the author's popular "Grammar and Composition" and embodying the improvements suggested by successful class room work. The general plan of the work and the development of the subject are in strict accordance with accepted pedagogical principles.

MAXWELL'S ADVANCED LESSONS IN ENGLISH GRAMMAR

60 cents

For use in Higher Grammar Grades and High Schools. It embraces all the theory and practice necessary during the last two years of a grammar school course or throughout a high school course. It is intended to serve two purposes ;—first, as a *text-book*, supplying the principles and rules of the science as well as their applications, and second as a *book of reference*, to be used whenever difficulties are presented either in the student's own compositions, or in literature that is subjected to critical study.

POWELL AND CONNOLLY'S RATIONAL GRAMMAR OF THE ENGLISH LANGUAGE . . . . 60 cents

This new grammar differs widely in treatment and terminology from other text-books in English. The subject is developed logically, and every point is made simple and clear. The practical side of the study—the correct use of language in speech and writing—is especially emphasized.

Copies of any of these books will be sent, prepaid, to any address on receipt of the price.

American Book Company

New York • Cincinnati • Chicago

(S. S. 83)

Text-Books in English

BUEHLER'S PRACTICAL EXERCISES IN ENGLISH

By H. G. BUEHLER, Master in English in the Hotchkiss School.

Cloth, 12mo, 152 pages , ... 50 cents

A drill-book for Grammar Schools and High Schools, containing a large number of exercises to be worked out by the student, with many definitions and discriminations in regard to the choice of words. The pupil is made to choose between the correct and incorrect forms of expression and to explain why he has done so. By this means he strengthens his own power of discrimination and acquires the principle of avoiding mistakes rather than correcting them.

BUTLER'S SCHOOL ENGLISH

By GEORGE P. BUTLER, formerly English Master in the Law-renceville School, Lawrenceville, N. J.

Cloth, 12mo, 272 pages . . . . . 75 cents

A brief, concise, and thoroughly practical manual for use in connection with the written English work of Secondary Schools. It has been prepared specially to secure definite results in the study of English, by showing the pupil how to review, criticise, and improve his own writing. The book is based on the following plan for teaching English: (1) The study and discussion of selections from standard English authors, (2) constant practice in composition, (3) the study of rhetoric for the purpose of cultivating the pupil's power of criticising and improving his own writing.

SWINTON'S SCHOOL COMPOSITION

By WILLIAM SWINTON. Cloth, 12mo, 113 pages . 32 cents

Prepared to meet the demand for a school manual of prose composition of medium size, arranged on a simple and natural plan, and designed not to teach the theory of style and criticism, but to give pupils in Intermediate or Grammar School grades a fair mastery of the art of writing good English.

Copies of any of these books will be sent, prepaid, to any address on receipt of the price by the Publishers:

American Book Company

New York • Cincinnati • Chicago

(S. S. 86)

cochlea

defunsses

ouchcofe

litany

Ararat

fanes

bacconts

losels

yew

bosky

glade

dell

wimple

Casement

antiphony

gules